Better Homes and Gardens®

PICTURE PERFECT

HOME COOKING

BETTER HOMES AND GARDENS® BOOKS
Des Moines, Iowa

BETTER HOMES AND GARDENS® BOOKS
An Imprint of Meredith® Books
President, Book Group: Joseph J. Ward
Vice President and Editorial Director: Elizabeth P. Rice
Managing Editor: Christopher Cavanaugh
Art Director: Ernest Shelton
Test Kitchen Director: Sharon Stilwell

Picture-Perfect Home Cooking
Produced by OTT Communications, Inc.
Food Marketing Division
President: Jerry Ott
Managing Editor: Paula Matthews
Graphic Designers: Woody Downer, John Schooley
Production: Glenda Bouressa, Linda Bouressa, Debbie Hardley, Sue Lea
Primary Food Photographer: Joyce Goldsmith
Photographer: David Kennedy
Assistant Photographer: Thearris Lawson
Food Stylist/Recipe Developer: Marilyn Rollins
Associate Food Stylist: Mary Ann Firth
Assistant Food Stylists: Doris Humpich, Barbara Welch

For Meredith® Books
Editors: Jennifer Darling, Lisa Mannes
Associate Art Director: Tom Wegner
Test Kitchen Product Supervisor: Marilyn Cornelius
Electronic Production Coordinator: Paula Forest
Production Manager: Douglas Johnston

On the cover: Vegetable-Stuffed Turkey Roll, page 50

Meredith Corporation Corporate Officers:
Chairman of the Executive Committee: E. T. Meredith III
Chairman of the Board, President and Chief Executive Officer: Jack D. Rehm
Group Presidents: Joseph J. Ward, Books; William T. Kerr, Magazines; Philip A. Jones, Broadcasting;
    Allen L. Sabbag, Real Estate
Vice Presidents: Leo R. Armatis, Corporate Relations; Thomas G. Fisher, General Counsel and Secretary;
    Larry D. Hartsook, Finance; Michael A. Sell, Treasurer; Kathleen J. Zehr, Controller and Assistant Secretary

WE CARE!

All of us at Better Homes and Gardens® Books are dedicated to providing you with the information and ideas you need to create tasty foods. We welcome your comments and suggestions. Write us at: Better Homes and Gardens® Books, Cookbook Editorial Department, RW-240, 1716 Locust St., Des Moines, IA 50309-3023

If you would like to order additional copies of any of our books, call 1-800-678-2803 or check with your local bookstore.

Our seal assures you that every recipe in *Picture-Perfect Home Cooking* has been tested in the Better Homes and Gardens® Test Kitchen. This means that each recipe is practical and reliable, and meets our high standards of taste appeal. We guarantee your satisfaction with this book for as long as you own it.

Who says no one cooks like Mom anymore?

If you missed out on your mother's or grandmother's cooking secrets, you're about to begin an adventure that will allow you to recapture—and pass along!—the irresistible aromas and flavors that make your childhood memories of home cooking so vivid and fond.

Picture-Perfect Home Cooking is a blue-ribbon collection of over 375 all-time favorite recipes that let you rediscover the pleasures of delicious home-cooked meals—without a doubt, the best of Mom's fare revisited and renewed for today's cook.

Glance over the pages here, and you'll be pleased as well as tempted by the appetizing assortment of the feel-good foods we all love and too often only dream of bringing to the table in our own homes. The experts at Better Homes and Gardens® share their most often requested tips, techniques, and shortcuts for perfecting the art of home cooking.

In addition to the hundreds of step-by-step photos that show you how to achieve the picture-perfect finished dish, you'll find a delicious array of beautifully photographed recipes—from favorites like Beef-Stuffed Peppers and Chicken Cacciatore to somewhat more adventurous dishes like Baked Halibut with Shrimp-Cucumber Sauce and Sesame Pork Tenderloin with Curried-Apricot Sauce.

With *Picture-Perfect Home Cooking* as your guide, you'll leave the guesswork behind—and embark on the lifelong journey of pleasure to be found in home cooking!

Introduction

TABLE OF CONTENTS

MEATS

Cranberry-Sauced Pork Roast

Cranberry-Sauced Pork Roast

1 3- to 3½-pound boneless
   pork top loin roast
   (double loin tied)
½ teaspoon salt
¼ teaspoon pepper
¼ teaspoon ground cumin
2 cups fresh cranberries
½ cup finely chopped onion
¼ cup water
1 tablespoon finely chopped
   jalapeño pepper*
¼ teaspoon ground cumin
⅔ cup currant jelly
2 teaspoons finely shredded
   orange peel

Trim fat from meat. Combine salt, pepper, and ¼ teaspoon cumin; rub over all sides of roast. Place meat on a rack in a shallow roasting pan. Insert a meat thermometer. Roast in a 325° oven for 1¾ to 2¼ hours or till thermometer registers 170°. Cover and let stand 15 minutes before carving.

Meanwhile, for sauce, in a medium saucepan combine cranberries, onion, water, jalapeño pepper, and ¼ teaspoon cumin. Cook and stir about 5 minutes or till berries pop. Stir in jelly till melted. Simmer, uncovered, about 4 to 5 minutes or till thick. Remove from heat and stir in orange peel. Cool slightly. Serve sauce with pork. Makes 10 to 12 servings.

*Note: Fresh jalapeño peppers contain oils that can burn your eyes, lips, and skin. Cover your hands with plastic bags or wear plastic gloves and wash your hands thoroughly before touching your eyes or face.

Per serving: 234 calories, 20 g protein, 18 g carbohydrate, 9 g total fat (3 g saturated), 61 mg cholesterol, 157 mg sodium, 308 mg potassium.

Rib Eye Roast with Blue Cheese Sauce

1 4- to 5-pound beef rib eye
   roast
3 cloves garlic, thinly sliced
2 cups sliced fresh
   mushrooms
½ cup finely chopped onion
3 tablespoons margarine *or*
   butter
½ cup whipping cream
¼ cup beef broth
2 tablespoons dry red wine
½ teaspoon coarsely ground
   pepper
1 4-ounce package crumbled
   blue cheese
⅔ cup toasted chopped
   pecans

Cut 1-inch-wide pockets into roast at 3-inch intervals. Insert a garlic slice into each pocket. Place meat, fat side up, on a rack in a shallow roasting pan. Insert a meat thermometer. Roast in a 350° oven for 1¼ to 2 hours for rare (140°), 1¾ to 2¼ hours for medium (160°), or 1½ to 2½ hours for well-done (170°). Cover with foil and let stand 15 minutes before carving.

Meanwhile, for sauce, in a large skillet cook mushrooms and onion in hot margarine or butter till tender. Stir in whipping cream, beef broth, wine, and pepper. Cook over medium heat for 4 to 5 minutes or till slightly thickened, stirring occasionally. Stir in blue cheese. Cook over low heat till cheese is melted, stirring occasionally. Stir in pecans. Serve sauce with meat. Makes 12 servings.

Per serving: 406 calories, 33 g protein, 3 g carbohydrate, 29 g total fat (11 g saturated), 110 mg cholesterol, 269 mg sodium, 535 mg potassium.

Cajun Steak Pinwheels

½ **cup chopped green pepper**
½ **cup chopped sweet red pepper**
½ **cup finely chopped onion**
½ **cup finely chopped celery**
½ **teaspoon dried thyme, crushed**
½ **teaspoon dried basil, crushed**
½ **teaspoon ground cumin**
½ **teaspoon garlic salt**
¼ **teaspoon ground red pepper**
1 **tablespoon cooking oil**
1 **1- to 1½-pound beef flank steak**

In a skillet cook green pepper, sweet red pepper, onion, celery, thyme, basil, cumin, garlic salt, and ground red pepper in hot oil for 5 minutes or till vegetables are tender, stirring frequently. Set vegetable mixture aside. **1**Score steak by making shallow cuts at 1-inch intervals across steak in a diamond pattern. Repeat on second side. Place meat between 2 sheets of heavy-duty plastic wrap. **2**With a meat mallet, pound steak into a 12x8-inch rectangle, working from center to edges. **3**Spread vegetable mixture over steak. Roll up from a short side. **4**Secure with wooden toothpicks at 1-inch intervals, starting ½ inch from one end. **5**Cut meat roll between toothpicks into eight 1-inch slices.

Place meat, cut side down, on the unheated rack of a broiler pan. Broil 3 inches from the heat for 6 minutes. Turn; broil 6 to 8 minutes more for medium doneness. Remove toothpicks. Makes 4 servings.

Per serving: 217 calories, 22 g protein, 5 g carbohydrate, 12 g total fat (4 g saturated), 53 mg cholesterol, 341 mg sodium, 470 mg potassium.

1Score the steak by making shallow diagonal cuts, about 1 inch apart, in a diamond pattern.

2Using a meat mallet, pound the steak into a 12x8-inch rectangle working from center to edge.

3Spread vegetable mixture over steak. Roll up steak, jelly-roll style, beginning from a short side.

4Secure rolled steak with wooden picks at 1-inch intervals.

5With a sharp knife, cut between picks into 8 slices.

Five-Spice Beef Ribs

3 **to 4 pounds beef short ribs**
½ **cup soy sauce**
¼ **cup dry sherry *or* orange**
    juice
6 **cloves garlic, minced**
1 **tablespoon sugar**
1 **tablespoon lemon juice**
½ **teaspoon fennel seed,**
    crushed
½ **teaspoon ground cinnamon**
½ **teaspoon aniseed, crushed**
½ **teaspoon Szechwan**
    peppercorns, crushed, *or*
    ¼ **teaspoon pepper**
¼ **teaspoon ground cloves**

Place ribs in a plastic bag set in a deep bowl. For marinade, combine soy sauce, sherry or orange juice, garlic, sugar, lemon juice, fennel seed, cinnamon, aniseed, pepper, and cloves. Pour mixture over ribs. Seal bag. Marinate in the refrigerator for 6 to 24 hours, turning bag occasionally.

Remove ribs from bag, reserving marinade. Place ribs, bone side down, in a shallow roasting pan. Pour marinade over ribs. Bake, covered, in a 350° oven for 2 to 2½ hours or till tender. Makes 6 servings.

Per serving: 573 calories, 26 g protein, 7 g carbohydrate, 48 g total fat (20 g saturated), 106 mg cholesterol, 1430 mg sodium, 327 mg potassium.

Beef and Brussels Sprouts Stir-Fry

1 **pound beef flank steak *or***
    boneless beef round
    steak
½ **cup water**
¼ **cup dry sherry**
2 **tablespoons soy sauce**
2 **teaspoons cornstarch**
1 **teaspoon grated gingerroot**
¼ **teaspoon dry mustard**
1 **tablespoon cooking oil**
2 **cloves garlic, minced**
2 **cups fresh brussels sprouts,**
    cut in half lengthwise *or*
    one 10-ounce package
    frozen brussels sprouts,
    thawed and cut in half
    lengthwise
2 **medium carrots, thinly**
    biased sliced
1 **small onion, sliced**
1 **sweet red pepper, cut into**
    thin strips
2 **cups hot cooked rice**

Trim fat from beef. Partially freeze beef for easier slicing. Thinly slice diagonally across the grain into thin strips. For sauce, stir together water, sherry, soy sauce, cornstarch, gingerroot, and dry mustard; set sauce aside.

Pour cooking oil into a wok or large skillet. (Add more oil as necessary during cooking.) Preheat over medium-high heat. Stir-fry garlic in hot oil for 15 seconds. Add brussels sprouts; stir-fry for 2 minutes. Add carrots and onion; stir-fry for 2 minutes. Add pepper strips; stir-fry for 1½ to 2 minutes or till vegetables are crisp-tender. Remove vegetables from the wok.

Add *half* of the beef to the hot wok or skillet. Stir-fry for 2 to 3 minutes or till done. Remove beef from wok. Repeat with remaining beef. Return all beef to the wok. Push beef from center of the wok. Stir sauce; add to center of the wok or skillet. Cook and stir till thickened and bubbly. Cook and stir for 1 minute more.

Return vegetables to the wok or skillet. Stir all ingredients together to coat with sauce. Cook and stir about 1 minute more or till heated through. Serve over hot cooked rice. Makes 4 servings.

Per serving: 417 calories, 28 g protein, 45 g carbohydrate, 12 g total fat (4 g saturated), 53 mg cholesterol, 340 mg sodium, 792 mg potassium.

Spicy London Broil

1 1- to 1½-pound beef flank steak
½ cup olive oil *or* cooking oil
¼ cup red wine vinegar
1 tablespoon lemon juice
½ teaspoon dried basil, crushed
½ teaspoon dried thyme, crushed
½ teaspoon dried oregano, crushed
1 teaspoon coarsely ground pepper
¼ teaspoon paprika
¼ teaspoon garlic salt

Score meat by making shallow cuts at 1-inch intervals diagonally across steak in a diamond pattern. Repeat on second side. **1** Place meat in a plastic bag set in a shallow dish.

For marinade, combine oil, vinegar, lemon juice, basil, thyme, and oregano; pour marinade over meat. Seal bag. Marinate in refrigerator for 4 hours, turning bag occasionally.

Remove meat from marinade, discarding marinade. **2** Combine pepper, paprika, and garlic salt; rub mixture over both sides of meat. Place meat on the unheated rack of a broiler pan. **3** Broil 3 inches from heat for 6 minutes. Turn and broil 5 to 6 minutes more for rare or 7 to 8 minutes more for medium-rare. **4** To serve, thinly slice diagonally across the grain. Makes 4 to 6 servings.

Per serving: 227 calories, 22 g protein, 0 g carbohydrate, 15 g total fat (4 g saturated), 53 mg cholesterol, 97 mg sodium, 340 mg potassium.

1 Place meat in a plastic bag set in a shallow dish. Pour marinade over meat.

2 Remove meat from marinade and rub spice mixture over both sides.

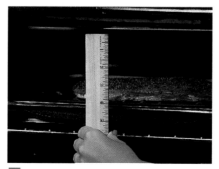
3 Place meat in oven with top surface of the meat 3 inches from the heating element.

4 To serve, slice diagonally across the grain in thin slices.

Creole Swiss Steak

- **1 pound beef round steak, cut ¾ inch thick**
- **2 tablespoons all-purpose flour**
- **¼ teaspoon salt**
- **¼ teaspoon pepper**
- **1 tablespoon cooking oil**
- **1 14½-ounce can tomatoes, cut up**
- **1 small onion, sliced**
- **1 cup sliced fresh *or* frozen okra**
- **½ cup sliced celery**
- **1 teaspoon dried basil, crushed**
- **¼ teaspoon garlic powder**
- **¼ teaspoon dry mustard**
- **⅛ teaspoon crushed red pepper**
- **2 cups hot cooked rice**

Cut meat into 4 serving-size pieces. Trim fat. Combine flour, salt, and pepper. With a meat mallet, pound flour mixture into meat. In a large skillet brown meat on both sides in hot oil. Drain fat.

Add *undrained* tomatoes, onion, okra, celery, basil, garlic powder, dry mustard, and red pepper. Cover and cook over low heat for 1¼ hours or till meat is tender. Skim fat. Serve with hot cooked rice.
Makes 4 servings.

Per serving: 368 calories, 32 g protein, 40 g carbohydrate, 8 g total fat (2 g saturated), 72 mg cholesterol, 374 mg sodium, 819 mg potassium.

Grilled Marinated Steak

- **1 2-pound boneless beef top sirloin steak (cut 1½ inches thick)**
- **¼ cup bourbon *or* apple juice**
- **¼ cup lemon juice**
- **¼ cup soy sauce**
- **2 tablespoons orange juice**
- **2 tablespoons cooking oil**
- **1 clove garlic, minced**
- **1 teaspoon ground ginger**
- **½ teaspoon coarsely ground pepper**

Trim fat from meat. Place steak in a plastic bag set in a shallow dish. For marinade, combine bourbon or apple juice, lemon juice, soy sauce, orange juice, oil, garlic, ginger, and pepper; pour over steak. Seal bag. Marinate in refrigerator for 4 to 24 hours, turning bag occasionally.

Remove steak from marinade; discard marinade. Grill on an uncovered grill directly over *medium* coals for 12 minutes. Turn and grill to desired doneness, allowing 8 to 10 minutes more for rare and 12 to 16 minutes more for medium. Makes 8 servings.

Per serving: 229 calories, 26 g protein, 1 g carbohydrate, 12 g total fat (4 g saturated), 76 mg cholesterol, 286 mg sodium, 361 mg potassium.

Autumn Pot Roast

1 **2- to 2½-pound beef chuck
   pot roast**
2 **tablespoons cooking oil**
¾ **cup beef broth**
¼ **cup dry red wine**
2 **medium onions, sliced and
   separated into rings**
½ **teaspoon paprika**
¼ **teaspoon ground allspice**
⅛ **teaspoon ground red
   pepper**
1 **pound sweet potatoes
   peeled and cut into
   1-inch slices**
1 **cup dried, pitted prunes**
1 **6-ounce package dried
   apricots**

Trim fat from roast. In a Dutch oven brown roast on both sides in hot oil. Drain fat. Add beef broth, wine, onions, paprika, allspice, and red pepper. Bring to boiling. Reduce heat and simmer, covered, for 1 hour. Add potatoes, prunes, and apricots. Cover and cook for 30 to 45 minutes more or till meat and potatoes are tender. Makes 8 servings.

Per serving: 402 calories, 35 g protein, 38 g carbohydrate, 12 g total fat (4 g saturated), 100 mg cholesterol, 151 mg sodium, 935 mg potassium.

Quick Sauerbraten

1 **3- to 4-pound boneless beef round rump roast**
2 **tablespoons cooking oil**
1 **large onion, sliced**
1 **cup water**
1 **8-ounce can tomato sauce**
⅓ **cup dry red wine *or* beef broth**
⅓ **cup red wine vinegar**
2 **teaspoons instant beef bouillon granules**
¼ **teaspoon pepper**
¼ **teaspoon ground allspice**
1 **bay leaf**
12 **gingersnaps, crushed**
5 **cups hot cooked spaetzle *or* noodles**

Trim fat from roast. In a Dutch oven brown roast on all sides in hot oil. Drain fat. Add onion to pan. Combine water, tomato sauce, wine or beef broth, vinegar, bouillon granules, pepper, allspice, and bay leaf. Pour over roast.

Bring to boiling. Reduce heat and simmer, covered, for 1¾ to 2¾ hours or till meat is tender. Remove meat from pan, reserving pan juices. Discard bay leaf.

For gravy, measure pan juices, skimming off fat. Reserve *3½ cups* of the pan juices; return to Dutch oven. Stir in crushed gingersnaps. Cook and stir till thickened and bubbly. Serve gravy with roast and hot cooked spaetzle or noodles. Makes 10 to 12 servings.

Per serving: 392 calories, 35 g protein, 31 g carbohydrate, 13 g total fat (4 g saturated), 119 mg cholesterol, 415 mg sodium, 454 mg potassium.

Burgundy Beef Patties

1 **beaten egg**
1 **tablespoon burgundy *or* other dry red wine**
1 **tablespoon Worcestershire sauce**
1 **tablespoon Dijon-style mustard**
¾ **cup soft bread crumbs**
2 **tablespoons snipped fresh parsley**
½ **teaspoon onion salt**
¼ **teaspoon pepper**
1 **pound lean ground beef**
½ **cup sliced fresh mushrooms**
½ **cup chopped red onion**
1 **tablespoon margarine *or* butter**
½ **cup burgundy *or* other dry red wine**
1 **tablespoon red wine vinegar**
¼ **teaspoon coarsely ground pepper**

In a mixing bowl combine egg, the 1 tablespoon burgundy or other dry red wine, Worcestershire sauce, and mustard. Stir in bread crumbs, parsley, onion salt, and ¼ teaspoon pepper. Add meat; mix well. Shape meat mixture into four ¾-inch-thick patties.

Place patties on the unheated rack of a broiler pan. Broil 3 to 4 inches from the heat for 15 to 18 minutes or till no pink remains, turning once.

Meanwhile, in a small skillet, cook mushrooms and onion in margarine or butter till tender. Stir in the ½ cup burgundy or other dry red wine, vinegar, and ¼ teaspoon pepper. Simmer for 3 to 5 minutes or till reduced and slightly thickened. Serve over beef patties. Makes 4 servings.

Per serving: 325 calories, 25 g protein, 8 g carbohydrate, 18 g total fat (6 g saturated), 124 mg cholesterol, 514 mg sodium, 435 mg potassium.

Meat Loaf

¾ **cup chili sauce**
¼ **cup packed brown sugar**
1 **teaspoon lemon juice**
¼ **teaspoon dry mustard**
¼ **teaspoon ground allspice**
1 **beaten egg**
1 **cup soft bread crumbs**
⅓ **cup milk**
¼ **cup finely chopped onion**
2 **tablespoons snipped fresh parsley**
½ **teaspoon salt**
½ **teaspoon dried sage, crushed**
¼ **teaspoon lemon-pepper seasoning**
1½ **pounds lean ground beef**

For sauce, in a small saucepan combine chili sauce, brown sugar, lemon juice, dry mustard, and allspice. Set aside.

In a mixing bowl combine egg, bread crumbs, milk, onion, parsley, salt, sage, and lemon-pepper seasoning. **1** Add ground beef and mix well. **2** In a shallow baking dish pat meat mixture into an 8x4x2-inch loaf. Spread *half* of the sauce over the top of the meat.

Bake in a 350° oven for 55 to 60 minutes or till no pink remains. **3** Transfer to a serving plate. **4** Heat remaining sauce and spoon over meat. Makes 6 servings.

Per serving: 325 calories, 24 g protein, 22 g carbohydrate, 15 g total fat (6 g saturated), 107 mg cholesterol, 743 mg sodium, 468 mg potassium.

1 Use a wooden spoon to thoroughly mix meat with seasoning mixture.

2 Shape meat mixture into an 8x4x2-inch loaf in a shallow baking dish.

3 Using two metal spatulas, transfer meat loaf to a serving plate.

4 Spoon remaining sauce over meat loaf before serving.

Stuffed Burgers

1 beaten egg
¼ cup fine dry bread crumbs
1 tablespoon milk
½ teaspoon salt
½ teaspoon dried basil,
   thyme, sage, *or* oregano,
   crushed
⅛ teaspoon pepper
1 pound lean ground beef,
   ground pork, ground
   veal, *or* ground lamb
¼ cup finely chopped
   pimiento-stuffed olives,
   pitted ripe olives, *or*
   green pepper; *or* ¼ cup
   shredded zucchini,
   carrot, *or* cheese
4 hamburger buns, split and
   toasted

In a mixing bowl combine egg, bread crumbs, milk, salt, basil, and pepper. Add ground meat and mix well. Shape meat mixture into eight ¼-inch-thick patties. Place about *1 tablespoon* olives, vegetables, or cheese atop each of *four* patties. Spread to within ½ inch of edges. Top with remaining patties. Press meat around edges to seal.

Place patties on the unheated rack of a broiler pan. Broil 3 inches from the heat for 15 to 18 minutes or till no pink remains, turning once. Serve patties on buns. Makes 4 servings.

Per serving: 387 calories, 27 g protein, 26 g carbohydrate, 19 g total fat (7 g saturated), 124 mg cholesterol, 713 mg sodium, 338 mg potassium.

Grilled Veal Chops with Mustard Sauce

4 veal loin chops *or* pork
   loin chops, cut 1 inch
   thick (about 2 pounds)
1 tablespoon lemon juice
2 teaspoons cooking oil
¼ teaspoon pepper
2 tablespoons chicken broth
1 tablespoon water
1 teaspoon Dijon-style
   mustard
1 teaspoon snipped fresh
   tarragon *or* ¼ teaspoon
   dried tarragon, crushed
1 tablespoon dairy sour
   cream

Trim fat from chops. Combine lemon juice, oil, and pepper; brush chops thoroughly with oil mixture. Grill veal chops directly over medium coals for 13 to 17 minutes (20 to 25 minutes for pork chops), turning chops once and brushing frequently with oil mixture. Transfer chops to a serving platter and keep warm.

For sauce, in a small saucepan combine chicken broth, water, mustard, and tarragon. Cook and stir over medium heat till hot. Remove from heat and stir in sour cream. Serve sauce with chops. Makes 4 servings.

Per serving: 238 calories, 31 g protein, 1 g carbohydrate, 11 g total fat (4 g saturated), 126 mg cholesterol, 171 mg sodium, 422 mg potassium.

Beef-Stuffed Peppers

6 **medium sweet red, green,**
   ***or* yellow peppers**
1 **pound lean ground beef**
½ **cup chopped onion**
1 **clove garlic, minced**
1 **8-ounce can tomato sauce**
1 **7½-ounce can tomatoes,**
   cut up
½ **cup couscous**
¼ **cup toasted slivered**
   almonds *or* peanuts
2 **tablespoons snipped fresh**
   parsley
½ **teaspoon dried oregano,**
   crushed
¼ **teaspoon salt**
¼ **teaspoon ground cumin**
¼ **teaspoon dry mustard**
¼ **teaspoon crushed red**
   pepper

1 Wash peppers. Cut a thin slice from the top of each pepper; save tops, if desired. Remove and discard seeds. In a saucepan cook peppers in boiling water for 3 minutes. **2** Invert and drain peppers on paper towels.

For filling, in a large skillet cook meat, onion, and garlic till meat is browned and onion is tender. Drain well. Combine meat mixture, tomato sauce, *undrained* tomatoes, couscous, nuts, parsley, oregano, salt, cumin, mustard, and crushed red pepper. **3** Fill peppers with meat mixture, and if desired, replace tops.

Place peppers in a 2-quart rectangular baking dish. Bake, covered, in a 350° oven about 25 minutes or till peppers are tender and filling is heated through. Makes 6 servings.

Per serving: 296 calories, 19 g protein, 29 g carbohydrate, 13 g total fat (4 g saturated), 47 mg cholesterol, 422 mg sodium, 706 mg potassium.

1 Cut tops from peppers and set aside. Remove and discard seeds.

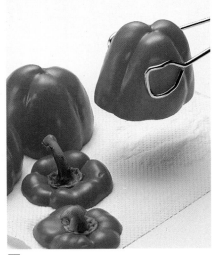

2 Invert partially cooked peppers on paper towels to drain.

3 Fill peppers with meat mixture. Replace reserved pepper tops, if desired. Set filled peppers in baking dish.

Breaded Veal

1 **pound veal leg sirloin steak *or* veal leg round steak, cut ½ inch thick**
⅔ **cup fine dry bread crumbs**
¼ **cup grated Parmesan cheese**
¼ **teaspoon dried basil, crushed**
¼ **teaspoon dried oregano, crushed**
⅛ **teaspoon dried marjoram, crushed**
⅛ **teaspoon garlic powder**
1 **beaten egg**
1 **tablespoon water**
¼ **cup all-purpose flour**
3 **tablespoons margarine *or* butter**

Cut veal into 4 serving-size pieces. Place meat between 2 pieces of heavy-duty plastic wrap. With a meat mallet, pound pieces to ¼-inch thickness.

In a shallow dish combine bread crumbs, Parmesan cheese, basil, oregano, marjoram, and garlic powder. In another shallow dish combine egg and water. Coat veal with flour. Dip veal in egg mixture, then coat both sides with bread crumb mixture.

In a large nonstick skillet cook veal in hot margarine or butter for 2 to 3 minutes on each side or till golden. Makes 4 servings.

Per serving: 359 calories, 32 g protein, 18 g carbohydrate, 17 g total fat (5 g saturated), 150 mg cholesterol, 417 mg sodium, 413 mg potassium.

Veal Paprika

1 **pound boneless veal leg round steak**
1 **tablespoon cooking oil**
1 **medium onion, thinly sliced**
1 **cup sliced fresh mushrooms**
1 **clove garlic, minced**
1 **8-ounce can tomato sauce**
½ **cup water**
2 **teaspoons paprika**
1 **teaspoon instant beef bouillon granules**
½ **teaspoon dried basil, crushed**
1 **8-ounce carton dairy sour cream**
2 **tablespoons all-purpose flour**
3 **cups hot cooked noodles**
2 **tablespoons snipped fresh parsley**

Partially freeze veal. Thinly slice veal across the grain into thin bite-size strips. In a large skillet cook and stir *half* of the veal in hot oil over medium-high heat for 2 to 3 minutes or till brown. Remove veal from skillet; repeat with remaining veal. Set all veal aside.

Add onion, mushrooms, and garlic to skillet; cook and stir for 3 to 4 minutes or till tender. Stir in tomato sauce, water, paprika, bouillon granules, basil, ½ teaspoon *salt*, and ¼ teaspoon *pepper*. Bring to boiling. Stir together sour cream and flour; add to skillet. Cook and stir till thickened and bubbly. Cook and stir 1 minute more. Return meat to skillet. Cook and stir till heated through. Serve over hot cooked noodles. Sprinkle each serving with parsley. Makes 4 servings.

Per serving: 451 calories, 33 g protein, 33 g carbohydrate, 21 g total fat (10 g saturated), 144 mg cholesterol, 926 mg sodium, 811 mg potassium.

Orange Barbecued Ribs

2½ **to 3 pounds pork loin back ribs** *or* **pork spareribs, cut into serving-size pieces**
½ **cup chopped onion**
1 **clove garlic, minced**
1 **tablespoon cooking oil**
1 **8-ounce can tomato sauce**
⅓ **cup orange marmalade**
2 **tablespoons frozen orange juice concentrate, thawed**
1 **tablespoon soy sauce**
1 **tablespoon lemon juice**
½ **teaspoon ground ginger**
¼ **teaspoon ground allspice**

Place ribs, bone side down, on a rack in a shallow roasting pan. Roast in a 350° oven for 1 hour. Drain.

Meanwhile, for sauce, in a medium saucepan cook onion and garlic in hot oil till tender but not brown. Stir in tomato sauce, marmalade, orange juice concentrate, soy sauce, lemon juice, ginger, and allspice. Simmer for 15 minutes, stirring occasionally.

Spoon some of the sauce over the ribs. Roast ribs, covered, for 30 to 45 minutes more or till tender, spooning sauce over ribs occasionally. Brush with any remaining sauce before serving. Makes 4 or 5 servings.

Per serving: 630 calories, 37 g protein, 29 g carbohydrate, 41 g total fat (15 g saturated), 149 mg cholesterol, 693 mg sodium, 721 mg potassium.

Country Pork Chop Skillet

4 **pork loin chops, cut ½ to ¾ inch thick**
½ **teaspoon dried tarragon, crushed**
¼ **teaspoon salt**
¼ **teaspoon pepper**
1 **tablespoon cooking oil**
¾ **cup water**
1 **teaspoon instant chicken bouillon granules**
2 **medium carrots, cut into julienne sticks (1 cup)**
½ **cup sliced green onion**
¼ **cup snipped fresh parsley**
½ **cup dairy sour cream**
2 **tablespoons all-purpose flour**
  Dash salt
  Dash pepper

Trim fat from meat. Combine tarragon, the ¼ teaspoon salt, and the ¼ teaspoon pepper; sprinkle over both sides of meat. In a large skillet cook chops in hot oil over medium heat for 3 minutes on each side or till browned. Drain off fat.

Combine water and bouillon granules; carefully pour over chops. Bring to boiling. Reduce heat and simmer, covered, for 15 minutes. Add carrots, green onion, and parsley. Simmer, covered, for 5 to 7 minutes more or till pork is tender. Transfer meat and vegetables to a serving platter, reserving the cooking liquid.

For sauce, measure reserved cooking liquid. Add water, if necessary, to make *1 cup*. Return cooking liquid to skillet. Stir together sour cream, flour, the dash salt, and the dash pepper; stir into the cooking liquid in skillet. Cook and stir till thickened and bubbly. Cook and stir for 2 minutes more. Serve sauce over chops and vegetables. Makes 4 servings.

Per serving: 264 calories, 20 g protein, 10 g carbohydrate, 16 g total fat (7 g saturated), 70 mg cholesterol, 476 mg sodium, 429 mg potassium.

Pork Chops Rosemary

4 **pork chops, cut ¾ inch thick**
1 **teaspoon dried rosemary *or* thyme, crushed**
¼ **teaspoon garlic powder**
¼ **teaspoon pepper**
1 **tablespoon margarine *or* butter**
1 **14½-ounce can tomatoes, cut up**
½ **of a small onion, sliced**
½ **cup sliced fresh mushrooms**
3 **tablespoons snipped fresh parsley**

Trim fat from meat. Combine rosemary or thyme, garlic powder, and pepper; sprinkle over chops.

In a large skillet cook chops in margarine or butter over medium-high heat for 3 to 4 minutes on each side or till browned. Add *undrained* tomatoes, onion, mushrooms, and parsley. Bring to boiling. Reduce heat and simmer, covered, for 20 to 25 minutes or till tender. Remove chops from skillet, reserving tomato mixture in skillet.

Bring tomato mixture in skillet to boiling. Boil, uncovered, for 5 to 8 minutes or till desired consistency. Serve over chops. Makes 4 servings.

Per serving: 259 calories, 26 g protein, 7 g carbohydrate, 14 g total fat (4 g saturated), 77 mg cholesterol, 262 mg sodium, 611 mg potassium.

Rice-Stuffed Pork Chops

4 **pork loin *or* rib chops,**
   cut 1¼ inches thick
   (about 2 pounds)
¾ **cup cooked rice**
¼ **cup chopped green onion**
¼ **cup toasted chopped**
   pecans
2 **tablespoons sliced**
   pimiento, drained
2 **teaspoons lemon juice**
⅛ **teaspoon salt**
⅛ **teaspoon ground sage**

Trim fat from chops. **1** Cut a pocket in each chop by cutting from fat side almost to bone.

For stuffing, combine cooked rice, green onion, pecans, pimiento, lemon juice, salt, and sage. **2** Spoon *one-fourth* of the stuffing into *each* pork chop. **3** Secure pocket opening with wooden toothpicks, if necessary. **4** Place chops on a rack in a shallow roasting pan.

Bake in a 375° oven for 40 to 50 minutes or till no pink remains. Remove wooden toothpicks. Makes 4 servings.

Per serving: 256 calories, 21 g protein, 13 g carbohydrate, 13 g total fat (3 g saturated), 60 mg cholesterol, 115 mg sodium, 299 mg potassium.

1 To make a pocket for the stuffing, cut from the fat side of the chop nearly to the bone.

2 Spoon one-fourth of the rice stuffing into each pork chop.

3 Securely close the pocket opening with one or two toothpicks inserted diagonally.

4 Place stuffed chops on a rack in a shallow roasting pan.

MEATS

Pork Chops with Maple-Orange Sauce

1 **medium onion, thinly
  sliced**
1 **tablespoon cooking oil**
4 **pork loin chops, cut ¾ inch
  thick (about 1¼ pounds)**
¼ **teaspoon salt**
¼ **teaspoon pepper**
½ **cup orange juice**
¼ **cup maple syrup *or* maple-
  flavored syrup**
1 **tablespoon cider vinegar**
¼ **teaspoon ground
  cinnamon**
¼ **cup raisins**
1 **tablespoon water**
2 **teaspoons cornstarch**
2 **cups hot cooked rice**

In a large skillet cook onion in hot oil till tender but not brown. Remove onion from skillet and set aside. Trim fat from meat. Brown chops in hot oil about 5 minutes on each side. Remove chops from skillet. Drain fat.

Sprinkle chops with salt and pepper. Return chops and onion to skillet. Combine orange juice, maple syrup, vinegar, and cinnamon; pour over chops. Sprinkle raisins over chops. Bring to boiling. Reduce heat and cook, covered, over medium-low heat about 25 minutes or till chops are tender. Transfer chops to a serving platter, reserving cooking liquid.

For sauce, stir together water and cornstarch; stir into reserved cooking liquid in skillet. Cook and stir till thickened and bubbly. Cook and stir 2 minutes more. Serve sauce with chops and hot cooked rice. Makes 4 servings.

Per serving: 381 calories, 18 g protein, 55 g carbohydrate, 10 g total fat (3 g saturated), 47 mg cholesterol, 176 mg sodium, 422 mg potassium.

Sesame Pork Tenderloins with Curried-Apricot Sauce

2 **pork tenderloins
  (about 1½ pounds total)**
¼ **cup soy sauce**
¼ **cup apricot nectar**
3 **tablespoons lemon juice**
½ **teaspoon ground ginger**
1 **clove garlic, minced**
2 **tablespoons sesame seed**
1 **cup apricot nectar**
1 **tablespoon cornstarch**
½ **teaspoon curry powder**
  **Dash bottled hot pepper
  sauce**
1 **teaspoon finely shredded
  lemon peel**

Trim fat from tenderloins, if necessary. Place tenderloins in a plastic bag set in a shallow dish. For marinade, combine soy sauce, the ¼ cup apricot nectar, *1 tablespoon* of the lemon juice, ginger, and garlic; pour over meat. Seal bag. Marinate in refrigerator for 4 to 12 hours, turning bag occasionally.

Remove meat from marinade; discard marinade. Sprinkle sesame seed evenly over pork. Place pork on a greased rack in a shallow roasting pan. Bake, uncovered, at 375° for 45 to 55 minutes or till meat thermometer registers 160°. Remove meat from oven and let stand 15 minutes before carving.

Meanwhile, for sauce, in small saucepan combine the 1 cup apricot nectar, remaining 2 tablespoons lemon juice, cornstarch, curry powder, and hot pepper sauce. Cook and stir over medium heat till thickened and bubbly. Cook and stir 2 minutes more. Remove from heat. Stir in the lemon peel. Serve sauce with pork. Makes 8 servings.

Per serving: 149 calories, 20 g protein, 7 g carbohydrate, 5 g total fat (2 g saturated), 61 mg cholesterol, 277 mg sodium, 416 mg potassium.

Vegetable-Stuffed Pork Tenderloin

2 **pork tenderloins (about 1½ pounds total)**
½ **cup dry sherry**
2 **tablespoons soy sauce**
¼ **teaspoon dried rosemary, crushed**
¼ **teaspoon dried thyme, crushed**
2 **cloves garlic, minced**
½ **cup shredded carrots**
¼ **cup finely chopped red onion**
¼ **cup chopped fresh mushrooms**
2 **teaspoons olive oil *or* cooking oil**
2 **tablespoons pine nuts**
¼ **teaspoon fennel seed, crushed**
¼ **teaspoon pepper**

Trim fat from tenderloins, if necessary. **1** Form a pocket in each tenderloin by cutting a lengthwise slit down the center to but not through the opposite side. **2** Place tenderloins in a shallow dish. For marinade, combine sherry, soy sauce, rosemary, thyme, and garlic; pour marinade into pockets and over tenderloins. Marinate at room temperature for 30 minutes.

Meanwhile, in a medium skillet cook carrots, onion, and mushrooms in hot oil till tender. Stir in pine nuts, fennel seed, and pepper.

Remove tenderloins from marinade; discard marinade. **3** Place meat on a rack in a shallow roasting pan. Divide vegetable mixture between tenderloin pockets. Close pockets and secure with wooden toothpicks. Roast in a 375° oven for 35 to 40 minutes or till meat thermometer registers 160°. Let stand for 10 minutes before carving. Makes 8 servings.

Per serving: 161 calories, 20 g protein, 4 g carbohydrate, 6 g total fat (1 g saturated), 60 mg cholesterol, 277 mg sodium, 428 mg potassium.

1 Form a pocket in each tenderloin by cutting a lengthwise slit down the center to but not through the bottom.

2 Place tenderloins in a shallow dish. Pour marinade into pockets and around tenderloins.

3 Spoon vegetable mixture evenly into tenderloin pockets. Close pockets and secure with toothpicks.

Roast Pork with Pineapple-Mustard Glaze

1   **4- to 5-pound pork loin center rib roast, backbone loosened (8 ribs)**
⅓ **cup pineapple-apricot preserves**
2   **tablespoons pineapple juice**
2   **tablespoons Dijon-style mustard**
1   **tablespoon soy sauce**
¼ **teaspoon ground ginger**

Trim fat from meat. If desired, sprinkle with *salt* and *pepper*. Place roast, rib side down, in a shallow roasting pan. Insert a meat thermometer. Roast in a 325° oven for 1½ to 3 hours or till thermometer registers 160° (medium-well) to 170° (well-done).

Meanwhile, for glaze, in a small saucepan combine preserves, pineapple juice, mustard, soy sauce, and ginger. Brush roast occasionally with glaze during last 30 minutes of roasting.

Cover roast with foil and let stand 15 minutes before carving. Makes 8 servings.

Per serving: 226 calories, 22 g protein, 10 g carbohydrate, 10 g total fat (3 g saturated), 68 mg cholesterol, 263 mg sodium, 300 mg potassium.

Pot Roasted Pork and Potatoes

1   **3- to 3½-pound boneless pork shoulder roast**
½ **teaspoon salt**
¼ **teaspoon ground ginger**
¼ **teaspoon pepper**
⅛ **teaspoon ground allspice**
2   **tablespoons cooking oil**
1   **cup orange juice**
½ **cup water**
1   **tablespoon finely shredded orange peel**
1   **teaspoon instant chicken bouillon granules**
3   **cups cubed, peeled sweet potatoes**
2   **medium apples, cored and cut into thin wedges**
½ **cup cold water**
¼ **cup all-purpose flour**

Trim fat from meat. Combine salt, ginger, pepper, and allspice; rub over all sides of meat. In a Dutch oven brown meat on all sides in hot oil. Drain fat. Add orange juice, water, orange peel, and bouillon granules. Bring to boiling. Reduce heat and simmer, covered, for 1¼ hours. Add potatoes. Return to boiling. Reduce heat and simmer, covered, for 20 minutes. Add apple wedges; continue cooking for 10 to 15 minutes more or till meat and potatoes are tender. Remove meat, potatoes, and apples from pan.

For sauce, skim fat from pan juices. Measure *1½ cups* juices. Combine water and flour; stir into reserved juices. Cook and stir till thickened and bubbly. Cook and stir 1 minute more. Pass sauce with meat. Makes 8 to10 servings.

Per serving: 376 calories, 31 g protein, 20 g carbohydrate, 19 g total fat (6 g saturated), 112 mg cholesterol, 336 mg sodium, 643 mg potassium.

Pork and Peanut Stir-Fry

1 **pound lean boneless pork**
½ **cup chicken broth**
2 **tablespoons hoisin sauce**
1 **tablespoon lemon juice**
2 **teaspoons cornstarch**
¼ **to ½ teaspoon bottled hot pepper sauce**
1 **tablespoon cooking oil**
2 **cloves garlic, minced**
2 **stalks celery, thinly bias sliced (1 cup)**
1 **small onion, sliced**
1 **medium sweet red pepper, cut into thin strips**
5 **cups coarsely shredded fresh spinach**
¼ **cup coarsely chopped unsalted peanuts**

Trim fat from pork. Partially freeze pork. Thinly slice across the grain into bite-size strips. For sauce, combine chicken broth, hoisin sauce, lemon juice, cornstarch, and hot pepper sauce. Set sauce aside.

Pour oil into a wok or large skillet. (Add more oil as necessary during cooking.) Preheat over medium-high heat. Stir-fry garlic in hot oil for 30 seconds. Add celery; stir-fry for 1 minute. Add onion; stir-fry for 1 minute. Add sweet red pepper; stir-fry for 1 to 2 minutes more or till vegetables are crisp-tender. Remove vegetables from wok.

Add *half* of the pork to the hot wok. Stir-fry for 2 to 3 minutes or till no pink remains. Remove from wok. Repeat with remaining pork. Return all pork to wok. Push meat from center of wok. Stir sauce; add to center of wok. Cook and stir till thickened and bubbly.

Return cooked vegetables to wok; add spinach. Stir all ingredients together to coat with sauce. Cover and cook for 1 to 2 minutes or till heated through and spinach is slightly wilted. Sprinkle with peanuts. Serve over *2 cups hot cooked rice*. Makes 4 or 5 servings.

Per serving: 403 calories, 25 g protein, 40 g carbohydrate, 16 g total fat (4 g saturated), 51 mg cholesterol, 741 mg sodium, 921 mg potassium.

MEATS

Curried Ham Loaf

2 eggs
1½ cups soft whole wheat *or*
    white bread crumbs
½ cup finely chopped onion
⅓ cup unsweetened
    pineapple juice
1 tablespoon Dijon-style
    mustard
1 teaspoon curry powder
¼ teaspoon pepper
1 pound ground fully
    cooked ham
¾ pound lean ground pork
2 8-ounce packages frozen
    peas with cream sauce
    (optional)

In a large bowl combine eggs, bread crumbs, onion, pineapple juice, mustard, curry powder, and pepper; add ham and pork and mix well.

Pack meat mixture lightly into an 8x4x2-inch loaf pan. Bake in a 350° oven for 1¼ to 1½ hours or to 170° (juices run clear). Pour off drippings.

Let meat stand for 10 minutes before removing from pan. If desired, cook peas with cream sauce according to package directions, and serve over sliced ham loaf. Makes 6 servings.

Per serving: 269 calories, 29 g protein, 10 g carbohydrate, 12 g total fat (4 g saturated), 131 mg cholesterol, 1,030 mg sodium, 481 mg potassium.

Ham with Mixed Fruit Salsa

⅔ cup chopped fresh pear
⅔ cup chopped fresh
    pineapple
⅔ cup chopped fresh plums
⅓ cup sliced green onion
2 teaspoons lemon juice
2 tablespoons unsweetened
    pineapple juice
2 teaspoons cider vinegar
½ teaspoon grated gingerroot
    or ⅛ teaspoon ground
    ginger
⅛ teaspoon ground
    cardamom
Dash ground allspice
1 1½-pound fully cooked
    center-cut ham slice, cut
    1 inch thick

For salsa, combine chopped pear, pineapple, plums, green onion, and lemon juice; mix well. Add pineapple juice, vinegar, gingerroot or ginger, cardamom, and allspice. Toss gently. Let salsa stand at room temperature for 1 hour.

Trim fat from ham. Slash edges of ham at 1-inch intervals. Place on a rack in a shallow baking pan. Bake in a 350° oven about 30 minutes or till heated through. Serve ham with salsa. Makes 6 servings.

Per serving: 174 calories, 21 g protein, 12 g carbohydrate, 5 g total fat (2 g saturated), 45 mg cholesterol, 1,077 mg sodium, 383 mg potassium.

Pepper Trio Pizza

2¾ to 3¼ cups all-purpose flour
1 package active dry yeast
½ teaspoon dried Italian
   seasoning, crushed
¼ teaspoon salt
1 cup warm water (120° to
   130°)
2 tablespoons cooking oil
   Cornmeal (optional)
   Red Pepper Sauce
1 pound bulk Italian sausage
   or lean ground beef,
   cooked and well drained
2 medium green sweet
   peppers, cut into thin
   strips
2 medium yellow sweet
   peppers, cut into thin
   strips
1 cup sliced fresh mushrooms
⅔ cup sliced pitted ripe olives
⅔ cup chopped onion
1 cup shredded cheddar
   cheese
1 cup shredded provolone
   cheese

In a large bowl combine *1¼ cups* of the flour, yeast, Italian seasoning, and salt. Add warm water and oil. Beat with an electric mixer on low speed for 30 seconds, scraping bowl constantly. Beat on high speed for 3 minutes. Using a spoon, stir in as much of the remaining flour as you can. Turn out onto a lightly floured surface. Knead in enough remaining flour to make a moderately stiff dough that is smooth and elastic (6 to 8 minutes total). Divide dough in half. Cover; let rest 10 minutes.

Grease two 12-inch pizza pans. Sprinkle with cornmeal, if desired. Roll each dough half into a 12-inch circle. **1 2** Transfer to prepared pans; build up edges slightly. *Do not let rise*. Bake in a 425° oven about 12 minutes or till lightly browned. **3** Spread Red Pepper Sauce evenly atop hot crusts to within ½ inch of edge. Top each pizza with meat, sweet peppers, mushrooms, olives, and onion. Sprinkle with cheeses. Bake for 10 to 15 minutes more or till heated through. Makes 8 servings.

Red Pepper Sauce: In a medium saucepan cook 2 cups finely chopped *sweet red pepper* and 2 cloves minced *garlic* in 1 tablespoon *olive oil or cooking oil* till tender. Stir in one 8-ounce can *tomato sauce*; 2 medium *tomatoes*, peeled, seeded, and chopped; 1 teaspoon *sugar*; 1 teaspoon dried *basil*, crushed; and ¼ teaspoon *crushed red pepper*. Bring to boiling. Reduce heat and simmer, uncovered, for 5 minutes. Cool slightly. Pour pepper mixture into a blender container; cover and blend till smooth.

Per serving: 495 calories, 22 g protein, 43 g carbohydrate, 27 g total fat (10 g saturated), 57 mg cholesterol, 900 mg sodium, 591 mg potassium.

1 Transfer dough to prepared pizza pans.

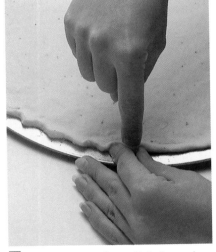

2 Build up the edges slightly and crimp by pinching the dough between fingers.

3 Spread Red Pepper Sauce evenly atop crust. Layer half of topping ingredients over each pizza.

Ham and Artichoke Bake

¼ **cup margarine** *or* **butter**
¼ **cup all-purpose flour**
¼ **teaspoon salt**
¼ **teaspoon ground nutmeg**
⅛ **teaspoon pepper**
2 **cups milk**
½ **cup grated Parmesan cheese**
2 **tablespoons dry white wine**
2 **13¾-ounce cans artichoke hearts, drained and quartered** *or* **two 9-ounce packages frozen artichoke hearts, thawed and quartered**
10 **ounces fully cooked ham, cut into julienne strips (2 cups)**
1 **4½-ounce can sliced mushrooms, drained**
1 **cup soft bread crumbs**
2 **tablespoons snipped fresh parsley**
1 **tablespoon margarine** *or* **butter, melted**

For sauce, in a medium saucepan melt the ¼ cup margarine or butter. Stir in the flour, salt, nutmeg, and pepper. Add milk all at once. Cook and stir over medium heat till thickened and bubbly. Stir in Parmesan cheese and wine.

Place artichokes in a single layer on the bottom of a lightly greased 3-quart rectangular baking dish. Sprinkle ham and mushrooms over artichokes. Pour sauce over all ingredients in dish. In a small bowl combine bread crumbs, parsley, and the 1 tablespoon melted margarine or butter; sprinkle evenly over casserole.

Bake in a 350° oven for 20 to 25 minutes or till golden brown and bubbly. Makes 6 servings.

Per serving: 292 calories, 20 g protein, 17 g carbohydrate, 16 g total fat (5 g saturated), 35 mg cholesterol, 1176 mg sodium, 567 mg potassium.

Italian Sausage-Stuffed Eggplant

2 **small eggplants (about ¾ pound each)**
¾ **pound bulk mild Italian sausage**
½ **cup chopped onion**
½ **cup chopped green pepper**
1 **clove garlic, minced**
1 **8-ounce can tomato sauce**
¼ **cup seasoned fine dry bread crumbs**
3 **tablespoons grated Parmesan cheese**
¼ **teaspoon pepper**
1 **cup shredded mozzarella cheese (4 ounces)**

Cut each eggplant in half lengthwise. Scoop out pulp, leaving about a ¼-inch-thick shell. Place eggplant shells in a 3-quart rectangular baking dish. Finely chop pulp; set aside.

In a skillet cook Italian sausage, onion, green pepper, and garlic till meat is browned and vegetables are tender. Drain off fat. Combine drained meat mixture, chopped eggplant pulp, tomato sauce, bread crumbs, Parmesan cheese, and pepper. Divide mixture evenly among eggplant shells. Cover.

Bake in a 350° oven about 45 minutes or till eggplant is tender. Uncover and sprinkle with mozzarella cheese. Bake, uncovered, about 5 minutes more or till cheese melts. Makes 4 servings.

Per serving: 391 calories, 25 g protein, 23 g carbohydrate, 23 g total fat (10 g saturated), 68 mg cholesterol, 1330 mg sodium, 837 mg potassium.

Lamb and Carrot Meatballs

1 **beaten egg**
¼ **teaspoon salt**
¼ **teaspoon dried thyme, crushed**
¼ **teaspoon pepper**
⅛ **teaspoon garlic powder**
1 **pound ground lamb**
½ **cup chopped onion**
½ **cup shredded carrot**
1 **8-ounce carton dairy sour cream**
3 **tablespoons all-purpose flour**
2 **teaspoons instant beef bouillon granules**
1½ **cups water**
¼ **cup snipped fresh parsley**
2 **cups hot cooked noodles**

In a mixing bowl combine egg, salt, thyme, pepper, and garlic powder; add lamb, onion, and carrot. Mix well. **1** Shape meat mixture into a 6x4-inch rectangle; divide into 24 pieces. **2** Roll into meatballs. Place meatballs in a shallow baking pan. Bake, uncovered, in a 375° oven about 20 minutes or till no pink remains.

Meanwhile, for sauce, in a medium saucepan combine sour cream, flour, and bouillon granules; stir in water. Cook and stir till thickened and bubbly. Cook and stir 1 minute more.

Drain fat from meatballs. Gently stir meatballs into sauce along with parsley. Serve over hot cooked noodles. Makes 4 servings.

Per serving: 507 calories, 28 g protein, 31 g carbohydrate, 30 g total fat (14 g saturated), 181 mg cholesterol, 690 mg sodium, 497 mg potassium.

1 To make meatballs of uniform size, shape meat mixture into a 6x4-inch rectangle on a sheet of waxed paper. Divide into 24 pieces.

2 Roll each piece into a ball between the palms of your hands.

Oriental Lamb Supper

4 lamb leg sirloin chops,
   cut ½ inch thick
   (about 1½ pounds)
¼ teaspoon pepper
¼ teaspoon ground ginger
1 tablespoon cooking oil
¼ cup water
1 tablespoon soy sauce
1 teaspoon brown sugar
1 teaspoon toasted sesame
   oil
1 medium onion, sliced
1 cup sliced celery
½ cup sliced fresh
   mushrooms
½ cup thinly sliced carrot
1 clove garlic, minced
2 tablespoons cold water
4 teaspoons cornstarch
2 cups hot cooked rice

Trim fat from meat. Combine pepper and ginger; sprinkle over both sides of lamb chops. In a large skillet brown chops on both sides in hot cooking oil. Drain off fat.

Combine the ¼ cup water, soy sauce, brown sugar, and sesame oil; pour over chops. Add onion, celery, mushrooms, carrot, and garlic. Cover and simmer for 20 to 25 minutes or till tender. Transfer chops and vegetables to a serving platter, reserving pan juices.

For sauce, combine the 2 tablespoons cold water and the cornstarch; add to pan juices. Cook and stir till thickened and bubbly. Cook and stir for 2 minutes more. Serve chops with sauce and hot cooked rice. Makes 4 servings.

Per serving: 415 calories, 34 g protein, 39 g carbohydrate, 13 g total fat (4 g saturated), 98 mg cholesterol, 364 mg sodium, 651 mg potassium.

Lamb Chops with Apple-Mint Glaze

2 tablespoons apple jelly
1 tablespoon lemon juice
1 tablespoon snipped fresh
   mint *or* ½ teaspoon dried
   mint, crushed
4 lamb loin chops, cut 1 inch
   thick
¼ teaspoon ground ginger
¼ teaspoon dried rosemary,
   crushed
⅛ teaspoon salt

For glaze, in a small saucepan combine jelly, lemon juice, and mint. Cook and stir over low heat till jelly melts. Set glaze aside. Trim fat from lamb chops. Combine ginger, rosemary, and salt; rub over lamb chops.

Place chops on the unheated rack of a broiler pan. Broil 3 inches from the heat for 5 minutes. Turn; broil 5 minutes more for medium. Brush chops with glaze. Broil 1 minute more. Brush any remaining glaze over chops before serving. Makes 2 servings.

Note: To micro-cook sauce, in a 1-cup glass measure combine jelly, lemon juice, and mint. Micro-cook on 100% power (high) about 1 minute or till jelly is melted.

Per serving: 226 calories, 23 g protein, 14 g carbohydrate, 8 g total fat (3 g saturated), 74 mg cholesterol, 195 mg sodium, 256 mg potassium.

Lamb and Ratatouille Kabobs

1¼ pounds boneless lamb round steak *or* sirloin steak, cut ¾ inch thick
¼ cup dry white wine
2 tablespoons cooking oil
2 cloves garlic, minced
1 tablespoon snipped fresh parsley
1 teaspoon dried oregano, crushed
¼ teaspoon pepper
⅛ teaspoon salt
1 large green pepper, cut into 1-inch pieces
1 medium eggplant, quartered and cut into 1-inch slices
8 cherry tomatoes

Trim fat from lamb. Cut lamb into ¾-inch cubes; set meat aside. For marinade, in a bowl combine wine, oil, garlic, parsley, oregano, pepper, and salt. Add meat to bowl. Cover and marinate in the refrigerator for 2 to 24 hours.

Cook green pepper pieces in boiling water for 1 minute. Drain meat, reserving marinade. On four long skewers alternately thread lamb, eggplant slices, and green pepper pieces. Place kabobs on the unheated rack of a broiler pan. Broil 4 to 5 inches from heat for 6 to 8 minutes for medium, brushing with marinade and turning skewers often. (*Do not* brush with marinade during the last 5 minutes of broiling.) Add *two* cherry tomatoes to *each* skewer the last 1 minute of broiling. Makes 4 servings.

Per serving: 275 calories, 25 g protein, 12 g carbohydrate, 14 g total fat (3 g saturated), 72 mg cholesterol, 132 mg sodium, 723 mg potassium.

MEATS

Vegetable-Lamb Skillet

1   9-ounce package frozen
    Italian-style green beans
    or frozen cut green beans
4   lamb shoulder chops, cut
    ½ inch thick
1   medium onion, sliced
1   tablespoon cooking oil
1   cup water
2   teaspoons instant chicken
    bouillon granules
¼   teaspoon dried basil,
    crushed
¼   teaspoon dried oregano,
    crushed
⅛   teaspoon pepper
2   cups sliced, peeled potatoes
1   2-ounce jar diced pimiento,
    drained
2   teaspoons cornstarch
¼   cup sliced pitted ripe
    olives

Place beans in sieve or strainer and hold under *cold running water* to separate; set aside. Trim fat from meat. If desired, sprinkle with *salt* and *pepper*. In a large skillet brown chops and onion in hot oil. Drain fat.

Combine water, bouillon granules, basil, oregano and pepper. Pour over chops. Add beans, potatoes, and pimiento. Cover; simmer for 20 to 25 minutes or till tender. Remove meat and vegetables.

For sauce, skim fat from pan juices. Add water to pan juices to equal ¾ *cup*. Return to skillet. Combine 1 tablespoon *cold water* and cornstarch; stir into juices. Cook and stir till thickened and bubbly. Cook and stir 2 minutes more. Pour sauce over chops; sprinkle with olives. Makes 4 servings.

Per serving: 300 calories, 22 g protein, 24 g carbohydrate, 13 g total fat (4 g saturated), 67 mg cholesterol, 608 mg sodium, 609 mg potassium.

Leg of Lamb with Chutney Mustard

1   5- to 7-pound leg of lamb
⅓   cup pear nectar
¼   cup Dijon-style mustard
2   tablespoons finely snipped
    chutney
¼   teaspoon garlic powder
¼   teaspoon pepper

Trim fat from meat. Pierce top side of lamb at 1-inch intervals with a meat fork. Place meat in a shallow baking dish. Combine pear nectar, mustard, chutney, garlic powder, and pepper; spoon *half* of the mustard mixture over lamb. Let stand in refrigerator for 2 hours. Cover remaining mustard mixture and refrigerate.

Place meat, bone side down, on a rack in a shallow roasting pan. Insert a meat thermometer into thickest portion. Roast in a 325° oven for 1½ to 2½ hours for rare (140°) and 2 to 3 hours for medium (160°). Brush with remaining mustard mixture after half the roasting time.

Let lamb stand for 15 minutes before carving. Makes 12 to 16 servings.

Per serving: 161 calories, 22 g protein, 3 g carbohydrate, 6 g total fat (2 g saturated), 67 mg cholesterol, 178 mg sodium, 267 mg potassium.

POULTRY

Spanish Chicken and Rice

Spanish Chicken and Rice

1 cup chopped onion
½ cup chopped green pepper
2 cloves garlic, minced
2 teaspoons cooking oil
1¾ cups chicken broth
1 cup long grain rice
¼ cup dry white wine
1 bay leaf
⅛ teaspoon ground saffron
1 cup frozen peas, thawed
½ cup sliced pimiento-
    stuffed olives
¼ cup snipped fresh parsley
2 to 2½ pounds meaty
    chicken pieces*
1 tablespoon cooking oil
¼ teaspoon garlic salt
⅛ teaspoon paprika

In a medium saucepan cook onion, green pepper, and garlic in 2 teaspoons hot oil over medium-high heat till tender. Add chicken broth, rice, wine, bay leaf, and saffron. Bring to boiling. Reduce heat; cover and simmer for 10 minutes. Remove bay leaf. Stir in peas, olives, and parsley. Transfer mixture to a 3-quart rectangular baking dish.

Skin chicken, if desired. Rinse chicken; pat dry with paper towels. In large skillet cook chicken in 1 tablespoon hot oil over medium-high heat about 10 minutes or till brown on all sides. Arrange chicken over rice in baking dish dish. Sprinkle chicken with garlic salt and paprika. Cover dish with foil. Bake in a 350° oven for 35 to 40 minutes or till chicken is tender and no longer pink. Makes 6 servings.

*Note: Use chicken breast halves, thighs, and/or drumsticks for meaty chicken pieces.

Per serving: 386 calories, 28 g protein, 33 g carbohydrate, 15 g total fat (3 g saturated), 69 mg cholesterol, 694 mg sodium, 396 mg potassium.

Glazed Chicken with Apple-Rice Stuffing

¼ cup wild rice
1¼ cups chicken broth
¼ cup long grain rice
1 medium red apple, chopped
¼ cup sliced green onions
¼ cup toasted chopped pecans
¼ cup raisins
2 tablespoons orange juice
½ teaspoon ground
    cardamom
¼ teaspoon ground ginger
1 2½- to 3-pound whole
    roasting chicken
¼ cup currant jelly
1 tablespoon margarine or
    butter
1 teaspoon Dijon-style
    mustard
    Dash ground allspice

For stuffing, rinse wild rice. In a small saucepan combine broth and wild rice. Bring to boiling; reduce heat. Cover and simmer for 25 minutes. Add long grain rice; cook for 15 to 20 minutes more or till wild rice and long grain rice are tender and liquid is absorbed. In a large mixing bowl combine rice mixture, apple, green onions, pecans, raisins, orange juice, cardamom, and ginger; mix well.

Rinse chicken; pat dry with paper towels. Season cavity with salt. Spoon some of the stuffing loosely into the neck cavity. Pull the neck skin to the back and fasten with a small skewer. Lightly spoon additional stuffing into the body cavity. (Put any remaining stuffing in a small casserole.) Tie the drumsticks securely to the tail. Twist the wing tips under the back. Place the bird, breast side up, on a rack in a shallow roasting pan. Brush with oil. Insert a meat thermometer into the center of one of the inside thigh muscles. The bulb should not touch bone. Roast, uncovered, in a 375° oven for 45 minutes. Add the casserole of additional stuffing to the oven. Roast for 15 more minutes.

Meanwhile, for glaze, in small saucepan combine jelly, margarine or butter, mustard, and allspice. Cook over medium-low heat till jelly melts, stirring frequently. Brush glaze over chicken. Roast for 15 to 30 minutes more or till thermometer registers 180° and drumsticks move easily, basting frequently. Makes 6 servings.

Per serving: 376 calories, 24 g protein, 30 g carbohydrate, 18 g total fat (4 g saturated), 66 mg cholesterol, 359 mg sodium, 367 mg potassium.

Fried Chicken with Lemon Gravy

1   2½-to 3-pound broiler-fryer
    chicken, cut up
⅓ cup fine dry bread crumbs
½ teaspoon lemon-pepper
    seasoning
½ teaspoon dried thyme,
    crushed
¼ teaspoon garlic powder
2   tablespoons cooking oil
2   tablespoons all-purpose
    flour
1   14½-ounce can chicken
    broth
1   tablespoon snipped fresh
    parsley
¼ teaspoon finely shredded
    lemon peel
1   tablespoon lemon juice

Skin chicken, if desired. Rinse chicken; pat dry with paper towels. **1 2** In a plastic bag combine bread crumbs, lemon-pepper seasoning, thyme, and garlic powder. Add chicken pieces, a few at a time, shaking to coat.

In a 12-inch skillet heat oil. **3** Add chicken, placing meaty pieces toward the center of the skillet, where heat is more intense. **4** Cook, uncovered, over medium heat for 15 minutes, turning to brown evenly. Reduce heat. Cover tightly. Cook for 25 minutes. Uncover; cook for 5 to 10 minutes more or till tender and no longer pink. Drain on paper towels. Transfer to a serving platter; keep warm.

For Lemon Gravy, pour off drippings reserving *2 tablespoons*. Return reserved drippings to skillet. Add flour; stir till smooth. Add chicken broth all at once. Cook and stir over medium heat till thickened and bubbly. Cook and stir for 2 minutes more. Stir in parsley, lemon peel, and lemon juice. Serve gravy with chicken. Makes 6 servings.

Per serving: 260 calories, 23 g protein, 7 g carbohydrate, 15 g total fat (4 g saturated), 70 mg cholesterol, 410 mg sodium, 246 mg potassium.

1 Combine bread crumbs and seasonings in a plastic bag. Add 2 or 3 chicken pieces at a time.

2 Close bag and shake to coat all pieces evenly with crumb mixture.

3 Place meaty pieces (breasts, thighs, and large ends of drumsticks) toward center of skillet.

4 Brown the chicken over medium heat. Turn pieces occasionally to brown evenly.

Fruitful Fried Chicken

1   2½- to 3-pound broiler-
    fryer chicken, cut-up
½   cup fine dry bread crumbs
½   teaspoon salt
¼   teaspoon ground ginger
¼   teaspoon pepper
⅛   teaspoon ground
    cinnamon
2   tablespoons cooking oil
4   green onions
2   medium pears, cored, and
    cut into wedges
½   cup chicken broth
½   cup apple juice
¼   cup raisins
1   tablespoon lemon juice
1½ teaspoons cornstarch
1   tablespoon water

Rinse chicken; pat dry with paper towels. In a plastic bag combine bread crumbs, salt, ginger, pepper, and cinnamon. Add chicken pieces, a few at a time, shaking to coat well.

In a 12-inch skillet cook chicken in hot oil over medium heat for 15 minutes, turning to brown evenly. Drain fat.

Meanwhile, cut the white portion of the green onions into ½-inch slices. Set aside the tops for garnish. Add sliced green onion, pears, chicken broth, apple juice, raisins, and lemon juice to skillet. Bring to boiling; reduce heat. Cover and simmer for 25 to 30 minutes or till chicken is tender and no longer pink. Transfer chicken and fruit to a serving platter; keep warm.

For sauce, stir together water and cornstarch. Add to juices in skillet. Cook and stir till thickened and bubbly. Cook and stir for 1 minute more. Slice green onion tops; sprinkle over chicken and fruit. Serve with sauce. Makes 6 servings.

Per serving: 320 calories, 22 g protein, 23 g carbohydrate, 16 g total fat (4 g saturated), 66 mg cholesterol, 366 mg sodium, 348 mg potassium.

Vintage Barbecued Drumsticks

⅓   cup chili sauce
¼   cup grape jelly
2   tablespoons red wine
    vinegar
½   teaspoon finely shredded
    lemon peel
1   teaspoon dry mustard
⅛   teaspoon garlic powder
    Dash bottled hot pepper
    sauce
8   chicken drumsticks
    (about 1½ pounds total)

For sauce, in a small saucepan stir together chili sauce, grape jelly, vinegar, lemon peel, dry mustard, garlic powder, and hot pepper sauce. Cook over low heat about 5 minutes or till jelly is melted, stirring occasionally. Remove from heat; set aside.

Rinse chicken; pat dry with paper towels.

For direct grilling, place chicken on the grill rack of an uncovered grill. Grill directly over medium coals for 30 to 35 minutes or till chicken is tender and no longer pink, turning once halfway through grilling and brushing frequently with sauce during the last 10 minutes of grilling.

For indirect grilling, in a covered grill arrange medium-hot coals around drip pan. Test for medium heat above the drip pan. Place chicken on the grill rack over drip pan. Cover and grill for 35 to 40 minutes or till chicken is tender and no longer pink, turning once halfway through grilling and brushing frequently with sauce during the last 10 minutes of grilling. Makes 4 servings.

Per serving: 271 calories, 22 g protein, 19 g carbohydrate, 12 g total fat (3 g saturated), 77 mg cholesterol, 342 mg sodium, 288 mg potassium.

Southern Stuffed Chicken Breasts

1 5-ounce can chunk-style ham, drained and flaked
½ cup frozen whole kernel corn, thawed
3 tablespoons finely chopped green onion
1 2-ounce jar sliced pimiento, drained
6 skinless, boneless medium chicken breast halves
½ cup cornflake crumbs
2 tablespoons yellow cornmeal
½ teaspoon poultry seasoning
⅛ to ¼ teaspoon ground red pepper
1 beaten egg
1 tablespoon water
2 tablespoons cooking oil

In a small bowl combine ham, corn, green onion, and pimiento; mix well. Set aside.

Rinse chicken; pat dry with paper towels. **1** Place *each* breast half, boned side up, between 2 pieces of clear plastic wrap. Working from the center to the edges, pound lightly with the flat side of a meat mallet to ⅛-inch thickness. Remove plastic wrap.

2 For *each* roll, place about *3 tablespoons* of the ham mixture at a short end of the breast half. **3 4** Fold in long sides of chicken and roll up jelly-roll style, starting from the end with the ham mixture. Secure with wooden toothpicks.

Combine cornflake crumbs, cornmeal, poultry seasoning, and ground red pepper; set aside. In a small bowl beat together egg and water. Dip each chicken roll in egg mixture. Roll in crumb mixture to coat all sides.

In a large skillet cook chicken in hot oil over medium-high heat about 5 minutes or till golden, turning to brown all sides. Transfer chicken rolls to a 2-quart rectangular baking dish. Bake in a 400° oven about 15 minutes or till chicken is tender and no longer pink. Makes 6 servings.

Per serving: 216 calories, 21 g protein, 10 g carbohydrate, 10 g total fat (4 g saturated), 75 mg cholesterol, 373 mg sodium, 200 mg potassium.

1 Place chicken between plastic wrap. Pound lightly with flat side of meat mallet till ⅛-inch thick.

2 Place about 3 tablespoons ham mixture at the short end of each chicken breast.

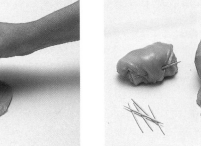

3 Fold in long sides and bottom edge of each chicken breast to help hold in filling.

4 Starting at the folded bottom edge, roll up jelly-roll style. Secure with wooden toothpicks.

Pineapple-Cheese Stuffed Chicken Breasts

**4 skinless, boneless large
  chicken breast halves
  (about 1 pound total)**
**1 3-ounce package cream
  cheese, softened**
**2 tablespoons drained canned
  crushed pineapple**
**2 tablespoons snipped fresh
  chives *or* thinly sliced
  green onion**
**1 tablespoon finely chopped
  green pepper**
¼ teaspoon salt
1 egg, slightly beaten
1 tablespoon water
¼ cup all-purpose flour
¼ teaspoon salt
¼ teaspoon ground ginger
¾ cup finely chopped pecans

Rinse chicken; pat dry with paper towels. Place *each* breast half, boned side up, between 2 pieces of clear plastic wrap. Working from the center to the edges, pound lightly with the flat side of a meat mallet to ⅛-inch thickness. Remove plastic wrap.

For filling, in a small bowl stir together cream cheese, pineapple, chives or green onion, green pepper, and ¼ teaspoon salt. Place *one-fourth* of the mixture in the center of each chicken breast; spread filling slightly. Fold in long sides. Roll up jelly-roll style, starting from a short end. Secure with wooden toothpicks.

Combine egg and water in a shallow pan or dish. In another pan or dish combine flour, ¼ teaspoon salt, and ginger. Coat rolls with flour; then dip into egg mixture. Roll in pecans to coat evenly. Place rolls in a 2-quart square baking dish. Bake, uncovered, in a 400° oven about 25 minutes, or till tender and no longer pink. Makes 4 servings.

Per serving: 382 calories, 27 g protein, 11 g carbohydrate, 26 g total fat (7 g saturated), 136 mg cholesterol, 400 mg sodium, 321 mg potassium.

Chicken Cordon Bleu

**2 whole medium chicken
  breasts (1½ pounds total),
  skinned, boned, and
  halved lengthwise**
**4 slices prosciutto *or* fully
  cooked ham**
**4 slices Swiss cheese
  (4 ounces)**
**5 tablespoons margarine *or*
  butter**
1 cup sliced fresh mushrooms
1 clove garlic, minced
**1 tablespoon all-purpose
  flour**
⅔ cup milk
½ cup dairy sour cream
**1 tablespoon all-purpose
  flour**
¼ teaspoon ground nutmeg
4 ounces wide noodles

Rinse chicken; pat dry with paper towels. Place 1 chicken piece, boned side up, between 2 pieces of clear plastic wrap. Working from the center to the edges, pound lightly with the flat side of a meat mallet to form a rectangle about ⅛ inch thick. Remove the plastic wrap. Repeat with remaining chicken pieces.

Place 1 slice of prosciutto or ham and 1 slice of cheese on each cutlet. Fold in the bottom and sides. Roll up jelly-roll style; secure with wooden toothpicks.

In a 10-inch skillet cook rolls in *3 tablespoons* of the hot margarine or butter over medium-low heat for 20 minutes or till tender. Turn to brown evenly. Remove toothpicks.

Meanwhile, for sauce, in a small saucepan melt the remaining *2 tablespoons* margarine or butter. Add mushrooms and garlic. Cook and stir till tender. Stir in 1 tablespoon flour. Add milk all at once. Stir together sour cream, 1 tablespoon flour, and nutmeg; stir into saucepan. Cook and stir till thickened and bubbly. Cook and stir 2 minutes more.

Meanwhile, cook noodles according to the package directions. Drain. Transfer noodles and chicken rolls to a serving platter; top with sauce. Makes 4 servings.

Per serving: 578 calories, 38 g protein, 27 g carbohydrate, 35 g total fat (13 g saturated), 126 mg cholesterol, 462 mg sodium, 408 mg potassium.

Chicken with Peppers and Tomatoes

6 **medium skinless, boneless
  chicken breast halves**
1 **tablespoon margarine *or*
  butter**
1 **8-ounce can stewed
  tomatoes**
1 **small onion, chopped**
½ **cup finely chopped sweet
  red pepper**
½ **cup finely chopped sweet
  green pepper**
½ **cup finely chopped sweet
  yellow pepper**
2 **tablespoons dry white wine**
1 **teaspoon chili powder**
¼ **teaspoon ground cumin**
3 **cups hot cooked rice**

Rinse chicken; pat dry with paper towels. Sprinkle both sides of chicken with ¼ teaspoon *salt* and ⅛ teaspoon *pepper*.

In a large skillet cook chicken in margarine or butter till brown on both sides, turning once. Drain off fat. Combine stewed tomatoes, onion, red pepper, green pepper, yellow pepper, wine, chili powder, and cumin. Pour over chicken. Cover and simmer for 10 to 12 minutes or till chicken is tender and no longer pink. Remove chicken; arrange on a serving platter; keep warm.

Heat the tomato mixture till boiling. Boil, uncovered, for 4 to 6 minutes or till desired consistency. Spoon tomato mixture over chicken. Serve with rice. Makes 6 servings.

Per serving: 274 calories, 22 g protein, 34 g carbohydrate, 5 g total fat (1 g saturated), 50 mg cholesterol, 260 mg sodium, 337 mg potassium.

Chicken Cacciatore

1   2½- to 3-pound broiler-
    fryer chicken, cut up
2   tablespoons olive oil
1   medium onion, sliced
1   clove garlic, minced
1   7½-ounce can tomatoes,
    cut up
1   6-ounce can tomato paste
¾   cup dry white wine
1   4-ounce can mushroom
    stems and pieces, drained
2   tablespoons snipped fresh
    parsley
1   teaspoon sugar
½   teaspoon salt
½   teaspoon dried rosemary,
    crushed
½   teaspoon dried thyme,
    crushed
¼   teaspoon dried oregano,
    crushed
⅛   teaspoon pepper
    Hot cooked spaghetti
    (optional)

Skin chicken, if desired. Rinse chicken; pat dry with paper towels. In a 12-inch skillet cook chicken in hot oil, uncovered, over medium heat for 10 to 15 minutes or till light brown, turning to brown evenly. Add onion and garlic the last 5 minutes of cooking. Drain fat.

In a medium bowl combine *undrained* tomatoes, tomato paste, wine, mushrooms, parsley, sugar, salt, rosemary, thyme, oregano, and pepper. Pour over chicken in skillet. Bring to boiling. Reduce heat and simmer, covered, for 35 to 40 minutes or till tender. Turn once during cooking. Serve over hot cooked spaghetti, if desired. Makes 6 servings.

Per serving: 284 calories, 22 g protein, 10 g carbohydrate, 15 g total fat (4 g saturated), 66 mg cholesterol, 389 mg sodium, 590 mg potassium.

Spicy Chicken Skillet

2   to 2½ pounds meaty
    chicken pieces
    (breasts, thighs, *and/or*
    drumsticks)
½   teaspoon garlic salt
¼   teaspoon pepper
2   tablespoons cooking oil
1   8-ounce jar picante sauce
½   cup chopped onion
¼   cup chopped green pepper
¼   cup sliced pitted ripe olives
2   teaspoons sugar
¼   teaspoon ground ginger
⅛   teaspoon ground red
    pepper
    Hot cooked rice *or* couscous
    (optional)

Skin chicken, if desired. Rinse chicken; pat dry with paper towels. Sprinkle both sides of chicken with garlic salt and pepper.

In a large skillet cook chicken in hot oil about 5 minutes on each side or till brown. Drain off fat. Combine picante sauce, onion, green pepper, olives, sugar, ginger, and ground red pepper. Pour over chicken. Heat to boiling; reduce heat. Cover and simmer for 15 to 20 minutes or till chicken is tender and no longer pink. Remove chicken; arrange on a serving platter; keep warm.

Heat the picante sauce mixture till boiling. Boil, uncovered, for 3 to 4 minutes or till slightly thickened. Skim any excess fat from sauce mixture. Spoon over chicken. Serve with rice or couscous, if desired. Makes 6 servings.

Per serving: 232 calories, 23 g protein, 8 g carbohydrate, 13 g total fat (3 g saturated), 69 mg cholesterol, 773 mg sodium, 378 mg potassium.

Baked Chicken Breasts Dijon

4 **skinless, boneless medium chicken breast halves**
2 **tablespoons Dijon-style mustard**
1 **tablespoon white wine vinegar**
¼ **cup fine dry bread crumbs**
2 **tablespoons grated Parmesan cheese**
¼ **teaspoon dried thyme, crushed**
⅛ **teaspoon garlic powder**
1 **tablespoon margarine or butter, melted**

1 To skin chicken breasts, pull the skin away from the meat. **2** Cut the meat away from the bone. **3** Pull the meat up and away from the rib bones. **4** Remove the long white tendon by pulling on the end of the tendon.

Rinse chicken; pat dry with paper towels. Place chicken in a greased shallow baking pan.

In a small bowl stir together mustard and vinegar. Brush the mustard mixture over chicken. In another small bowl toss together bread crumbs, Parmesan cheese, thyme, garlic powder, and ⅛ teaspoon *pepper*. Stir in margarine or butter. Sprinkle crumb mixture over chicken. Press crumb mixture slightly into chicken. Bake in a 350° oven for 20 to 25 minutes or till chicken is tender and no longer pink. Makes 4 servings.

Per serving: 165 calories, 19 g protein, 6 g carbohydrate, 7 g total fat (2 g saturated), 47 mg cholesterol, 367 mg sodium, 161 mg potassium.

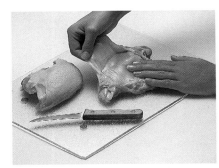

1 To skin chicken breasts, pull the skin away from the meat. Discard the skin.

2 Starting to one side of the breastbone, use a thin sharp knife to cut the meat away from the bone.

3 Continue cutting, using a sawing motion. Press the flat side of the knife against the rib bones. As you cut, pull the meat up and away from the rib bones.

4 Remove the long white tendon from each breast half by pulling on the end of the tendon. Use a knife to scrape against the tendon, freeing the surrounding meat.

Crunchy Baked Chicken with Raisin Sauce

2 to 2½ pounds meaty
    chicken pieces
    (breasts, thighs, *and/or*
    drumsticks)
½ cup all-purpose flour
½ cup finely chopped
    peanuts
½ teaspoon salt
½ teaspoon paprika
¼ teaspoon curry powder
⅛ teaspoon ground ginger
⅓ cup milk
¼ cup margarine *or* butter,
    melted
    Raisin Sauce

Remove skin from chicken, if desired. Rinse chicken; pat dry with paper towels. In a shallow dish combine flour, peanuts, salt, paprika, curry powder, and ginger. Dip chicken pieces in milk. Then roll in flour mixture to coat both sides. In a 13x9x2-inch baking pan arrange chicken, skin side up and so the pieces do not touch each other. Drizzle with melted margarine or butter.

Bake in a 375° oven for 45 to 55 minutes or till chicken is tender and no longer pink. *Do not* turn chicken during baking. Serve with Raisin Sauce. Makes 6 servings.

Raisin Sauce: In a small saucepan combine ½ cup *water*, ½ cup *orange juice*, 1 tablespoon *cornstarch*, and 1 tablespoon *lemon juice*. Cook and stir over medium heat till thickened and bubbly. Cook and stir for 2 minutes more. Stir in ⅓ cup *raisins*, ¼ cup *orange marmalade*, and ⅛ teaspoon ground *allspice*. Heat through.

Per serving: 427 calories, 27 g protein, 30 g carbohydrate, 22 g total fat (5 g saturated), 70 mg cholesterol, 339 mg sodium, 405 mg potassium.

Baked Chicken and Dressing

1 8-ounce package herb
    seasoned stuffing mix
1 cup sliced fresh mushrooms
½ cup chopped celery
¼ cup chopped onion
1 2-ounce jar sliced pimiento,
    drained
3 tablespoons snipped fresh
    parsley
1½ cups water
2 to 2½ pounds meaty
    chicken pieces
    (breast halves, thighs,
    and/or drumsticks)
1 tablespoon melted
    margarine *or* butter
    Salt
    Pepper
    Paprika

In a large bowl, combine stuffing mix, mushrooms, celery, onion, pimiento, parsley, and water. Mix well. Spoon mixture into a lightly greased 2-quart rectangular baking dish.

Skin chicken, if desired. Rinse chicken; pat dry with paper towels. Arrange chicken over dressing. Brush chicken with melted margarine or butter. Sprinkle with salt, pepper, and paprika. Cover dish with foil. Bake in a 375° oven for 45 minutes. Remove foil; bake for 15 to 20 minutes more or till chicken is tender and no longer pink. Makes 6 servings.

Per serving: 336 calories, 29 g protein, 32 g carbohydrate, 10 g total fat (2 g saturated), 69 mg cholesterol, 648 mg sodium, 330 mg potassium.

Chicken and Asparagus Lasagna

6 lasagna noodles

½ pound asparagus, washed, trimmed, and cut into ½-inch pieces

¼ cup chopped onion

1 clove garlic, minced

2 tablespoons margarine

2 tablespoons all-purpose flour

¼ teaspoon pepper

1⅔ cups milk

1 cup shredded mozzarella cheese (4 ounces)

2 tablespoons dry white wine (optional)

⅛ teaspoon ground nutmeg

1 beaten egg

2 cups ricotta cheese

½ cup grated Parmesan cheese

¼ teaspoon dried thyme, crushed

2 cups chopped cooked chicken

2 tablespoons snipped fresh parsley

Cook noodles according to package directions; drain. Rinse with cold water; drain again. Set aside.

Meanwhile, cook asparagus, covered, in a small amount of *boiling water* for 8 to 10 minutes or till crisp-tender. Drain; set aside.

For sauce, in a medium saucepan cook onion and garlic in margarine till tender, but not brown. Stir in flour and pepper. Add milk. Cook and stir till thickened and bubbly. Cook and stir for 1 minute more. Over low heat, add mozzarella cheese, wine, and nutmeg, stirring till cheese melts.

For filling, in a medium bowl stir together egg, ricotta cheese, ¼ *cup* of the Parmesan cheese, and the thyme. **1**Layer three of the cooked noodles in a 2-quart rectangular baking dish. **2**Spread with *half* of filling. **3**Layer *half* of the chicken and *half* of the asparagus over filling. **4**Top with *half* of the sauce. Repeat layers. Sprinkle with the remaining Parmesan cheese.

Bake in a 375° oven for 30 to 35 minutes or till heated through. Let stand 10 minutes before serving. Sprinkle with parsley. Makes 8 servings.

Per serving: 350 calories, 29 g protein, 20 g carbohydrate, 17 g total fat (8 g saturated), 96 mg cholesterol, 360 mg sodium, 359 mg potassium.

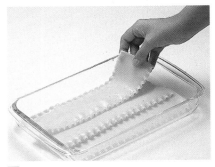

1Place half of the cooked lasagna noodles lengthwise in baking dish.

2Spread half of the ricotta filling mixture over noodles.

3Layer half of the chopped, cooked chicken and asparagus pieces over filling.

4Pour half of sauce over chicken and asparagus, spreading evenly. Repeat layers.

Chicken-Spinach Pot Pie

1 **cup chopped onion**
1 **cup shredded carrot**
1 **cup chopped celery**
½ **cup chopped red, yellow,**
    or **green sweet pepper**
2 **tablespoons margarine** *or*
    butter
3 **cups chopped, cooked**
    chicken
1 **10-ounce package frozen**
    chopped spinach, thawed
    and well drained
1 **8-ounce container sour**
    cream dip with chives
1 **cup shredded creamy**
    havarti *or* **Swiss cheese**
    (4 ounces)
1 **egg, slightly beaten**
½ **teaspoon salt**
¼ **teaspoon pepper**
¼ **teaspoon ground nutmeg**
½ **of a 17¼-ounce package**
    frozen puff pastry
    (1 sheet), thawed
1 **egg, slightly beaten**
1 **teaspoon water**

In a large skillet cook onion, carrot, celery, and sweet pepper in margarine or butter till tender. Stir in chicken, spinach, sour cream dip, cheese, 1 egg, salt, pepper, and nutmeg. Spoon mixture into a 2-quart rectangular baking dish.

On a lightly floured surface roll puff pastry to a 12x9-inch rectangle. Place pastry over chicken mixture in baking dish. Trim edges of pastry to fit dish. If desired, cut remaining pastry into shapes with small cookie cutters. Place cutouts on top of pastry in the baking dish. Stir together 1 egg and the water. Brush pastry with egg mixture. Cut slits in pastry. Bake in a 350° oven for 30 minutes or till pastry is golden. Makes 6 to 8 servings.

Per serving: 567 calories, 33 g protein, 28 g carbohydrate, 36 g total fat (3 g saturated), 162 mg cholesterol, 846 mg sodium, 534 mg potassium.

Chicken Patties with Chutney Sauce

1 **beaten egg**
½ **cup chopped green onion**
¼ **cup fine dry bread crumbs**
1 **teaspoon finely shredded**
    lemon peel
¼ **teaspoon salt**
¼ **teaspoon ground**
    cardamom
⅛ **teaspoon ground ginger**
⅛ **teaspoon pepper**
1 **pound ground raw chicken**
2 **tablespoons all-purpose**
    flour
1 **tablespoon cooking oil**
½ **cup chutney**
¼ **cup orange juice**

In a large bowl combine egg, green onion, bread crumbs, lemon peel, salt, cardamom, ginger, and pepper. Add ground chicken; mix well. (Mixture will be sticky.) Shape chicken mixture into four ¾-inch-thick patties. Place flour in a shallow dish. Coat both sides of patties with flour.

In a large skillet cook patties in hot oil over medium heat for 6 minutes, turning once. Cover and cook for 3 to 5 minutes more or till no longer pink and juices run clear.

Meanwhile, for sauce, cut up any large pieces of chutney. In a small bowl combine chutney and orange juice. Serve sauce with patties. Makes 4 servings.

Per serving: 295 calories, 19 g protein, 29 g carbohydrate, 11 g total fat (3 g saturated), 108 mg cholesterol, 258 mg sodium, 249 mg potassium.

Gingered Chicken

1 **20-ounce can pineapple chunks**
2 **tablespoons orange juice**
2 **tablespoons soy sauce**
2 **cloves garlic, minced**
2 **teaspoons grated gingerroot**
1 **teaspoon honey**
¼ **teaspoon ground coriander**
12 **ounces skinless, boneless chicken breast halves**
1 **tablespoon cooking oil**
2 **cups thinly sliced carrots**
2 **cups fresh pea pods, tips and strings removed**
2 **teaspoons cornstarch**
2 **teaspoons finely chopped crystallized ginger**
½ **cup coarsely chopped red sweet pepper**

Drain pineapple, reserving ⅓ *cup* juice. Set pineapple chunks aside. For marinade, in a bowl stir together reserved pineapple juice, orange juice, soy sauce, garlic, gingerroot, honey, and coriander. Rinse chicken and pat dry. Cut chicken lengthwise into ½-inch wide strips. Add chicken to marinade; stir to coat. Marinate in the refrigerator for 1 hour. Drain chicken, reserving marinade.

Pour oil into a wok or skillet. (Add more oil as necessary during cooking.) Preheat wok or skillet over medium-high heat. Add carrots to wok; stir-fry for 4 minutes. Add pea pods; stir-fry 1 minute more or till crisp-tender. Remove vegetables from wok. Add chicken; stir-fry for 3 to 4 minutes or till tender and no longer pink. Push chicken to sides of wok.

Stir together the reserved marinade and cornstarch; add to center of wok. Cook and stir till thickened and bubbly. Return vegetables to wok. Add reserved pineapple and crystallized ginger; stir all ingredients together to coat with sauce. Cook and stir about 1 minute more or till heated through. Serve with *3 cups hot cooked rice*. Sprinkle with chopped red pepper. Makes 4 or 5 servings.

Per serving: 440 calories, 23 g protein, 72 g carbohydrate, 7 g total fat (1 g saturated), 45 mg cholesterol, 529 mg sodium, 691 mg potassium.

Chicken and Green Bean Stir-Fry

3 tablespoons soy sauce
2 tablespoons dry sherry
1 tablespoon hoisin sauce
2 teaspoons cornstarch
2 teaspoons lemon juice
1 teaspoon brown sugar
1 teaspoon grated gingerroot
1 pound skinless, boneless
   chicken breast halves
1 tablespoon cooking oil
2 cloves garlic, minced
½ pound fresh green beans,
   washed, trimmed, and
   cut in half crosswise
1 cup sliced fresh
   mushrooms
1 small red sweet pepper, cut
   into thin strips
1 8-ounce can bamboo
   shoots, drained
½ cup coarsely chopped
   cashews
3 cups hot cooked brown
   rice

For sauce, in a small bowl combine soy sauce, sherry, hoisin sauce, cornstarch, lemon juice, brown sugar, and gingerroot; stir well. Set aside. Rinse chicken; pat dry with paper towels. Cut into 1-inch pieces.

Pour oil into a wok or large skillet. (Add more oil as necessary during cooking.) Preheat wok or skillet over medium-high heat. Stir-fry garlic in hot oil for 30 seconds. Add green beans to wok; stir-fry for 2 minutes. Add mushrooms and red pepper; stir-fry for 1 to 2 minutes or till vegetables are crisp-tender. Remove vegetables from wok. Add *half* of the chicken to the wok; stir-fry for 2 to 3 minutes or till tender and no longer pink. Remove cooked chicken. Repeat with remaining chicken. Stir the sauce; add to the wok. Cook and stir till thickened and bubbly. Return the cooked vegetables and cooked chicken to wok. Add the bamboo shoots. Cook about 1 minute more or till heated through, stirring constantly. Stir in cashews. Serve over hot cooked brown rice. Makes 4 servings.

Per serving: 479 calories, 31 g protein, 51 g carbohydrate, 16 g total fat (3 g saturated), 59 mg cholesterol, 1197 mg sodium, 664 mg potassium.

Tequila Chicken

¾ pound skinless, boneless
   chicken breast halves
1 tablespoon cooking oil
1 12-ounce jar chunky salsa
3 tablespoons snipped fresh
   cilantro
2 tablespoons tequila
1 tablespoon lime juice
2 teaspoons finely shredded
   lime peel
2 teaspoons sugar
¼ teaspoon ground
   cinnamon
¼ teaspoon ground red
   pepper
⅛ teaspoon garlic powder
2 cups hot cooked rice

Rinse chicken; pat dry with paper towels. Cut chicken into ½-inch strips.

In a large skillet cook chicken strips in hot oil till light brown; drain cooking liquid from skillet.

Meanwhile, in a medium bowl combine salsa, cilantro, tequila, lime juice, lime peel, sugar, cinnamon, red pepper, and garlic powder. Pour over chicken in skillet. Bring to boiling. Reduce heat. Simmer, uncovered, for 8 to 10 minutes or till chicken is tender and no longer pink. Serve over hot cooked rice. Makes 4 servings.

Per serving: 310 calories, 20 g protein, 38 g carbohydrate, 8 g total fat (1 g saturated), 45 mg cholesterol, 376 mg sodium, 446 mg potassium.

Honey-Glazed Duckling

3 tablespoons honey
3 tablespoons dry sherry
2 tablespoons frozen orange
    juice concentrate,
    thawed
2 tablespoons soy sauce
¼ teaspoon ground ginger
⅛ teaspoon garlic powder
⅛ teaspoon ground red
    pepper
1 3- to 5-pound domestic
    duckling

For glaze, in a small bowl combine honey, sherry, orange juice concentrate, soy sauce, ginger, garlic powder, and red pepper. Stir well; set aside.

Rinse duckling; pat dry with paper towels. Pull the neck skin to the back and fasten with a small skewer. Tie the drumsticks securely to the tail. Twist the wing tips under the back. **1** Prick the skin all over with a fork to allow fat to drain during roasting.

Place duckling, breast side up, on a rack in a shallow roasting pan. Insert a meat thermometer into the center of one of the inside thigh muscles. The bulb should not touch the bone.

Roast in a 375° oven, uncovered, for 1¾ to 2¼ hours or till thermometer registers 180° or the drumsticks move easily in their sockets and duck is no longer pink. **2 3** Remove excess fat occasionally during roasting. Baste with glaze during the last 30 minutes. Heat remaining glaze and pass with duckling. Makes 4 servings.

Per serving: 521 calories, 26 g protein, 18 g carbohydrate, 37 g total fat (13 g saturated), 109 mg cholesterol, 537 mg sodium, 360 mg potassium.

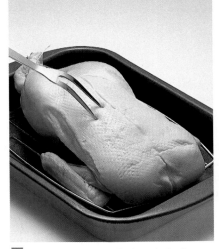

1 Using a kitchen fork, prick the skin well all over so that fat can drain off the bird while it cooks.

2 To remove excess fat during roasting, take the roasting pan out of the oven and set it on a heat-proof surface. Using a pot holder, tilt the pan slightly so that the fat runs to one corner.

3 Use a meat baster to take up the fat. Empty the fat into a glass measuring cup or metal can. Remove excess fat several times during roasting.

Citrus-Herb Chicken

2 tablespoons finely
    chopped onion
1 teaspoon olive oil *or*
    cooking oil
1½ teaspoons finely shredded
    orange peel
¼ cup orange juice
2 tablespoons lemon juice
1 tablespoon dry sherry
1½ teaspoons snipped fresh
    mint *or* ½ teaspoon dried
    mint, crushed
1 teaspoon honey
⅛ teaspoon ground ginger
⅛ teaspoon dried rosemary,
    crushed
2 to 2½ pounds meaty
    chicken pieces
    (breasts, thighs, *and/or*
    drumsticks)

For glaze, in a small saucepan cook onion in hot oil till tender. Add orange peel, orange juice, lemon juice, sherry, mint, honey, ginger, and rosemary. Bring to boiling; reduce heat. Simmer, uncovered, for 5 minutes. Remove from heat.

Rinse chicken; pat dry with paper towels. Place chicken, skin side down, on the unheated rack of a broiler pan. Broil 4 to 5 inches from the heat about 20 minutes or till lightly browned. Brush chicken with glaze. Turn chicken, skin side up; brush again with glaze. Broil for 5 to 15 minutes more or till chicken is tender and no longer pink, brushing often with glaze during the last 5 minutes of cooking. Makes 6 servings.

Per serving: 192 calories, 22 g protein, 3 g carbohydrate, 9 g total fat (2 g saturated), 69 mg cholesterol, 61 mg sodium, 201 mg potassium.

Grilled Chicken and Pineapple

¼ cup pineapple juice
2 tablespoons lemon juice
2 tablespoons cooking oil
2 tablespoons soy sauce
1 teaspoon ground ginger
½ teaspoon garlic powder
½ teaspoon dry mustard
2 to 2½ pounds meaty
    chicken pieces
    (breasts, thighs, *and/or*
    drumsticks)
6 slices fresh pineapple, cut
    ½ inch thick

For marinade, stir together pineapple juice, lemon juice, oil, soy sauce, ginger, garlic powder, and dry mustard; set aside.

Skin chicken, if desired. Rinse chicken; pat dry with paper towels. Place in a plastic bag, set into a deep bowl. Pour marinade over chicken. Seal bag and turn to coat chicken well. Marinate in the refrigerator for 2 to 4 hours, turning bag occasionally.

Drain chicken, reserving marinade. Place chicken, skin side down, on an uncovered grill. Grill directly over medium coals for 20 minutes. Turn; brush with marinade. Grill for 15 to 25 minutes more or till tender and no longer pink, brushing often with marinade. (Do not brush with marinade during the last 5 minutes of grilling.) Add pineapple slices to grill during the last 5 minutes of grilling, turning once to brown both sides. Makes 6 servings.

Per serving: 249 calories, 23 g protein, 9 g carbohydrate, 13 g total fat (3 g saturated), 69 mg cholesterol, 405 mg sodium, 262 mg potassium.

Turkey Tamale Pie

12 ounces ground raw turkey
½ cup chopped onion
1 tablespoon cooking oil
⅓ cup salsa-style catsup
1 10-ounce package corn bread mix
½ cup shredded American cheese
¼ cup salsa-style catsup
2 teaspoons cornstarch
1 7½-ounce can tomatoes, cut up

1 In a skillet cook turkey and onion in hot oil till meat is browned and no pink remains. Drain. Return mixture to skillet. Stir in the ⅓ cup salsa-style catsup. Set aside.

In a medium mixing bowl prepare corn bread mix according to package directions. **2** Spread *half* of the batter in a greased 2-quart square baking dish. **3** Spoon meat mixture over batter in dish; drop remaining batter by spoonfuls over meat mixture. Bake, uncovered, in a 350° oven for 30 to 35 minutes or till corn bread is done. Sprinkle with cheese. Bake 2 to 3 minutes more or till cheese is melted. Let stand 5 minutes before serving.

Meanwhile, in a small saucepan combine the ¼ cup salsa-style catsup and cornstarch. Stir in *undrained* tomatoes. Cook and stir till thickened and bubbly. Cook and stir for 2 minutes more.

To serve, cut into squares. Spoon tomato mixture atop each serving. Makes 6 servings.

Per serving: 374 calories, 15 g protein, 43 g carbohydrate, 16 g total fat (4 g saturated), 68 mg cholesterol, 1226 mg sodium, 373 mg potassium.

1 Brown the turkey and onion in hot oil till the turkey is lightly browned and no pink remains.

2 Spread half the corn bread batter in a greased 2-quart square baking dish.

3 Spoon turkey mixture over batter in dish. Drop spoonfuls of remaining batter over turkey mixture.

Turkey Picadillo

1 **pound ground raw turkey**
½ **cup chopped onion**
1 **clove garlic, minced**
½ **cup chili sauce**
½ **cup water**
¼ **cup raisins**
¼ **cup chopped pitted ripe olives**
1 **teaspoon chili powder**
½ **teaspoon ground cumin**
¼ **teaspoon salt**
¼ **teaspoon ground cinnamon**
¼ **teaspoon crushed red pepper**
10 **6-inch corn tortillas**
   Shredded lettuce (optional)
   Dairy sour cream (optional)

In a medium skillet cook turkey, onion, and garlic over medium-high heat till turkey is brown; drain. Stir in chili sauce, water, raisins, olives, chili powder, cumin, salt, cinnamon, and crushed red pepper. Bring to boiling. Reduce heat. Simmer, uncovered, for 10 minutes or till most of the liquid has evaporated.

Meanwhile, wrap the tortillas in foil. Heat in a 300° oven about 10 minutes or till softened. Spoon turkey mixture down center of tortillas. Top with lettuce and sour cream, if desired. Fold tortillas over filling. Makes 5 servings.

Per serving: 313 calories, 18 g protein, 40 g carbohydrate, 10 g total fat (2 g saturated), 34 mg cholesterol, 615 mg sodium, 428 mg potassium.

Turkey Meatballs in Creamy Herb Sauce

1 **beaten egg**
1¼ **cups soft bread crumbs**
¼ **cup finely chopped onion**
2 **tablespoons diced pimiento**
2 **tablespoons snipped fresh parsley**
1 **pound ground raw turkey**
1 **clove garlic, minced**
1 **tablespoon margarine *or* butter**
2 **tablespoons all-purpose flour**
1 **teaspoon instant chicken bouillon granules**
¼ **teaspoon dried thyme, crushed**
¼ **teaspoon dried rosemary, crushed**
⅛ **teaspoon poultry seasoning**
1⅔ **cups milk**
3 **cups hot cooked noodles**

In a medium bowl combine egg, bread crumbs, onion, pimiento, parsley, ½ teaspoon *salt,* and ¼ teaspoon *pepper.* Add turkey; mix well. Shape into 30 meatballs about 1 inch in diameter. Place in an ungreased shallow baking pan. Bake in a 375° oven for 15 to 20 minutes or till no longer pink. Drain meatballs on paper towels.

In a large saucepan cook garlic in margarine or butter for 2 minutes. Stir in flour, bouillon granules, thyme, rosemary, and poultry seasoning. Add milk all at once. Cook and stir over medium heat till thickened and bubbly. Cook and stir for 1 minute more. Gently stir meatballs into sauce. Heat through. Serve over hot cooked noodles. Makes 6 servings.

Per serving: 357 calories, 20 g protein, 41 g carbohydrate, 12 g total fat (3 g saturated), 108 mg cholesterol, 480 mg sodium, 304 mg potassium.

Vegetable-Stuffed Turkey Roll

1 egg, beaten
½ cup fine dry bread crumbs
½ cup finely chopped onion
¼ cup milk
½ teaspoon dried thyme, crushed
¼ teaspoon dried rosemary, crushed
¼ teaspoon garlic salt
¼ teaspoon pepper
1½ pounds ground raw turkey
1 cup chopped fresh broccoli
⅔ cup shredded carrot
⅓ cup chopped sweet red pepper
2 tablespoons grated Parmesan cheese
2 tablespoons currant jelly, melted

In a medium mixing bowl combine egg, bread crumbs, onion, milk, thyme, rosemary, garlic salt, and pepper. Add turkey; mix well. **1** On waxed paper pat turkey mixture into a 12x8-inch rectangle; set aside.

For vegetable stuffing, in a saucepan cook broccoli, carrot, and red pepper, covered, in a small amount of boiling water for 3 to 4 minutes or till crisp-tender. Drain well. Stir in Parmesan cheese.

2 Spread vegetable stuffing over turkey mixture to within 1 inch of sides. **3** Beginning at a short end, roll turkey tightly using waxed paper to lift mixture. Peel waxed paper away as you roll. Place in a 9x5x3-inch loaf pan. Bake in a 350° oven for 1 to 1¼ hours or till no longer pink (meat thermometer registers 180°). Remove from pan; transfer to a serving platter. Brush with melted jelly. Makes 6 servings.

Note: To micro-cook stuffing, combine broccoli, carrot, and red pepper in a 1-quart microwave-safe casserole. Micro-cook on 100% power (high) for 2 to 3 minutes or till crisp-tender; drain. Stir in Parmesan cheese.

Per serving: 242 calories, 20 g protein, 17 g carbohydrate, 11 g total fat (3 g saturated), 80 mg cholesterol, 273 mg sodium, 368 mg potassium.

Vegetable-Stuffed Turkey Roll *(continued)*

1 On waxed paper, use your fingertips to pat the meat mixture into a 12x8-inch rectangle.

2 Use a spoon or spatula to spread the vegetable stuffing over the meat mixture to within 1 inch of all of the sides.

3 Beginning at one of the short ends, roll up the meat mixture jelly-roll style. Use the waxed paper to lift the mixture.

Hot Turkey Salad Oriental

2 cups cubed cooked turkey
1 cup fresh bean sprouts *or*
    ½ of a 16-ounce can bean
    sprouts, rinsed and
    drained
1 cup chopped celery
½ cup sliced water chestnuts
½ cup sliced green onion
1 4-ounce jar sliced
    pimiento, drained
1 cup mayonnaise
1 tablespoon finely shredded
    lemon peel
1 tablespoon soy sauce
2 teaspoons lemon juice
1 teaspoon grated gingerroot
    ***or* ¼ teaspoon ground**
    ginger
⅓ cup sliced toasted almonds

In a large bowl combine turkey, bean sprouts, celery, water chestnuts, green onion, and pimiento.

For dressing, stir together mayonnaise, lemon peel, soy sauce, lemon juice, and gingerroot or ginger. Pour over turkey mixture. Toss to coat. Spoon turkey mixture into an ungreased 2-quart square baking dish. Sprinkle with almonds. Bake in a 350° oven about 25 minutes or till heated through. Makes 4 servings.

Note: To reduce fat and calories, substitute a reduced fat mayonnaise or salad dressing.

Per serving: 587 calories, 20 g protein, 13 g carbohydrate, 52 g total fat (9 g saturated), 70 mg cholesterol, 1063 mg sodium, 553 mg potassium.

Roast Turkey with Leek and Pecan Stuffing

**2 cups thinly sliced leeks
(white portion only)**
½ cup chopped onion
½ cup shredded carrot
½ cup margarine *or* butter
½ cup snipped fresh parsley
**1 teaspoon dried marjoram,
crushed**
**¼ teaspoon dried thyme,
crushed**
¼ teaspoon pepper
8 cups dry bread cubes*
**1 cup toasted pecans,
chopped**
**6 slices bacon, crisp-cooked,
drained, and crumbled**
¾ to 1 cup chicken broth
1 8- to 10-pound turkey

For stuffing, in a medium saucepan cook leeks, onion, and carrot in margarine or butter till tender but not brown; remove from heat. Stir in parsley, marjoram, thyme, and pepper; set aside. In a large bowl combine bread cubes, pecans, and crumbled bacon. Add onion mixture. Drizzle with enough broth to moisten, tossing lightly till well mixed.

To stuff turkey, rinse turkey well on the outside as well as inside body and neck cavities. Pat dry with paper towels. **1** Spoon some of stuffing loosely into the neck cavity. **2** Pull the neck skin to the back; fasten with a small skewer. **3** Lightly spoon stuffing into the body cavity. (Place any remaining stuffing in a small casserole. Cover and chill. Bake alongside the turkey for 30 to 35 minutes or till heated through.) **4** Tuck the ends of the drumsticks under the band of skin across the tail. If the band of skin is not present, tie the drumsticks securely to the tail. **5** Twist the wing tips under the back.

Place turkey, breast side up, on a rack in a shallow roasting pan. **6** If using a meat thermometer, insert it into the center of one of the inside thigh muscles. The bulb should not touch the bone.

Roast, uncovered, in a 325° oven for 3½ to 4½ hours, basting occasionally with pan drippings. When the bird is two-thirds done, cut the skin band or string between the drumsticks so that the thighs will cook evenly. Continue roasting till the meat thermometer registers 180° to 185°. Drumsticks should move very easily in their sockets and the thickest part of the drumsticks will feel very soft when pressed. Remove from oven, cover with foil and let stand 15 to 20 minutes before carving. Makes 8 to 10 servings.

*Note: To make dry bread cubes, cut 16 slices of bread into ½-inch cubes. Spread in a single layer in a 15½x10½x2-inch baking pan. Bake in a 350° oven for 10 to 15 minutes or till dry, stirring twice during baking.

Per serving: 571 calories, 35 g protein, 32 g carbohydrate, 34 g total fat (7 g saturated), 125 mg cholesterol, 1785 mg sodium, 715 mg potassium.

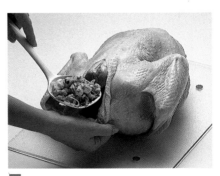

1 To stuff the bird, lightly spoon some of the stuffing mixture into the neck cavity.

2 Pull the neck skin over the stuffing to the back of the bird. Fasten securely to the back with a small wooden or metal skewer.

3 Loosely fill the body cavity with stuffing, allowing room for expansion during cooking.

Roast Turkey with Leek and Pecan Stuffing *(continued)*

  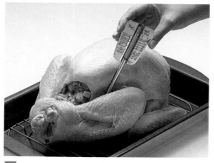

4 Tuck the ends of the drumsticks under the band of skin across the tail. If the band of skin is not present, tie the legs securely to the tail with string.

5 Twist the tips of the wings under the back of the bird to keep the wings from overbrowning during roasting.

6 Insert a meat thermometer in the center of the inside thigh muscle making sure the bulb of the thermometer does not touch the bone.

Turkey Breasts with Oranges and Olives

1½ **pounds turkey breast slices**
½ **teaspoon celery salt**
¼ **teaspoon garlic powder**
¼ **teaspoon pepper**
1 **tablespoon olive oil *or* cooking oil**
2 **small oranges, peeled and sectioned**
   Orange juice
⅓ **cup sliced pitted ripe olives**
¼ **cup thinly sliced celery**
2 **tablespoons dry white wine**
¼ **teaspoon dried rosemary, crushed**

Rinse turkey; pat dry with paper towels. Stir together celery salt, garlic powder, and pepper. Sprinkle both sides of turkey with seasoning mixture, pressing into the surface of the meat.

In a large skillet cook turkey in hot oil till brown on both sides, turning once.

Meanwhile, over a small bowl section oranges, catching all of the juice in the bowl. Measure juice and add additional orange juice, if necessary, to make ¼ cup.

In a small bowl combine the ¼ cup juice, olives, celery, wine, and rosemary. Pour over turkey in skillet. Bring to boiling; reduce heat. Cover and simmer for 10 to 12 minutes or till turkey is tender and no longer pink. Add orange sections to skillet. Heat through. Makes 6 servings.

Per serving: 162 calories, 22 g protein, 4 g carbohydrate, 6 g total fat (1 g saturated), 50 mg cholesterol, 221 mg sodium, 302 mg potassium.

Tropical Turkey Kabobs

½ cup pineapple juice
1 tablespoon lime juice
1 tablespoon cooking oil
1 tablespoon soy sauce
1 teaspoon grated gingerroot
1½ pounds turkey breast
    tenderloins
12 pearl onions, peeled
1 large green sweet pepper,
    cut into 1½-inch pieces
1 large red sweet pepper, cut
    into 1½-inch pieces
2 papayas, peeled, seeded,
    and cut into 1½-inch
    pieces

For marinade, in a 1-cup glass measure combine pineapple juice, lime juice, oil, soy sauce, and gingerroot; set aside.

Rinse turkey; pat dry with paper towels. Cut into 1-inch pieces. **1** Place turkey in a plastic bag set into a deep bowl. **2** Pour marinade over turkey. Seal bag and turn bag to coat turkey well. Marinate in the refrigerator for 2 to 4 hours, turning bag occasionally.

In a small saucepan cook pearl onions, covered, in a small amount of *boiling water* for 2 minutes. Add green and red sweet peppers; cook for 1 minute more. Drain vegetables.

Remove turkey from bag, reserving marinade. **3** On six long metal skewers, alternately thread turkey, onions, green pepper, red pepper, and papaya, leaving about ¼ inch between pieces.

Grill kabobs on the grill rack of an uncovered grill directly over medium-hot coals for 12 to 14 minutes or till turkey is tender and no longer pink, turning kabobs and brushing with reserved marinade once after 6 minutes. Makes 6 servings.

Per serving: 252 calories, 23 g protein, 28 g carbohydrate, 5 g total fat (1 g saturated), 50 mg cholesterol, 210 mg sodium, 632 mg potassium.

1 Place turkey breast pieces in a plastic bag set in a deep bowl.

2 Pour the marinade mixture over the turkey pieces. Close the bag.

3 On six 12-inch metal skewers alternately thread the turkey, onions, green pepper, red pepper, and papaya pieces, leaving ¼ inch between pieces.

Chicken and Asparagus Turnovers

1 **10-ounce package frozen asparagus spears**
3 **cups diced cooked chicken**
1 **4½-ounce jar sliced mushrooms, drained**
3 **tablespoons margarine *or* butter**
3 **tablespoons all-purpose flour**
¼ **teaspoon onion powder**
¼ **teaspoon dry mustard**
¼ **teaspoon pepper**
1 **cup milk**
½ **cup chicken broth**
¼ **cup grated Parmesan cheese**
3 **cups all-purpose flour**
¾ **teaspoon salt**
¾ **cup vegetable shortening**
1 **8-ounce package cream cheese**
½ **to ⅔ cup cold water**

Cook asparagus according to package directions; drain well and cut into ½-inch pieces. In a medium bowl combine asparagus, chicken, and mushrooms; set aside.

In a small saucepan melt margarine or butter. Combine 3 tablespoons flour, onion powder, dry mustard, and pepper. Stir into margarine till smooth. Combine milk and chicken broth; gradually add to flour mixture. Cook over medium heat till thickened and bubbly, stirring constantly. Remove from heat. Stir in Parmesan cheese. Add to asparagus-chicken mixture; combine thoroughly.

In a mixing bowl combine 3 cups flour and salt. Cut in shortening and cream cheese with pastry blender till pieces are the size of small peas. Add water, a little at a time, till mixture is moistened. Turn dough out onto lightly floured surface. Flatten and roll into an 18x12-inch rectangle. Cut into six 6-inch squares.

Spoon about *½ cup* chicken-asparagus mixture onto half of each pastry square. Moisten edges of pastry and fold unfilled side over filling to form a triangle. Seal edges with a fork. Cut slits in pastry to vent. Place on ungreased baking sheet and bake in a 375° oven for 35 to 40 minutes or till golden brown. Makes 6 servings.

Per serving: 836 calories, 36 g protein, 53 g carbohydrate, 53 g total fat (19 g saturated), 116 mg cholesterol, 768 mg sodium, 495 mg potassium.

Apple-Glazed Cornish Hens

2 **tablespoons finely chopped onion**
4 **teaspoons cooking oil**
¼ **cup apple jelly**
1 **teaspoon lemon juice**
2 **1¼- to 1½-pound Cornish game hens, halved**
½ **teaspoon salt**
½ **teaspoon dried thyme, crushed**
¼ **teaspoon dried sage, crushed**
¼ **teaspoon pepper**

For apple glaze, in a small saucepan cook onion in *2 teaspoons* hot oil till tender. Add apple jelly; cook and stir till jelly melts. Add lemon juice; mix well. Set aside.

Cut Cornish hens in half lengthwise with poultry shears. Cut on each side of the back bone and discard bone. Rinse hens; pat dry with paper towels. Rub hens with the remaining oil. Combine salt, thyme, sage, and pepper. Sprinkle both sides of hen halves evenly with herb mixture.

Place hen halves, skin side down, on the unheated rack of a broiler pan. Place under broiler about 5 inches from the heat. Broil for 15 minutes. Turn hen halves, skin side up, and broil for 10 to 20 minutes more or till meat is no longer pink and juices run clear when thighs are pierced with a fork, brushing occasionally with apple glaze during the last 5 minutes of cooking. Makes 4 servings.

Per serving: 382 calories, 30 g protein, 14 g carbohydrate, 23 g total fat (5 g saturated), 100 mg cholesterol, 345 mg sodium, 27 mg potassium.

Cornish Hens with Couscous

¼ **cup chopped onion**
1 **tablespoon margarine *or* butter**
⅔ **cup water**
½ **teaspoon instant chicken bouillon granules**
¼ **teaspoon ground cinnamon**
¼ **teaspoon ground ginger**
⅛ **teaspoon ground turmeric**
½ **cup couscous**
3 **tablespoons currants**
2 **tablespoons pine nuts**
1 **teaspoon finely shredded lemon peel**
2 **1¼- to 1½-pound Cornish game hens**
1 **tablespoon margarine *or* butter, melted**

For stuffing, in a medium saucepan cook onion in 1 tablespoon margarine or butter till tender. Add water, bouillon granules, cinnamon, ginger, and turmeric. Bring to boiling. Stir in couscous. Cover; remove from heat. Let stand for 5 minutes. Stir in currants, pine nuts, and lemon peel. Set aside.

Rinse hens; pat dry with paper towels. Season cavities with *salt* and *pepper*. Lightly stuff hens with couscous mixture. Pull neck skin, if present, to back of each hen. Twist wing tips under back, holding skin in place. Tie legs to tail. Place hens, breast side up, on a rack in a shallow roasting pan. Brush 1 tablespoon melted margarine or butter over hens; cover loosely with foil. Roast in a 375° oven for 30 minutes. Uncover and roast 1 hour more or till tender and no longer pink, brushing occasionally with additional margarine or butter, if necessary. To serve, cut hens in half lengthwise; spoon stuffing onto a serving platter. Place hens atop stuffing. Makes 4 servings.

Per serving: 476 calories, 35 g protein, 25 g carbohydrate, 27 g total fat (6 g saturated), 100 mg cholesterol, 388 mg sodium, 157 mg potassium.

Grilled Chicken with Peppery Glaze

2 to 2½ pounds meaty
   chicken pieces
   (breasts, thighs, *and/or*
   drumsticks)
¼ cup jalapeño pepper jelly
¼ cup chili sauce
1 clove garlic, minced

Skin chicken, if desired. Rinse chicken; pat dry with paper towels. In a covered grill arrange medium-hot coals around a drip pan. Test for medium heat above the drip pan. Place chicken, bone side up, on the grill rack over the drip pan. Cover and grill for 30 minutes.

Meanwhile, in a small saucepan stir together pepper jelly, chili sauce, and garlic. Cook over medium-low heat, stirring occasionally, till the jelly is melted. Remove from heat.

Turn chicken; grill for 20 to 30 minutes more or till chicken is tender and no longer pink, brushing with glaze 2 or 3 times during the last 10 minutes of grilling. Makes 6 servings.

Note: To check temperature of coals, hold your hand, palm side down, over the drip pan at the height chicken will be placed. Start counting one-thousand-one, etc. If you have to remove your hand after three seconds, the coals are medium-hot.

Per serving: 216 calories, 23 g protein, 11 g carbohydrate, 8 g total fat (2 g saturated), 69 mg cholesterol, 198 mg sodium, 215 mg potassium.

Sesame-Citrus Chicken

2 to 2½ pounds meaty
   chicken pieces (breast
   halves, thighs, *and/or*
   drumsticks)
½ cup finely chopped onion
¼ cup lime or lemon juice
2 tablespoons lower-sodium
   soy sauce
2 tablespoons dry sherry
2 tablespoons frozen orange
   juice concentrate,
   thawed
2 garlic cloves, minced
½ teaspoon hot chili oil *or*
   ¼ teaspoon bottled hot
   pepper sauce
1 tablespoon toasted sesame
   seeds

Remove skin from chicken. Rinse chicken; pat dry with paper towels. In bowl combine onion, lime juice, soy sauce, sherry, orange juice concentrate, garlic, and chili oil or hot pepper sauce. Place chicken in a plastic bag in a bowl; pour marinade mixture over chicken to coat. Close bag; refrigerate 12 or 24 hours, turning chicken pieces occasionally. Drain, reserving marinade. Place chicken, skinned side down, on the unheated rack of a broiler pan. Broil 4 to 5 inches from the heat for 20 minutes, brushing with marinade once or twice, brush again. Turn chicken and brush with marinade. Broil for 5 to 15 minutes more or till meat is tender and no longer pink. Sprinkle with sesame seeds. Makes 4 servings.

Per serving: 250 calories, 28 g protein, 9 g carbohydrate, 10 g total fat (2 g saturated), 81 mg cholesterol, 352 mg sodium, 382 mg potassium.

FISH AND SEAFOOD

Baked Salmon Steaks and Julienne Vegetables

Baked Salmon Steaks and Julienne Vegetables

4 **fresh or frozen salmon steaks, cut 1 inch thick (1¼ pounds)**
2 **medium carrots, cut into julienne strips (1 cup)**
1 **medium red sweet pepper, cut into julienne strips (1 cup)**
1 **medium zucchini, cut into julienne strips (1 cup)**
¼ **cup margarine *or* butter, melted**
1 **tablespoon snipped fresh dill *or* 1 teaspoon dried dillweed**
1 **tablespoon lemon juice**
⅛ **teaspoon garlic powder**
Lemon wedges (optional)

Thaw salmon, if frozen. In a small saucepan cook carrot strips in a small amount of boiling water for 2 minutes; drain well. Stir in red sweet pepper and zucchini strips. Place vegetables in the bottom of a 2-quart rectangular baking dish. Place salmon steaks atop vegetables.

Stir together melted margarine or butter, dill, lemon juice, and garlic powder; drizzle over salmon and vegetables. Bake, covered, in a 400° oven for 15 to 20 minutes or till fish flakes easily when tested with a fork. Serve vegetables with fish. Drizzle pan juices over all. Serve with lemon wedges, if desired. Makes 4 servings.

Per serving: 258 calories, 21 g protein, 6 g carbohydrate, 16 g total fat (3 g saturated), 25 mg cholesterol, 244 mg sodium, 387 mg potassium.

Mushroom-Stuffed Fish Fillets

8 **fresh or frozen skinless sole or flounder fillets (1 to 1½ pounds)**
1½ **cups chopped fresh mushrooms**
½ **cup shredded carrot**
1 **tablespoon snipped fresh parsley**
1 **clove garlic, minced**
2 **teaspoons cooking oil**
½ **cup soft bread crumbs**
½ **teaspoon lemon-pepper seasoning**
Lemon-Chive Sauce

Thaw fish, if frozen. For stuffing, cook mushrooms, carrot, parsley, and garlic in hot oil till tender. Stir in bread crumbs and lemon-pepper seasoning. Spoon *one-eighth* of the stuffing onto one end of *each* fish fillet. Roll up; secure rolls with wooden toothpicks.

Place fish rolls in a 2-quart rectangular baking dish. Bake, covered, in a 350° oven for 30 to 35 minutes or till fish flakes easily when tested with a fork. Serve with Lemon-Chive Sauce. Makes 4 servings.

Lemon-Chive Sauce: In a small saucepan melt 1 tablespoon *margarine* or *butter*. Stir in 1 tablespoon *all-purpose flour*, 1 tablespoon *snipped fresh chives*, ½ teaspoon finely shredded *lemon peel*, ⅛ teaspoon *salt*, and dash *pepper*. Add ¾ cup *milk* all at once. Cook and stir over medium heat till thickened and bubbly. Cook and stir 1 minute more. Makes ¾ cup sauce.

Per serving: 209 calories, 24 g protein, 10 g carbohydrate, 8 g total fat (2 g saturated), 64 mg cholesterol, 386 mg sodium, 539 mg potassium.

Poached Fish with Dill Sauce

**1 3-pound fresh or frozen
  dressed fish**
3 lemon slices
1 bay leaf
½ teaspoon salt
**¼ teaspoon dried tarragon,
  crushed**
**2 tablespoons margarine *or*
  butter**
4 teaspoons all-purpose flour
½ teaspoon sugar
**½ teaspoon dried dillweed
  Dash salt**
1 beaten egg yolk

Thaw fish, if frozen. **1** Wrap fish in a single layer of 100% cotton cheesecloth. In a fish poacher or a large roasting pan that has a wire rack with handles, add enough water to almost reach the rack. Remove and grease rack; set aside.

Add lemon slices, bay leaf, the ½ teaspoon salt, and tarragon to water. Place pan over two burners on range top. Bring to boiling. Reduce heat. **2** Lower fish on rack into pan. **3 4** Simmer, covered, for 35 to 40 minutes or till fish flakes easily when tested with a fork. **5** Remove fish; keep warm.

For dill sauce, strain cooking liquid; reserve *1 cup*. Melt margarine or butter; stir in flour, sugar, dillweed, and the dash salt. Add reserved cooking liquid. Cook and stir till bubbly. Gradually stir about *½ cup* of the hot mixture into the beaten egg yolk; return to saucepan. Cook and stir 1 minute more. Pass sauce with fish. Makes 6 servings.

Per serving: 203 calories, 32 g protein, 2 g carbohydrate, 7 g total fat (1 g saturated), 91 mg cholesterol, 179 mg sodium, 627 mg potassium.

1 Wrap fish in a single layer of cheesecloth to keep it in one piece as it cooks. Bring edges of cheesecloth up to overlap on top of fish.

2 Place the wrapped fish on the rack of a poaching pan. Carefully lower fish into pan.

3 Cover pan and place it across two burners of the range.

4 To test for doneness, pull cheesecloth away from fish. Insert fork into thickest part of the fish. When done, the fish flakes easily.

5 Remove fish from the pan by lifting out of the rack.

Baked Halibut with Shrimp-Cucumber Sauce

1 **pound fresh or frozen halibut steaks, cut ¾ inch thick**
2 **tablespoons margarine or butter**
½ **teaspoon dried dillweed**
½ **teaspoon lemon-pepper seasoning**
¼ **teaspoon garlic powder**
Shrimp-Cucumber Sauce

Thaw fish, if frozen. Arrange halibut steaks in an 8x8x2-inch baking dish. Combine 2 tablespoons melted margarine or butter, dill, lemon-pepper seasoning, and garlic powder. Pour over fish. Bake, covered, in a 400° oven for 15 to 20 minutes or till fish flakes easily when tested with a fork. Serve with Shrimp-Cucumber Sauce. Makes 4 servings.

Shrimp-Cucumber Sauce: Meanwhile, in a small saucepan melt 2 tablespoons *margarine* or *butter*. Stir in 4 teaspoons *all-purpose flour*, ⅛ teaspoon *salt*, ⅛ teaspoon *pepper*, and dash ground *nutmeg* till smooth. Add 1 cup *milk* all at once. Cook and stir over medium-high heat till thickened and bubbly. Cook and stir 1 minute more. Stir in one 4½-ounce can *shrimp*, drained and chopped; ¼ cup shredded *cucumber*; 1 tablespoon *dry sherry*; and dash bottled *hot pepper sauce*. Makes 1⅔ cups.

Per serving: 311 calories, 33 g protein, 6 g carbohydrate, 16 g total fat (3 g saturated), 96 mg cholesterol, 498 mg sodium, 697 mg potassium.

Baked Red Snapper with Onion Sauce

1 **pound fresh or frozen red snapper fillets**
1 **tablespoon margarine or butter, melted**
½ **cup chopped onion**
¼ **cup finely chopped red or yellow sweet pepper**
2 **tablespoons margarine or butter**
¼ **cup water**
¼ **cup dry white wine**
1 **teaspoon finely shredded lemon peel**
1 **tablespoon lemon juice**
¼ **teaspoon salt**
¼ **teaspoon dried thyme, crushed**
⅛ **teaspoon pepper**
1 **tablespoon snipped fresh parsley**
4 **cups coarsely shredded fresh spinach**

Thaw fish, if frozen. Arrange snapper fillets in the bottom of a 2-quart rectangular baking dish. Drizzle with the 1 tablespoon melted margarine or butter. Bake, covered, in a 450° oven for 10 to 12 minutes or till fish flakes easily when tested with a fork.

Meanwhile, for sauce, in a small saucepan cook onion and sweet pepper in the 2 tablespoons margarine or butter till tender. Stir in water, wine, lemon peel, lemon juice, salt, thyme, and pepper. Bring to boiling. Reduce heat and simmer, uncovered, for 5 minutes. Stir in parsley.

Line a serving platter with shredded spinach. Arrange baked fish fillets atop spinach. Pour sauce over fish. Makes 4 servings.

Per serving: 217 calories, 25 g protein, 3 g carbohydrate, 10 g total fat (2 g saturated), 42 mg cholesterol, 330 mg sodium, 817 mg potassium.

Pan-Fried Fish

1 **pound fresh** *or* **frozen fish
   fillets (½ to 1 inch thick)**
1 **beaten egg**
2 **tablespoons water**
⅔ **cup cornmeal** *or* **fine dry
   bread crumbs**
½ **teaspoon salt**
   Dash pepper
   Shortening *or* **cooking oil
   for frying**

Thaw fish, if frozen. Measure thickness of fish. Cut into serving-size portions. Pat dry. In a shallow dish combine egg and water. In another dish mix cornmeal or bread crumbs, salt, and dash pepper. **1** Dip fish into egg mixture, then coat with cornmeal mixture.

In a large skillet heat ¼ inch melted shortening or oil. **2** Add half of the fish in a single layer. (If fillets have skin, fry skin side last.) Fry fish on one side till golden. Allow 3 to 4 minutes per side for ½-inch-thick fillets (5 to 6 minutes per side for 1-inch-thick fillets). **3** Turn carefully. Fry till golden and fish flakes easily when tested with a fork. **4** Drain on paper towels. Keep warm in a 300° oven while frying remaining fish. Makes 4 servings.

Per serving: 260 calories, 25 g protein, 18 g carbohydrate, 9 g total fat (2 g saturated), 98 mg cholesterol, 327 mg sodium, 347 mg potassium.

1 Dip both sides of the fish fillets into the egg mixture, then into the cornmeal mixture.

2 To fry fish, place the fish in hot oil in a single layer.

3 When ready to turn, gently slip a wide spatula under the fillet and turn over carefully.

4 Using the spatula, transfer fried fish to paper towels to drain off the excess fat.

Oven-Fried Catfish with Spicy Hot Mayonnaise

1 **pound fresh *or* frozen catfish fillets, cut ½ to ¾ inch thick**
¼ **cup mayonnaise *or* salad dressing**
¼ **cup plain yogurt**
2 **tablespoons snipped fresh cilantro**
1 **tablespoon chopped onion**
1 **jalapeño pepper*, seeded and chopped**
½ **teaspoon chili powder**
¼ **teaspoon ground cumin**
¼ **cup cornflake crumbs**
¼ **cup cornmeal**
½ **teaspoon paprika**
¼ **teaspoon salt**
¼ **teaspoon garlic powder**
⅛ **teaspoon ground red pepper**
2 **lightly beaten egg whites**

Thaw catfish, if frozen. For Spicy Hot Mayonnaise, combine mayonnaise or salad dressing, yogurt, cilantro, onion, jalapeño pepper, chili powder, and cumin in a blender container. Cover and blend till smooth. Cover and chill.

In a shallow dish combine cornflake crumbs, cornmeal, paprika, salt, garlic powder, and ground red pepper. Dip catfish fillets into egg whites; coat with crumb mixture.

Place catfish on a greased baking sheet. Bake, uncovered, in a 450° oven for 8 to 12 minutes or till fish flakes easily when tested with a fork. Serve with Spicy Hot Mayonnaise. Makes 4 servings.

*Note: Fresh jalapeño peppers contain oils that can burn your eyes, lips, and skin. Cover your hands with plastic bags or wear plastic gloves and wash your hands thoroughly before touching your eyes or face.

Per serving: 272 calories, 23 g protein, 13 g carbohydrate, 14 g total fat (2 g saturated), 53 mg cholesterol, 353 mg sodium, 323 mg potassium.

Baked Fish Rockefeller

6 **4-ounce fresh *or* frozen skinless fish fillets (white fish, cod, *or* orange roughy)**
2 **10-ounce packages frozen chopped spinach, thawed and well drained**
1 **10¾-ounce can condensed cream of mushroom soup**
1 **cup shredded sharp cheddar cheese (4 ounces)**
2 **tablespoons dry sherry *or* milk**
¼ **teaspoon pepper**
¾ **cup soft bread crumbs**
1 **tablespoon margarine *or* butter, melted**
Paprika

Thaw fish, if frozen. Place spinach in a 2-quart rectangular baking dish. Arrange fish fillets over spinach. For sauce, in a saucepan combine mushroom soup, cheese, dry sherry or milk, and pepper. Cook and stir over medium heat about 5 minutes or till cheese melts. Pour sauce over fish fillets.

Toss bread crumbs with melted margarine or butter. Sprinkle over sauce. Sprinkle with paprika. Bake in a 400° oven for 30 to 35 minutes or till fish flakes easily when tested with a fork. Makes 6 servings.

Per serving: 261 calories, 26 g protein, 10 g carbohydrate, 13 g total fat (6 g saturated), 64 mg cholesterol, 694 mg sodium, 531 mg potassium.

Thai Sweet-Sour Scallops

¼ **cup rice vinegar**
2 **tablespoons hoisin sauce**
2 **teaspoons cornstarch**
2 **teaspoons sugar**
2 **teaspoons finely shredded**
   lemon peel
3 **tablespoons cooking oil**
1 **medium onion, thinly**
   sliced
1 **small jalapeño pepper*,**
   finely chopped
2 **cloves garlic, minced**
1½ **cups thinly sliced carrots**
1 **medium red sweet pepper,**
   cut into strips
1 **pound fresh *or* frozen sea**
   scallops, thawed
1 **6-ounce package frozen**
   pea pods, thawed
2 **cups hot cooked rice**

For sauce, in a small bowl stir together the rice vinegar, hoisin sauce, cornstarch, sugar, and lemon peel; set aside.

Pour *1 tablespoon* cooking oil into a wok or large skillet. (Add more oil as necessary during cooking.) Preheat wok or skillet over medium-high heat. Stir-fry onion, jalapeño pepper (see Note page 63), and garlic in hot oil for 30 seconds. Add carrots; stir-fry for 2 minutes. Add sweet red pepper strips; stir-fry for 2 minutes more or till vegetables are crisp-tender. Remove the vegetables from the wok.

Add *half* of the scallops to the hot wok. Stir-fry 3 minutes or till scallops turn opaque. Remove from wok. Repeat with remaining scallops. Return all scallops to wok. Push scallops from the center of the wok.

Stir sauce; add to the center of the wok. Cook and stir till thickened and bubbly. Return the cooked vegetables to the wok; add thawed pea pods. Stir all ingredients together to coat with sauce. Cook and stir about 1 minute more or till heated through. Serve immediately over hot cooked rice. Makes 4 servings. * See note page 63.

Per serving: 401 calories, 20 g protein, 60 g carbohydrate, 12 g total fat (2 g saturated), 34 mg cholesterol, 440 mg sodium, 887 mg potassium.

FISH AND SEAFOOD

Crabmeat Imperial

¼ **cup finely chopped green pepper**
¼ **cup finely chopped red sweet pepper**
¼ **cup chopped green onion**
2 **tablespoons finely chopped celery**
1 **tablespoon margarine *or* butter**
¾ **cup mayonnaise**
1 **tablespoon Dijon-style mustard**
1 **tablespoon dry white wine**
¼ **teaspoon salt**
¼ **teaspoon white pepper**
  Dash hot pepper sauce
16 **ounces coarsely flaked, cooked crabmeat**
4 **patty shells**

In a small saucepan cook green pepper, sweet pepper, onion, and celery in margarine or butter till tender. Remove from heat.

In a bowl combine mayonnaise, mustard, wine, salt, pepper, and dash hot pepper sauce; stir till smooth. Gently stir vegetable mixture and crabmeat into mayonnaise mixture. Spoon crabmeat mixture into 4 patty shells on a baking sheet. Bake in a 375° oven for 20 to 25 minutes or till bubbly. Sprinkle with snipped fresh parsley, if desired. Makes 4 servings.

Per serving: 451 calories, 24 g protein, 3 g carbohydrate, 38 g total fat (6 g saturated), 137 mg cholesterol, 819 mg sodium, 447 mg potassium.

Mixed Seafood Grill

1 **pound fresh *or* frozen tuna steaks, cut 1 inch thick**
½ **pound fresh *or* frozen large shrimp (12)**
½ **pound fresh *or* frozen sea scallops**
¼ **cup olive oil**
¼ **cup dry white wine**
3 **tablespoons finely chopped onion**
½ **teaspoon dried dillweed**
½ **cup mayonnaise *or* salad dressing**
½ **cup shredded cucumber**
1 **2-ounce jar sliced pimiento, drained and chopped**
½ **teaspoon dried dillweed**
2 **red sweet peppers, cut into 1-inch pieces**

Thaw tuna and seafood, if frozen. Cut tuna into 1-inch pieces. Peel and devein shrimp, leaving tails intact. Place tuna, shrimp, and scallops in a plastic bag set in a bowl. For marinade, combine olive oil, wine, onion, and ½ teaspoon dillweed; pour marinade over tuna and seafood. Close bag and marinate in refrigerator for 30 minutes, turning bag occasionally.

Meanwhile, for sauce, combine mayonnaise, cucumber, pimiento, and ½ teaspoon dillweed. Cover and chill.

Remove tuna and seafood from marinade, reserving marinade. Thread tuna, seafood, and sweet pepper pieces onto six 12-inch skewers. Grill directly over medium coals for 10 to 12 minutes or till tuna and seafood are done, turning once and brushing occasionally with marinade. (Do not brush with marinade the last 5 minutes of grilling.) Serve with sauce. Makes 6 servings.

Per serving: 350 calories, 29 g protein, 4 g carbohydrate, 24 g total fat (4 g saturated), 97 mg cholesterol, 247 mg sodium, 446 mg potassium.

Grilled Swordfish with Citrus Salsa

1 **pound fresh *or* frozen swordfish steak, cut 1 inch thick**
¼ **cup orange juice**
2 **tablespoons lemon juice**
2 **tablespoons lime juice**
1 **tablespoon cooking oil**
½ **teaspoon ground ginger**
1 **clove garlic, minced**
1 **orange, peeled and chopped**
⅓ **cup finely chopped fresh *or* canned pineapple**
2 **tablespoons finely chopped onion**
2 **tablespoons finely chopped red sweet pepper**
2 **tablespoons snipped fresh parsley**
2 **tablespoons lime juice**
1 **jalapeño pepper*, seeded and finely chopped**

Thaw swordfish, if frozen. **1** Measure fish thickness. Place swordfish steaks in a plastic bag set in a bowl. For marinade, combine orange juice, lemon juice, 2 tablespoons lime juice, oil, ginger, and garlic; pour over fish in bag. Close bag and marinate in refrigerator for 1 hour, turning bag occasionally.

Meanwhile, for salsa, stir together chopped orange, pineapple, onion, sweet pepper, parsley, 2 tablespoons lime juice, and jalapeño pepper (See Note page 63). Cover and chill.

Remove fish from marinade; discard marinade. **2 3** Place fish in a well-greased wire grill basket directly over medium coals. Grill for 8 to 12 minutes or till fish flakes easily when tested with a fork, turning once. Cut into 4 pieces and serve with salsa. Makes 4 servings.

Per serving: 154 calories, 23 g protein, 4 g carbohydrate, 5 g total fat (1 g saturated), 45 mg cholesterol, 106 mg sodium, 407 mg potassium.

1 For best results when grilling, fish steaks should be between ½ and 1 inch thick.

2 To test the temperature of the coals, hold your palm over the coals at the height the fish will cook. If you need to withdraw your hand after four seconds, coals are medium.

3 Place the fish in a well-greased wire grill basket.

Grilled Grouper with Red Pepper Sauce

1 pound fresh *or* frozen
grouper fillets
1 large sweet red pepper,
chopped (1½ cups)
1 tablespoon margarine *or*
butter
2 medium tomatoes, peeled,
seeded, and chopped
(1¼ cups)
1 tablespoon sugar
1 teaspoon red wine vinegar
¼ teaspoon salt
⅛ teaspoon garlic powder
Dash ground red pepper
2 tablespoons lemon juice
1 tablespoon olive oil
¼ teaspoon dried rosemary,
crushed

Thaw fish, if frozen. Cut fish into 4 serving-size portions. Set aside.
For Red Pepper Sauce, in a saucepan cook sweet red pepper in margarine or butter over medium heat till tender. Stir in tomatoes, sugar, vinegar, salt, garlic powder, and ground red pepper. Cook over medium heat for 5 minutes, stirring occasionally. Transfer mixture to blender container or food processor bowl. Cover and blend or process till smooth. Return sauce to saucepan; keep warm.

Combine lemon juice, olive oil, and rosemary; brush over fish. Place fish in a well-greased grill basket. Place grill basket on grill rack directly over medium coals. Grill for 4 to 6 minutes per ½-inch thickness or fish or till fish flakes easily when tested with a fork. Turn fish over halfway through grrilling time. Serve with Red Pepper Sauce. Makes 4 servings.

Per serving: 200 calories, 23 g protein, 10 g carbohydrate, 8 g total fat (1 g saturated), 42 mg cholesterol, 223 mg sodium, 659 mg potassium.

Creamed Scallops

1 pound fresh *or* frozen bay
scallops
1 cup sliced fresh
mushrooms
½ cup thinly sliced celery
½ cup chopped onion
1 tablespoon margarine *or*
butter
1 10¾-ounce can condensed
cream of shrimp soup
2 tablespoons dry sherry
(optional)
¼ teaspoon pepper
4 baked patty shells *or*
8 ounces hot cooked
pasta
⅓ cup toasted sliced almonds
2 tablespoons snipped fresh
parsley
Lemon wedges (optional)

Thaw scallops, if frozen. In a large skillet cook mushrooms, celery, and onion in margarine or butter till tender. Stir in shrimp soup, sherry (if desired), and pepper; mix well. Gently fold in the scallops. Cook and stir till bubbly. Cook and stir 3 minutes more.

To serve, spoon scallop mixture over patty shells or cooked pasta. Sprinkle with almonds and parsley. Serve with lemon wedges, if desired. Makes 4 servings.

Per serving: 442 calories, 21 g protein, 29 g carbohydrate, 28 g total fat (3 g saturated), 44 mg cholesterol, 996 mg sodium, 563 mg potassium.

Shrimp and Vegetable Stir-Fry

1 **pound medium fresh
 shrimp**
¼ **cup dry white wine**
2 **tablespoons lemon juice**
1 **teaspoon cornstarch**
1 **teaspoon grated gingerroot**
½ **teaspoon curry powder**
¼ **teaspoon crushed red
 pepper**
2 **teaspoons cooking oil**
2 **small zucchini, cut into
 bite-size chunks**
1 **8-ounce package frozen
 baby corn, thawed *or*
 one 15-ounce can baby
 corn, drained**
1 **small red onion, thinly
 sliced**
2 **cloves garlic, minced**
2 **cups hot cooked rice**

1 Peel shrimp and gently pull off tail portion. **2 3** Devein shrimp and discard black sand vein. Rinse shrimp; set aside.

For sauce, in a small bowl combine wine, lemon juice, cornstarch, gingerroot, curry powder, and red pepper; stir well. Set sauce aside.

Pour oil in a wok or large skillet. Preheat wok over medium-high heat. Add zucchini, corn, onion, and garlic to wok; stir-fry for 2 to 3 minutes or till crisp-tender. Remove vegetables from wok. Add shrimp and sauce to wok. Simmer, stirring constantly, for 3 to 4 minutes or till shrimp turn opaque.

Return vegetables to wok. Stir all ingredients together to coat with sauce. Heat through. Serve over rice. Makes 4 servings.

Per serving: 273 calories, 19 g protein, 38 g carbohydrate, 3 g total fat (1 g saturated), 131 mg cholesterol, 199 mg sodium, 698 mg potassium.

1 To peel the shrimp, open the shell lengthwise down the body, using your fingers. Starting at the head end, peel back the shell. Gently pull off the tail portion of the shell.

2 Devein the shrimp by making a shallow slit along its back from the head end to the tail end.

3 Using the tip of a knife, carefully remove and discard the black sand vein that runs along the center back. Rinse under cold running water, if desired.

Shrimp Enchiladas

8 10-inch flour tortillas
1 pound fresh *or* frozen
    shrimp, cooked and
    chopped
1 10¾-ounce can condensed
    cream of chicken soup
2 medium tomatoes, peeled,
    seeded, and chopped
1 8-ounce carton dairy sour
    cream
2 cups shredded cheddar,
    Cojack, *or* Monterey Jack
    cheese
1 4-ounce can diced green
    chili peppers, drained
¼ teaspoon dried oregano,
    crushed
⅛ teaspoon ground red
    pepper
¼ cup finely chopped green
    onion

Stack tortillas and wrap tightly in foil. Heat in a 350° oven for 10 minutes to soften.

Meanwhile, for filling, in a mixing bowl stir together chopped shrimp, chicken soup, *half* of the chopped tomatoes, the sour cream, *half* of the shredded cheese, the green chili peppers, oregano, and red pepper. Spoon about *½ cup* of the filling onto *each* tortilla just below center. Fold bottom edge up and over filling. Fold in opposite sides of each tortilla; roll up tortillas from bottom.

Place tortillas, seam side down, in a greased 3-quart rectangular baking dish. Bake, covered, in a 350° oven for 25 minutes. Sprinkle with remaining 1 cup cheese, remaining chopped tomato, and green onion. Bake about 5 minutes more or till cheese is melted. Makes 8 servings.

Per serving: 393 calories, 24 g protein, 29 g carbohydrate, 20 g total fat (11 g saturated), 154 mg cholesterol, 816 mg sodium, 354 mg potassium.

Tuna Patties with Dill Sauce

½ cup mayonnaise *or* salad
    dressing
1 tablespoon Dijon-style
    mustard
¼ teaspoon dried basil,
    crushed *or* ¼ teaspoon
    dried dillweed
    Dash pepper
1 beaten egg
1 cup soft bread crumbs
1 cup shredded carrots
½ cup finely chopped celery
¼ cup sliced green onion
¼ cup milk
¼ teaspoon salt
¼ teaspoon pepper
1 12¼-ounce can tuna
    (water-pack), drained

For Dill Sauce, stir together mayonnaise or salad dressing, mustard, basil or dillweed, and the dash pepper. Cover and chill.

In a large mixing bowl combine, egg, bread crumbs, carrots, celery, green onion, milk, salt, and the ¼ teaspoon pepper. Add tuna; mix well. Shape mixture into four 4-inch patties (about ½ inch thick). Place patties on the unheated rack of a broiler pan. Broil 4 inches from the heat for 8 to 10 minutes or till heated through, turning once. Serve patties with Dill Sauce. Makes 4 servings.

Per serving: 377 calories, 26 g protein, 13 g carbohydrate, 26 g total fat (4 g saturated), 86 mg cholesterol, 548 mg sodium, 354 mg potassium.

SOUPS AND STEWS

Curried Lamb and Vegetables

Curried Lamb and Vegetables

1½ **pounds lean boneless lamb, cut into ¾-inch cubes**
1 **tablespoon cooking oil**
1 **cup chopped onion**
2 **cloves garlic, minced**
1 **tablespoon curry powder**
1 **cup water**
1 **teaspoon instant chicken bouillon granules**
½ **teaspoon ground ginger**
¼ **teaspoon pepper**
¼ **cup water**
2 **tablespoons all-purpose flour**
2 **cups broccoli flowerets**
1 **red sweet pepper, cut into julienne strips**
1 **small yellow summer squash, cut into ¼-inch slices**

In a large saucepan or Dutch oven brown *half* of the meat in hot oil. Remove meat from saucepan. Add remaining meat, onion, garlic, and curry powder to saucepan. Cook and stir till meat is browned and onion is tender. Return all meat to pan.

Stir in the 1 cup water, bouillon granules, ginger, and pepper. Simmer, covered, for 30 to 40 minutes or till meat is tender. Stir together the ¼ cup water and flour; stir into saucepan. Cook and stir till thickened and bubbly. Stir in broccoli, red sweet pepper, and squash. Cook, covered, for 5 to 10 minutes more or till vegetables are crisp-tender. Makes 5 main-dish servings.

Per serving: 224 calories, 25 g protein, 11 mg carbohydrate, 9 gm total fat (3 gm saturated), 69 mg cholesterol, 241 mg sodium, 536 mg potassium.

Pork and Cabbage Stew

1 **2-pound boneless pork shoulder roast**
1 **tablespoon cooking oil**
1½ **cups sliced carrots**
1 **12-ounce can beer**
1 **large onion, thinly sliced**
1 **cup water**
¼ **cup cider vinegar**
1 **tablespoon instant beef bouillon granules**
1 **teaspoon caraway seed**
¼ **teaspoon crushed red pepper**
1 **bay leaf**
2 **cups shredded cabbage**
2 **cups thinly sliced celery**

Trim fat from pork roast; cut meat into 1-inch cubes. In a large saucepan or Dutch oven brown pork, *half* at a time, in hot oil. Drain off fat.

Return pork to saucepan. Stir in carrots, beer, onion, water, vinegar, bouillon granules, caraway seed, red pepper, and bay leaf. Bring to boiling. Reduce heat and simmer, covered, for 45 minutes. Stir in cabbage and celery. Cover and simmer about 15 minutes more or till pork is tender. Discard bay leaf. Makes 6 main-dish servings.

Per serving: 334 calories, 28 g protein, 11 g carbohydrate, 18 g total fat (6 g saturated), 99 mg cholesterol, 553 mg sodium, 603 mg potassium.

Rich and Hearty Beef Stew

¼ **cup all-purpose flour**
1½ **pounds beef stew meat,
    cut into 1-inch cubes**
2 **tablespoons cooking oil**
3 **cups water**
½ **cup dry red wine *or* water**
1 **large onion, sliced**
1 **tablespoon instant beef
    bouillon granules**
2 **cloves garlic, minced**
1 **bay leaf**
½ **teaspoon dried tarragon,
    crushed**
¼ **teaspoon dried thyme,
    crushed**
¼ **teaspoon pepper**
⅛ **teaspoon ground cloves**
2 **cups sliced carrots**
2 **cups sliced fresh
    mushrooms**
1 **10-ounce package frozen
    lima beans**

1 Place flour in a plastic bag. Add meat cubes, a few at a time, shaking to coat. **2** In a large saucepan or Dutch oven brown *half* of the stew meat in *1 tablespoon* hot oil. Remove meat from pan; drain. Repeat with remaining stew meat and oil. Return all meat to saucepan.

Stir in water, wine, onion, bouillon granules, garlic, bay leaf, tarragon, thyme, pepper, and cloves. Bring to boiling. Reduce heat and simmer, covered, for 1 to 1¼ hours or till meat is nearly tender. Stir in carrots, mushrooms, and lima beans. Simmer, covered, about 30 minutes more or till meat and vegetables are tender. **3** Skim off excess fat. Remove bay leaf. Makes 6 main-dish servings.

Per serving: 349 calories, 32 g protein, 22 g carbohydrate, 13 g total fat (4 g saturated), 82 mg cholesterol, 559 mg sodium, 688 mg potassium.

1 Place flour in a plastic bag. Add meat cubes, a few pieces at a time, shaking to coat.

2 In a Dutch oven, brown about half of the meat in hot oil, turning to brown evenly on all sides. Drain meat, using papertowels, if desired. Repeat with remaining meat.

3 To remove excess fat from stew, tilt the pan slightly to collect the liquid fat at the edge of the pan. Skim off fat with a metal spoon.

SOUPS AND STEWS

Savory Sausage Ragout

1 pound fresh Italian sausage links
1 cup chopped onion
1 cup chopped green pepper
2 cloves garlic, minced
1 14½-ounce can whole Italian-style tomatoes
1 8-ounce can tomato sauce
1 cup sliced fresh mushrooms
2 tablespoons snipped fresh parsley
1 teaspoon dried basil, crushed
½ teaspoon dried oregano, crushed
1 14-ounce can artichoke hearts
8 ounces hot cooked cavatelli *or* mostaccioli
¼ cup grated Parmesan cheese

Slice sausage links into ½-inch thick slices. In a large saucepan or Dutch oven cook sausage over medium heat till browned. Drain sausage on paper towels, reserving *2 tablespoons* drippings. Set sausage aside.

Cook onion, green pepper, and garlic in reserved drippings till tender. Drain off fat. Stir in *undrained* tomatoes, tomato sauce, mushrooms, parsley, basil, oregano, and sausage. Bring to boiling. Reduce heat and simmer, covered, for 10 minutes, stirring occasionally. Stir in *drained* artichoke hearts. Simmer about 5 minutes more or till heated through. Serve over hot cooked pasta. Sprinkle each serving with Parmesan cheese. Makes 4 main-dish servings.

Per serving: 625 calories, 32 g protein, 70 g carbohydrate, 25 g total fat (9 g saturated), 70 mg cholesterol, 1,595 mg sodium, 1,221 mg potassium.

Cajun Seafood Stew

1 pound fresh *or* frozen medium shrimp
¾ pound fresh *or* frozen whitefish fillets, cut into 1-inch pieces
2 cups sliced fresh mushrooms
1 cup chopped onion
1 cup chopped green pepper
1 cup thinly sliced celery
2 cloves garlic, minced
1 tablespoon cooking oil
2 14½-ounce cans Cajun-style stewed tomatoes
1 8-ounce can tomato sauce
½ teaspoon dried thyme, crushed
½ teaspoon dried oregano, crushed
¼ teaspoon dried basil, crushed

Thaw shrimp and fish, if frozen. Peel and devein shrimp, if necessary. In a large saucepan or Dutch oven cook mushrooms, onion, green pepper, celery, and garlic in hot oil till tender. Stir in *undrained* tomatoes, tomato sauce, thyme, oregano, basil, and ¼ teaspoon *pepper*. Bring to boiling. Reduce heat and simmer, covered, for 15 minutes. Stir in shrimp and fish. Cook about 5 minutes more or till shrimp turn pink and the fish flakes easily when tested with a fork. Makes 6 to 8 main-dish servings.

Per serving: 206 calories, 25 g protein, 19 g carbohydrate, 4 g total fat (1 g saturated), 139 mg cholesterol, 895 mg sodium, 1,022 mg potassium.

73

Chicken and Succotash Stew with Cheddar Dumplings

3½ **cups chicken broth**
1 **cup frozen whole kernel corn**
1 **cup frozen baby lima beans**
1 **carrot, thinly sliced**
½ **cup chopped onion**
1 **clove garlic, minced**
½ **teaspoon dried thyme, crushed**
¼ **teaspoon pepper**
⅓ **cup all-purpose flour**
2 **cups cubed cooked chicken**
1 **cup packaged biscuit mix**
⅓ **cup milk**
¼ **cup shredded sharp cheddar cheese**
1 **tablespoon snipped fresh parsley**

In a large saucepan or Dutch oven combine *2½ cups* of the chicken broth, corn, lima beans, carrot, onion, garlic, thyme, and pepper. Bring to boiling. **1 2**Combine remaining chicken broth and flour; stir into vegetable mixture. Stir in chicken. **3**Cook and stir till thickened and bubbly.

Meanwhile, for dumplings, combine biscuit mix, milk, cheese, and parsley. **4**Drop dumpling mixture from a tablespoon into 8 mounds atop bubbling stew. **5**Simmer, covered, over low heat about 13 minutes or till a toothpick inserted into dumplings comes out clean. Makes 4 main-dish servings.

Per serving: 467 calories, 36 g protein, 49 g carbohydrate, 14 g total fat (4 g saturated), 77 mg cholesterol, 1,175 mg sodium, 768 mg potassium.

1To thicken stew mixture, combine 1 cup chicken broth and flour, stirring till smooth.

2Gradually add flour mixture to stew, stirring to blend.

3Cook and stir stew mixture over medium heat till thickened and bubbly.

4Drop dumpling mixture from a tablespoon atop bubbling stew.

5To check the dumplings for doneness, insert a wooden toothpick into one of the dumplings. When done, toothpick will come out clean.

Vegetable and Rice Ragout

½ **pound fresh green beans**
1 **large onion, finely chopped**
2 **cloves garlic, minced**
1 **tablespoon cooking oil**
2 **cups thinly sliced carrots**
1 **14½-ounce can tomatoes,**
   cut up
⅓ **cup slivered almonds**
2 **teaspoons instant chicken**
   bouillon granules
2 **teaspoons finely shredded**
   lemon peel
1 **teaspoon ground ginger**
½ **teaspoon ground cinnamon**
¼ **teaspoon crushed red**
   pepper
1 **15-ounce can kidney beans,**
   rinsed and drained
2 **yellow summer squash, cut**
   into ½-inch-thick slices
1 **medium red sweet pepper,**
   coarsely chopped
1½ **cups cooked rice**
¼ **cup snipped fresh parsley**

Wash green beans; remove ends and strings. Cut green beans into 2-inch pieces; set aside. In a large saucepan or Dutch oven cook onion and garlic in hot oil till tender. Add 2½ cups *water*, carrots, green beans, *undrained* tomatoes, almonds, bouillon granules, lemon peel, ginger, cinnamon, and crushed red pepper. Bring to boiling. Reduce heat and simmer, covered, for 10 minutes.

Stir in kidney beans, sliced squash, and sweet red pepper. Simmer, covered, for 7 to 10 minutes more or till squash is just tender. Combine 1 tablespoon *cornstarch* and 1 tablespoon *water*. Stir into vegetable mixture along with rice and parsley. Cook and stir till thickened and bubbly. Cook and stir 1 minute more. Makes 6 main-dish servings.

Per serving: 259 calories, 11 g protein, 45 g carbohydrate, 6 g total fat (1 g saturated), 0 mg cholesterol, 555 mg sodium, 717 mg potassium.

Turkey and Two Bean Chili

½ **pound ground raw turkey**
1 **cup chopped onion**
½ **cup chopped carrot**
2 **cloves garlic, minced**
1 **tablespoon cooking oil**
1 **15-ounce can pinto beans**
1 **15-ounce can garbanzo**
   beans
1 **14½-ounce can tomatoes,**
   cut up
1 **14½-ounce can chicken**
   broth
1 **cup water**
1 **4-ounce can diced green**
   chili peppers, drained
2 **tablespoons tomato paste**
2 **teaspoons chili powder**
1 **teaspoon ground cumin**

In a large saucepan or Dutch oven cook turkey, onion, carrot, and garlic in hot oil till turkey is no longer pink and onion is tender. Drain fat, if necessary.

Stir in *rinsed* and *drained* pinto and garbanzo beans, *undrained* tomatoes, chicken broth, water, chili peppers, tomato paste, chili powder, and cumin. Bring to boiling. Reduce heat and simmer, uncovered, for 20 to 25 minutes or till mixture thickens slightly. Makes 4 main-dish servings.

Per serving: 339 calories, 22 g protein, 47 g carbohydrate, 8 g total fat (2 g saturated), 22 mg cholesterol, 1,552 mg sodium, 1,148 mg potassium.

Beef and Bean Soup

**1 pound beef stew meat,
   cut into ¾-inch cubes**
1 tablespoon cooking oil
⅓ cup chopped onion
**1 14½-ounce can tomatoes,
   cut up**
1 14½-ounce can beef broth
1½ cups water
¼ cup snipped fresh parsley
2 teaspoons paprika
**1 teaspoon dried mint,
   crushed**
¼ teaspoon pepper
⅛ teaspoon garlic powder
**1 15-ounce can kidney beans,
   rinsed and drained**
1 cup frozen cut green beans
1 cup frozen baby lima beans

In a 4 to 6 quart Dutch oven brown *half* of the beef stew meat in hot oil. Remove meat from pan. Brown remaining meat and onion. Drain off fat. Return all meat to pan.

Stir in *undrained* tomatoes, beef broth, water, parsley, paprika, mint, pepper, and garlic powder. Bring to boiling. Reduce heat and simmer, covered, for 45 minutes. Stir in kidney beans, green beans, and lima beans. Return to boiling. Reduce heat and simmer, covered, for 20 to 25 minutes more or till meat and vegetables are tender. Makes 4 main-dish servings.

Per serving: 372 calories, 35 g protein, 41 g carbohydrate, 10 g total fat (3 g saturated), 57 mg cholesterol, 734 mg sodium, 1,097 mg potassium.

Winter Vegetable and Sausage Soup

½ of a 16-ounce package (4)
   fully cooked smoked
   sausage links, sliced
   ¼ inch thick
4 cups water
2 cups peeled, finely chopped
   parsnips *or* rutabaga
2 cups peeled, finely chopped
   potatoes
1 cup peeled, finely chopped
   turnips *or* carrots
1 cup chopped onion
1 tablespoon instant chicken
   bouillon granules
¾ teaspoon dried thyme,
   crushed
½ teaspoon dried marjoram,
   crushed
¼ teaspoon pepper
3 tablespoons snipped fresh
   parsley

In a large saucepan or Dutch oven cook sausage over medium heat till browned. Drain sausage on paper towels; set aside. Drain off fat.

In same saucepan or Dutch oven combine water, parsnips or rutabaga, potatoes, turnips or carrots, onion, bouillon granules, thyme, marjoram, and pepper. Bring to boiling. Reduce heat and simmer, covered, for 40 to 45 minutes or till vegetables are tender. Stir in sausage. Cook and stir till heated through. Sprinkle each serving with parsley. Makes 4 side-dish servings.

Per serving: 249 calories, 9 g protein, 36 g carbohydrate, 9 g total fat (3 g saturated), 22 mg cholesterol, 1,026 mg sodium, 755 mg potassium.

Hearty Lentil Soup

2 cups chopped onion
2 cloves garlic, minced
2 teaspoons cooking oil
1½ pounds meaty ham bone
6 cups chicken broth
1 cup chopped, peeled
   potatoes
1 cup chopped celery
1 cup chopped carrots
1 cup dry lentils, rinsed and
   drained
2 teaspoons dried basil,
   crushed
1 teaspoon dried oregano,
   crushed
½ teaspoon dried thyme,
   crushed
¼ teaspoon coarsely ground
   pepper
1 cup shredded cabbage
1 8-ounce can tomato sauce

In a Dutch oven cook onion and garlic in hot oil till tender. Add ham bone, chicken broth, 1 cup *water*, potatoes, celery, carrots, lentils, basil, oregano, thyme, and pepper. Bring to boiling. Reduce heat and simmer, covered, about 35 minutes or till lentils and vegetables are tender.

Remove ham bone. When cool enough to handle, cut meat off bone and coarsely chop. Discard bone. Stir meat into pan along with cabbage and tomato sauce. Simmer, uncovered, about 15 minutes more or till cabbage is tender. Makes 8 main-dish servings.

Per serving: 246 calories, 23 g protein, 29 g carbohydrate, 5g total fat (2 g saturated), 24 mg cholesterol, 1,516 mg sodium, 920 mg potassium.

Beef Broth

4 **pounds meaty beef**
soupbones
(shank crosscuts, short
ribs, *or* arm bones)
½ **cup water**
3 **carrots, cut up**
2 **medium onions, cut up**
2 **stalks celery with leaves,**
cut up
8 **sprigs parsley**
10 **whole black peppercorns**
4 **bay leaves**
1 **tablespoon dried basil *or***
thyme, crushed
2 **cloves garlic, halved**
1 **teaspoon salt**
10 **cups water**

Place soupbones in a large shallow roasting pan. Bake in a 450° oven about 30 minutes or till well browned, turning once. Place soupbones in a large Dutch oven. Pour the ½ cup water into the roasting pan, scraping up crusty browned bits. Add water mixture to Dutch oven. Add carrots, onions, celery, parsley, peppercorns, bay leaves, basil, garlic, and salt. Add the 10 cups water. Bring to boiling. Reduce heat and simmer, covered, for 3½ hours. Remove soupbones.

1 To strain, pour broth through a large sieve or colander lined with 2 layers of 100% cotton cheesecloth. Discard vegetables and seasonings. If desired, clarify broth (see Note page 79). **2** If using the broth while hot, skim fat from top. **3** *Or* chill broth, then lift off fat.

If desired, when bones are cool enough to handle, remove meat from bones and reserve meat for another use. Discard bones. Store broth and reserved meat, if any, in separate covered containers in the refrigerator up to 3 days or in the freezer up to 6 months. Makes about 8 cups broth.

Per cup: 0 calories, 0 g protein, 0 g carbohydrate, 0 g total fat (0 g saturated), 0 mg cholesterol, 266 mg sodium, 0 mg potassium.

1 To strain the stock, line a large colander with two layers of clean cheesecloth. Set colander in a large heat-proof bowl or container. Pour stock through the lined colander.

2 Using a large metal spoon, skim off the fat that rises to the top of the hot stock.

3 If desired, chill stock in the refrigerator for 6 to 8 hours. Use a spoon to lift solid fat off top of stock.

SOUPS AND STEWS

Chicken Broth

2½ pounds bony chicken pieces (backs, necks, and wings from 2 chickens)
3 stalks celery with leaves, cut up
2 carrots, cut up
1 large onion, cut up
2 sprigs parsley
1 teaspoon salt
½ teaspoon dried thyme, sage, *or* basil, crushed
¼ teaspoon pepper
2 bay leaves
6 cups cold water

In a large Dutch oven or kettle place chicken pieces, celery, carrots, onion, parsley, salt, thyme, sage or basil, pepper, and bay leaves. Add water. Bring to boiling. Reduce heat and simmer, covered, for 2 hours. Remove chicken pieces.

To strain, pour broth through a large sieve or colander lined with 2 layers of 100% cotton cheesecloth. Discard vegetables and seasonings. If desired, clarify broth (see Note below). If using the broth while hot, skim fat. *Or* chill broth, then lift off fat.

If desired, when bones are cool enough to handle, remove meat from bones and reserve meat for another use. Discard bones. Store broth and reserved meat, if any, in separate covered containers in the refrigerator up to 3 days or in the freezer up to 6 months. Makes about 5 cups broth and 2½ cups meat.

Note: To clarify broth, separate an egg, saving the yolk for another use. In a Dutch oven or kettle combine the strained broth, ¼ cup cold water, and the egg white. Bring to boiling. Remove from heat and let stand for 5 minutes. Strain the broth through a large sieve or colander lined with several layers of damp, 100% cotton cheesecloth.

Per cup: 0 calories, 0 g protein, 0 g carbohydrate, 0 g total fat (0 g saturated), 0 mg cholesterol, 426 mg sodium, 0 mg potassium.

Turkey Marsala Soup

2 turkey thighs (about 2¾ pounds), skinned, boned, and cut into 1-inch pieces
1 cup chopped onion
2 cloves garlic, minced
1 tablespoon olive oil
3 cups water
1½ cups sliced carrots
1½ cups sliced celery
1 cup Marsala *or* white wine
1 tablespoon instant chicken bouillon granules
¼ teaspoon pepper
2 cups sliced fresh mushrooms
¼ cup all-purpose flour
¼ cup water

In a large saucepan or Dutch oven cook turkey, onion, and garlic in hot oil about 8 minutes or till turkey is lightly browned. Stir in water, carrots, celery, Marsala or white wine, bouillon granules, and pepper. Bring to boiling. Reduce heat and simmer, covered, 20 minutes. Stir in mushrooms. Cover and simmer about 10 minutes more or till mushrooms are tender.

Stir together flour and water; gradually stir into turkey mixture. Cook and stir over medium heat till thickened and bubbly. Cook and stir 1 minute more. Makes 8 main-dish servings.

Per serving: 184 calories, 18 g protein, 9 g carbohydrate, 6 g total fat (2 g saturated), 48 mg cholesterol, 400 mg sodium, 383 mg potassium.

Chilled Beet-Apple Borscht

2¼ cups water
1½ cups apple juice
¼ cup packed brown sugar
2 teaspoons instant chicken bouillon granules
2 teaspoons finely shredded lemon peel
3 inches stick cinnamon
4 whole cloves
4 whole allspice
1 16-ounce can sliced beets, drained
1½ cups chopped, peeled apple
1 tablespoon lemon juice
2 tablespoons dairy sour cream *or* plain yogurt

In a large saucepan or Dutch oven combine water, apple juice, brown sugar, bouillon granules, lemon peel, cinnamon, cloves, and allspice. Bring to boiling. Reduce heat and simmer, covered, for 15 minutes. 1 Strain mixture through a sieve, discarding spices and lemon peel. Return mixture to saucepan.

Stir in beets and chopped apple. Bring to boiling. Reduce heat and simmer, covered, for 15 minutes or till apples are tender. Cool slightly. 2 Place *half* of the beet mixture in a blender container or food processor bowl. Cover and blend or process till smooth. Repeat with remaining beet mixture. 3 Transfer mixture to a bowl; stir in lemon juice. Cover and chill for 2 to 24 hours. Ladle into serving bowls. Dollop with sour cream or yogurt. 4 5 *Or* to create a design, drizzle yogurt in a spiral pattern atop soup. 6 Draw the tip of a toothpick through the circles. Makes 6 side-dish servings.

Per serving: 116 calories, 1 g protein, 27 g carbohydrate, 1 g total fat (1 g saturated), 2 mg cholesterol, 434 mg sodium, 243 mg potassium.

1 Strain soup mixture through a sieve to remove spices.

2 Process soup mixture in a food processor or blender till smooth.

3 Pour pureed mixture into a bowl. Cover and chill in the refrigerator.

4 For design, fill a small plastic bag with sour cream or yogurt . Cut the corner off of bag, leaving a small hole.

5 Gently squeeze the sour cream or yogurt out of the bag, forming a spiral pattern atop each bowl of soup.

6 Create a design by drawing the tip of a toothpick through circles.

Spiced Carrot and Apple Soup

1 **cup chopped onion**
1 **tablespoon margarine *or* butter**
2½ **cups sliced carrots**
2 **cups chicken broth**
1 **large apple, peeled and coarsely chopped (1 cup)**
½ **cup apple juice**
½ **teaspoon ground coriander**
¼ **teaspoon ground cardamom**
⅛ **teaspoon ground cumin**
⅛ **teaspoon ground ginger**
⅛ **teaspoon salt**
  Snipped fresh parsley (optional)

In a large saucepan or Dutch oven cook onion in margarine or butter till tender but not brown. Stir in carrots, chicken broth, chopped apple, apple juice, coriander, cardamom, cumin, ginger, and salt. Bring to boiling. Reduce heat and simmer, covered, for 12 to 15 minutes or till carrots are very tender. Cool slightly.

Place *2 cups* of the carrot mixture in a blender container or food processor bowl. Cover and blend or process till smooth. Repeat with remaining carrot mixture. Return all of the mixture to the saucepan; heat through. Ladle into serving bowls and sprinkle with parsley, if desired. Makes 4 to 6 side-dish servings.

Per serving: 134 calories, 4 g protein, 22 g carbohydrate, 4 g total fat (1 g saturated), 1 mg cholesterol, 548 mg sodium, 450 mg potassium.

Sweet Potato Soup

2 **pounds sweet potatoes**
½ **cup chopped onion**
2 **tablespoons margarine *or* butter**
2 **cups water**
2½ **teaspoons instant chicken bouillon granules**
¼ **teaspoon ground cinnamon**
⅛ **teaspoon ground cardamom**
2 **tablespoons brandy (optional)**
1 **cup whipping cream**

Wash and peel sweet potatoes. Cut off woody portions and ends; cut into quarters. In a large saucepan cook potatoes, covered, in enough boiling water to cover for 25 to 35 minutes or till tender; drain.

Meanwhile, in a medium saucepan cook onion in margarine or butter till tender. Stir in water, bouillon granules, cinnamon, cardamom, and brandy, if desired. Bring to boiling. Cook, covered, for 5 minutes, stirring occasionally. Remove from heat. Cool slightly.

Combine *half* of the cooked sweet potatoes and *half* of the onion mixture in a blender container or food processor bowl. Cover and blend or process till smooth. Repeat with remaining sweet potatoes and onion mixture. Return mixture to a large saucepan. Stir in whipping cream. Cook and stir over medium-low heat till heated through. *Do not boil.* Makes 6 side-dish servings.

Per serving: 288 calories, 3 g protein, 28 g carbohydrate, 19 g total fat (10 g saturated), 54 mg cholesterol, 433 mg sodium, 429 mg potassium.

Corn and Wild Rice Chowder

**5 fresh ears of corn *or* one
    10-ounce package frozen
    whole kernel corn**
3 slices bacon
½ cup chopped onion
1½ cups water
**1 tablespoon snipped fresh
    parsley**
**½ teaspoon dried thyme,
    crushed**
**2 teaspoons instant chicken
    bouillon granules**
1 bay leaf
¼ teaspoon pepper
2 cups milk
¼ cup all-purpose flour
**¾ cup cooked wild rice
    (¼ cup uncooked*)**

Use a sharp knife to cut off kernels from ears of corn. Set aside.
  Meanwhile, in a large saucepan cook bacon over medium heat till crisp. Drain bacon on paper towels, reserving *1 tablespoon* drippings. Crumble bacon and set aside.
  Cook onion in reserved bacon drippings till tender but not brown. Stir in water, parsley, thyme, bouillon granules, bay leaf, pepper, and corn. Bring to boiling. Reduce heat and simmer, covered, for 15 minutes, stirring occasionally. Stir in *1¾ cups* of the milk. Combine flour with remaining milk; stir into corn mixture. Cook and stir till thickened and bubbly. Cook and stir for 1 minute more. Stir in wild rice. Cook and stir till heated through. Remove bay leaf. Garnish each serving with crumbled bacon. Makes 6 side-dish servings.
  *Note: In saucepan combine wild rice and *½ cup* water. Bring to boiling, reduce heat. Cover and simmer for 40 minutes or till water is absorbed.

Per serving: 174 calories, 8 g protein, 30 g carbohydrate, 4 g total fat (2 g saturated), 9 mg cholesterol, 393 mg sodium, 358 mg potassium.

Oyster Chowder

6 **slices bacon**
2 **cups cubed potatoes**
1 **cup sliced fresh**
   mushrooms
½ **cup chopped onion**
½ **cup chopped celery**
1 **clove garlic, minced**
3 **tablespoons margarine** *or*
   butter
3 **tablespoons all-purpose**
   flour
3 **cups milk**
¼ **cup snipped fresh parsley**
½ **teaspoon dried thyme,**
   crushed
¼ **teaspoon salt**
2 **8-ounce cans whole**
   oysters, rinsed and
   drained
¼ **cup dry sherry**

In a large saucepan or Dutch oven cook bacon over medium heat till crisp. Drain on paper towels, reserving *2 tablespoons* drippings. Crumble bacon and set aside.

Stir potatoes, mushrooms, onion, celery, and garlic into reserved drippings. Cook, covered, about 15 minutes or till potatoes are tender, stirring occasionally. Remove potato mixture from saucepan and set aside.

In the same pan melt margarine or butter; stir in flour. Stir in milk, parsley, thyme, salt, dash *ground red pepper*, and potato mixture. Cook and stir over medium heat till thickened and bubbly. Cook and stir 1 minute more. Stir in oysters and dry sherry. Heat through. Makes 4 main-dish servings.

Per serving: 485 calories, 20 g protein, 38 g carbohydrate, 26 g total fat (9 g saturated), 90 mg cholesterol, 528 mg sodium, 1,091 mg potassium.

Cheddar Cheese Chowder Florentine

½ **cup chopped onion**
½ **cup chopped carrot**
⅓ **cup sliced celery**
3 **tablespoons margarine** *or*
   butter
3 **tablespoons all-purpose**
   flour
½ **teaspoon dry mustard**
¼ **teaspoon pepper**
1 **14½-ounce can chicken**
   broth
1½ **cups milk**
1 **10-ounce package frozen**
   chopped spinach, thawed
   and well drained
2 **cups shredded sharp**
   cheddar cheese
   (8 ounces)

In a large saucepan or Dutch oven cook onion, carrot, and celery in margarine or butter about 5 minutes or till crisp-tender. Stir in flour, dry mustard, and pepper. Add chicken broth and milk all at once. Cook and stir over medium heat till thickened and bubbly. Cook and stir 1 minute more.

Stir in spinach and shredded cheese. Cook and stir over low heat till cheese melts and soup is heated through. Makes 6 side-dish servings.

Per serving: 275 calories, 15 g protein, 10 g carbohydrate, 20 g total fat (10 g saturated), 45 mg cholesterol, 584 mg sodium, 339 mg potassium.

PASTA AND GRAINS

Chicken and Pasta Toss

Chicken and Pasta Toss

2 **whole medium chicken breasts (1½ pounds total), skinned, boned, and halved lengthwise**
1 **tablespoon olive oil**
1 **cup thinly sliced carrots**
1 **cup chopped fresh broccoli**
1 **small onion, sliced**
⅓ **cup chicken broth**
¼ **cup dry white wine**
½ **cup chopped oil-packed dried tomatoes, drained**
1 **teaspoon dried basil, crushed**
¼ **teaspoon dried thyme, crushed**
1 **clove garlic, minced**
4 **cups hot cooked angel hair pasta (capellini)**
Grated Parmesan cheese

Cut chicken into bite-size pieces; set aside. Pour oil into a large skillet; preheat skillet over medium-high heat. Add carrots to skillet; cook and stir carrots in hot oil for 2 minutes. Add broccoli and onion; cook and stir for 2 to 3 minutes more till crisp-tender. Remove vegetables from skillet.

If necessary, add more oil to skillet. Add chicken pieces to skillet. Cook and stir chicken for 4 to 5 minutes or till no longer pink. Stir in chicken broth, white wine, tomatoes, basil, thyme, and garlic; cook and stir for 1 minute. Return vegetables to skillet; add pasta. Toss gently about 1 minute or till heated through. Sprinkle with Parmesan cheese. Serve immediately. Makes 4 main-dish servings.

Per serving: 395 calories, 27 g protein, 48 g carbohydrate, 10 g total fat (2 g saturated), 47 mg cholesterol, 235 mg sodium, 640 mg potassium.

Spaghetti with Mushroom-Pepper Sauce

3 **cups sliced fresh mushrooms**
1 **medium green sweet pepper, chopped**
1 **medium red sweet pepper, chopped**
3 **cloves garlic, minced**
1 **tablespoon olive oil *or* cooking oil**
1 **14½-ounce can whole Italian-style tomatoes, cut up**
½ **of a 6-ounce can (⅓ cup) tomato paste**
1 **teaspoon sugar**
1 **teaspoon dried basil, crushed**
¼ **teaspoon pepper**
¼ **cup sliced pitted ripe olives**
8 **ounces packaged spaghetti**

For sauce, in a large saucepan cook mushrooms, green and red sweet peppers, and garlic in hot oil till tender. Stir in undrained tomatoes, tomato paste, sugar, basil, and pepper. Bring to boiling. Reduce heat and simmer, uncovered, about 15 minutes or to desired consistency. Stir in olives.

Meanwhile, cook pasta according to package directions. Drain well. Spoon sauce over pasta. Makes 4 to 6 side-dish servings.

Per serving: 346 calories, 11 g protein, 64 g carbohydrate, 6 g total fat (1 g saturated), 0 mg cholesterol, 570 mg sodium, 824 mg potassium.

Macaroni Ring with Vegetables

2 **tablespoons fine dry bread crumbs**
¼ **cup finely chopped onion**
2 **tablespoons margarine *or* butter, melted**
3 **beaten eggs**
1 **cup hot cooked macaroni**
1 **cup shredded sharp cheddar cheese (4 ounces)**
1 **cup soft bread crumbs (about 1⅓ slices)**
1 **cup milk**
¼ **cup snipped fresh parsley**
1 **2-ounce jar sliced pimiento, drained**
¼ **teaspoon pepper**
1 **cup sliced zucchini**
1 **cup frozen peas**
¼ **teaspoon dried thyme, crushed**
1 **tablespoon margarine *or* butter**

Grease a 5-cup ring mold. Sprinkle bottom and sides with fine dry bread crumbs; set aside.

In a small saucepan cook onion in the 2 tablespoons margarine or butter till tender but not brown. In a large mixing bowl stir together onion mixture, eggs, macaroni, cheese, soft bread crumbs, milk, parsley, pimiento, and pepper. **1** Spoon mixture into prepared mold.

Bake, uncovered, in a 350° oven for 30 minutes or till firm and heated through. Let stand 10 minutes. **2** Invert onto a serving dish.

Meanwhile, in a medium saucepan cook zucchini, peas, and thyme in the 1 tablespoon margarine or butter, covered, over medium heat about 4 minutes or till just tender. **3** Spoon vegetables into center of macaroni ring. Makes 6 main-dish servings.

Per serving: 311 calories, 14 g protein, 27 g carbohydrate, 16 g total fat (6 g saturated), 130 mg cholesterol, 313 mg sodium, 269 mg potassium.

1 Spoon macaroni mixture into a greased 5-cup ring mold.

2 Place serving dish atop ring mold. Carefully invert ring mold and plate to release baked macaroni ring onto serving dish.

3 Fill center of macaroni ring with cooked vegetables.

Texas Macaroni and Cheese

1   7-ounce package elbow
    macaroni
½   cup chopped onion
1   clove garlic, minced
2   tablespoons cooking oil
2   tablespoons all-purpose
    flour
½   teaspoon ground cumin
¼   teaspoon salt
2½ cups milk
8   ounces Mexican-style
    cheese spread, cut up
1   large tomato, peeled,
    seeded, and chopped
½   cup chopped pitted ripe
    olives
2   tablespoons chopped fresh
    parsley
½   cup crushed corn chips

Cook macaroni according to package directions. Drain well; set aside.

In a large saucepan cook onion and garlic in hot oil over medium heat till tender. Stir in flour, cumin, and salt; add milk all at once. Cook and stir over medium heat till slightly thickened and bubbly.

Remove saucepan from heat. Add cheese and stir till melted. Stir in cooked macaroni, chopped tomato, olives, and parsley. Transfer to a 2-quart rectangular baking dish. Top with crushed corn chips. Bake in a 350° oven for 25 to 30 minutes or till bubbly. Makes 6 main-dish servings.

Per serving: 432 calories, 18 g protein, 41 g carbohydrate, 22 g total fat (10 g saturated), 40 mg cholesterol, 420 mg sodium, 297 mg potassium.

Classic Lasagna

¼   pound bulk pork sausage
1   cup sliced fresh
    mushrooms
⅓   cup chopped onion
1   clove garlic, minced
1   14½-ounce can tomatoes,
    cut up
1   15-ounce can tomato sauce
1   teaspoon sugar
1½ teaspoons dried Italian
    seasoning, crushed
⅛   teaspoon pepper
1   beaten egg
1   cup ricotta cheese
¼   cup grated Parmesan
    cheese
6   packaged lasagna noodles
1   cup shredded mozzarella
    cheese (4 ounces)
¼   cup grated Parmesan
    cheese

For sauce, in a saucepan cook sausage, mushrooms, onion, and garlic till sausage is brown and onion is tender. Drain off fat. Stir in undrained tomatoes, tomato sauce, sugar, Italian seasoning, and pepper. Bring to boiling. Reduce heat and simmer, uncovered, for 35 to 40 minutes or to desired consistency.

Meanwhile, in a small mixing bowl stir together egg, ricotta cheese, and ¼ cup Parmesan cheese. Set aside.

Cook lasagna noodles according to package directions. Drain well. Arrange 3 lasagna noodles in a greased 2-quart square baking dish. Trim to fit. Spread with *half* of the ricotta cheese mixture. Spoon *half* of the sauce over top. Sprinkle with *half* of the mozzarella cheese. Repeat layers of noodles, cheese mixture, and sauce; reserve remaining mozzarella cheese. Sprinkle ¼ cup Parmesan cheese over all.

Bake lasagna, covered, in a 350° oven for 30 minutes. Uncover and sprinkle remaining mozzarella cheese on top. Bake about 5 minutes more or till heated through. Let stand for 10 minutes before serving. Makes 6 main-dish servings.

Per serving: 308 calories, 20 g protein, 29 g carbohydrate, 13 g total fat (7 g saturated), 73 mg cholesterol, 971 mg sodium, 631 mg potassium.

Stuffed Manicotti with Primavera Sauce

12 packaged manicotti shells
 1 cup sliced fresh
      mushrooms
 1 cup chopped fresh broccoli
 ½ cup chopped onion
 1 medium carrot, shredded
 2 cloves garlic, minced
 1 tablespoon olive oil
 1 15-ounce can tomato sauce
 1 14½-ounce can tomatoes,
      drained and chopped
 1 6-ounce can tomato paste
1½ teaspoons dried Italian
      seasoning, crushed
 ⅛ to ¼ teaspoon crushed red
      pepper
 2 cups ricotta cheese
 1 cup shredded mozzarella
      cheese
 ½ cup grated Romano cheese
 3 tablespoons snipped fresh
      parsley
 1 slightly beaten egg
 ½ cup shredded mozzarella
      cheese

1 Cook manicotti according to package directions. **2** Drain and cool cooked manicotti.

For sauce, in a large saucepan cook mushrooms, broccoli, onion, carrot, and garlic in hot oil till tender. Stir in tomato sauce, tomatoes, tomato paste, Italian seasoning, and crushed red pepper. Bring to boiling. Reduce heat and simmer, uncovered, over medium heat for 15 minutes, stirring occasionally. Remove from heat; set aside.

For filling, in a medium bowl combine ricotta cheese, the 1 cup mozzarella cheese, Romano cheese, parsley, and egg; mix well. **3** Using a small spoon, carefully fill manicotti shells with cheese mixture, using about ¼ *cup* filling in *each* shell. Spread half of the sauce in bottom of a 3-quart rectangular baking dish. Place filled manicotti shells in a single layer atop sauce. Pour remaining sauce over manicotti.

Cover and bake in a 350° oven for 35 to 40 minutes or till bubbly. Sprinkle with the ½ cup shredded mozzarella cheese. Let stand 5 minutes before serving. Makes 6 main-dish servings.

Per serving: 462 calories, 29 g protein, 49 g carbohydrate, 18 g total fat (9 g saturated), 86 mg cholesterol, 934 mg sodium, 1,035 mg potassium.

1 Slowly add manicotti to rapidly boiling water 2 or 3 pieces at a time.

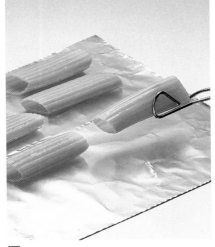

2 Cool cooked manicotti in a single layer on greased foil.

3 Using a small spoon, fill each manicotti with about ¼ cup of the cheese mixture.

Ham and Cheese Tortellini

1 cup sliced fresh
    mushrooms
½ teaspoon dried thyme,
    crushed
¼ teaspoon pepper
1 tablespoon margarine *or*
    butter
1 9-ounce package
    refrigerated cheese-filled
    tortellini
1 cup frozen peas
1 cup diced fully cooked
    ham
¾ cup half-and-half *or* light
    cream
½ cup grated Parmesan
    cheese

In a small saucepan cook mushrooms, thyme, and pepper in hot margarine or butter till tender; set aside.

Cook tortellini according to package directions *except* add the frozen peas the last 2 minutes of cooking. Drain well. Return tortellini and peas to hot saucepan. Stir in ham, half-and-half or light cream, Parmesan cheese, and mushroom mixture. Toss gently. Cook and stir over low heat for 1 to 2 minutes or till mixture thickens slightly. Transfer to a warm serving dish. Serve immediately. Makes 6 main-dish servings.

Per serving: 237 calories, 15 g protein, 18 g carbohydrate, 11 g total fat (5 g saturated), 25 mg cholesterol, 666 mg sodium, 220 mg potassium.

Pasta with Peppery Salsa

2 cloves garlic, minced
¼ teaspoon crushed red
    pepper
1 tablespoon cooking oil
½ cup chopped green sweet
    pepper
½ cup chopped red sweet
    pepper
½ cup frozen whole kernel
    corn
½ teaspoon ground cumin
¼ teaspoon salt
2 large tomatoes, peeled,
    seeded, and chopped
1 tablespoon red wine
    vinegar
4 ounces packaged angel
    hair pasta (capellini)

For salsa, in a saucepan cook garlic and crushed red pepper in hot oil over medium heat about 1 minute or till tender. Stir in green and red sweet peppers, corn, cumin, and salt. Cover and cook for 5 minutes. Stir in chopped tomatoes and vinegar. Cook, uncovered, for 5 minutes more.

Meanwhile, cook pasta according to package directions. Drain well. Return pasta to hot saucepan. Add salsa. Toss gently till well coated. Serve immediately. Makes 4 side-dish servings.

Per serving: 193 calories, 6 g protein, 34 g carbohydrate, 5 g total fat (1 g saturated), 0 mg cholesterol, 144 mg sodium, 321 mg potassium.

Linguine with Creamy Spinach Pesto

½ **cup firmly packed fresh spinach**
⅓ **cup semi-soft cheese with spiced garlic and herbs**
¼ **cup grated Parmesan cheese**
3 **tablespoons toasted pine nuts**
2 **tablespoons snipped fresh basil** *or* **2 teaspoons dried basil, crushed**
2 **tablespoons olive oil** *or* **cooking oil**
¼ **teaspoon salt**
1 **clove garlic, minced**
8 **ounces hot cooked linguine**

In a blender container or food processor bowl combine spinach, semi-soft cheese, Parmesan cheese, pine nuts, basil, oil, salt, and garlic. Cover and blend or process till smooth.

Place linguine in a warm serving bowl. Add spinach mixture; toss gently till coated. Makes 8 side-dish servings.

Per serving: 215 calories, 7 g protein, 24 g carbohydrate, 11 g total fat (4 g saturated), 14 mg cholesterol, 161 mg sodium, 93 mg potassium.

Rice Cakes

1 14 ½-ounce can pasta-style
    chunky tomatoes
    (optional)
⅔ cup long grain rice
½ cup chopped onion
½ cup shredded carrot
2 tablespoons cooking oil
1 egg, slightly beaten
½ cup shredded mozzarella
    cheese
⅓ cup fine dry bread crumbs
3 tablespoons grated
    Parmesan cheese
1 tablespoon milk
½ teaspoon dried thyme,
    crushed

For sauce, in a small saucepan heat chunky tomatoes over low heat, if desired. Cover and keep warm. Cook long grain rice according to package directions. (You should have 2 cups hot cooked rice.)

Meanwhile, cook onion and carrot in *2 teaspoons* of the oil over medium heat till tender. In a medium bowl combine egg, mozzarella cheese, bread crumbs, Parmesan cheese, milk, and thyme. Add hot cooked rice and mix well. Let rice mixture stand 10 minutes.

Shape rice mixture into eight ¾-inch-thick patties that are about 3-inches in diameter, using about ¼ cup mixture for each patty. In a large skillet cook rice patties, 4 at a time, in remaining hot oil about 4 minutes on each side or till patties are golden brown and heated through. Serve with warm sauce, if desired. Makes 5 side-dish servings.

Per serving: 255 calories, 9 g protein, 31 g carbohydrate, 10 g total fat (3 g saturated), 52 mg cholesterol, 197 mg sodium, 130 mg potassium.

Brown Rice Pilaf

1¾ cups water
¾ cup brown rice
¼ teaspoon salt
½ pound fresh asparagus,
    cut into 1-inch pieces
2 tablespoons margarine *or*
    butter
1 cup sliced fresh
    mushrooms
¼ cup thinly sliced green
    onion
½ cup chopped walnuts
3 tablespoons snipped fresh
    parsley
1 tablespoon dry sherry
2 teaspoons soy sauce

In a large saucepan bring water, brown rice, and salt to boiling. Reduce heat and simmer, covered, for 35 to 40 minutes or till rice is tender and liquid is absorbed.

Meanwhile, in a large skillet cook asparagus in margarine or butter for 3 minutes. Add mushrooms and green onion. Cook and stir for 3 minutes more. Stir in cooked rice, walnuts, parsley, sherry, and soy sauce. Cook till heated through, stirring often. Makes 6 side-dish servings.

Per serving: 189 calories, 4 g protein, 21 g carbohydrate, 10 g total fat (1 g saturated), 0 mg cholesterol, 162 mg sodium, 216 mg potassium.

Polenta with Two-Tomato Topping

2¾ cups water
2 teaspoons instant chicken bouillon granules
1 cup yellow cornmeal
1 cup cold water
3 tablespoons grated Parmesan cheese
2 medium red tomatoes, seeded and chopped
2 medium yellow tomatoes, seeded and chopped
¼ cup chopped green onion
3 tablespoons snipped fresh basil *or* 3 teaspoons dried basil, crushed
2 teaspoons snipped fresh oregano *or* ½ teaspoon dried oregano, crushed
1 teaspoon balsamic vinegar *or* wine vinegar
¼ teaspoon garlic salt
⅛ to ¼ teaspoon crushed red pepper
⅓ cup grated Parmesan cheese

For polenta, bring the 2¾ cups water and bouillon granules to boiling. Meanwhile, in a bowl combine cornmeal, the 1 cup water, and the 3 tablespoons Parmesan cheese. Slowly add cornmeal mixture to boiling water, stirring constantly. Cook and stir till mixture returns to boiling.
1 Reduce heat; cook over low heat for 10 to 15 minutes or till mixture is very thick, stirring occasionally. Remove from heat.
2 Pour cornmeal mixture into a greased 9-inch pie plate, spreading evenly. Cover with foil and set aside about 30 minutes or till firm. Bake, covered, in a 350° oven about 10 minutes or till hot.

Meanwhile, for topping, in a bowl combine chopped tomatoes, green onion, basil, oregano, vinegar, garlic salt, and red pepper. Cover and let stand at room temperature for 30 minutes.
3 To serve, cut polenta into wedges. Top with tomato mixture. Sprinkle with the ⅓ cup Parmesan cheese. Makes 6 side-dish servings.

Per serving: 144 calories, 7 g protein, 23 g carbohydrate, 3 g total fat (2 g saturated), 7 mg cholesterol, 548 mg sodium, 248 mg potassium.

1 Cook and stir cornmeal mixture over low heat till very thick.

2 Using a small spatula, spread mixture evenly in pie plate.

3 To serve, cut baked polenta into wedges.

PASTA AND GRAINS

Creamy Olive Risotto

½ **cup chopped onion**
½ **cup chopped celery**
½ **cup sliced fresh mushrooms**
2 **cloves garlic, minced**
3 **tablespoons margarine *or* butter**
1 **cup long grain rice**
3 **cups chicken broth**
⅔ **cup chopped pitted ripe olives**
½ **cup whipping cream**
½ **cup grated Parmesan cheese**
1 **2-ounce jar sliced pimiento, drained**
3 **tablespoons snipped fresh parsley**

In a large saucepan cook onion, celery, mushrooms, and garlic in margarine or butter over medium heat till tender. Add rice; cook and stir for 2 to 3 minutes. Stir in *1½ cups* of the chicken broth. Cook, uncovered, over medium-high heat about 5 minutes or till liquid is absorbed, stirring frequently.

Stir in remaining chicken broth and cook, uncovered, for 25 to 30 minutes or till liquid is absorbed, stirring frequently. Stir in olives, whipping cream, Parmesan cheese, pimiento, and parsley. Cook for 2 to 3 minutes more or till heated through. Makes 6 to 8 side-dish servings.

Per serving: 324 calories, 10 g protein, 30 g carbohydrate, 19 g total fat (8 g saturated), 34 mg cholesterol, 706 mg sodium, 299 mg potassium.

Cheese and Sausage Grits

4 **cups water**
1½ **teaspoons instant chicken bouillon granules**
1 **cup quick-cooking grits**
¾ **cup shredded Swiss cheese**
4 **beaten eggs**
½ **pound bulk pork sausage, cooked and drained**
⅓ **cup sliced green onion**
¼ **teaspoon dry mustard**
⅛ **teaspoon pepper**
¾ **cup shredded cheddar cheese**
2 **tablespoons snipped fresh parsley**

In a saucepan bring water and bouillon granules to boiling. Slowly add quick-cooking grits, stirring constantly. Cook and stir till boiling. Reduce heat; cook and stir for 6 to 7 minutes or till water is absorbed and mixture is thick.

Stir Swiss cheese into hot grits till melted. Gradually stir about *½ cup* grits mixture into beaten eggs. Return egg mixture to saucepan. Stir in sausage, green onion, dry mustard, and pepper; mix well. Spoon grits mixture into a greased 2-quart rectangular baking dish.

Bake in a 325° oven for 25 to 30 minutes or till a knife inserted off center comes out clean. Sprinkle with cheddar cheese and parsley. Let stand 5 minutes before serving. Makes 6 main-dish servings.

Per serving: 325 calories, 18 g protein, 22 g carbohydrate, 18 g total fat (8 g saturated), 185 mg cholesterol, 615 mg sodium, 187 mg potassium.

Vegetable Couscous

1 **small red sweet pepper,
    coarsely chopped**
½ **cup chopped onion**
½ **cup sliced carrots**
1 **tablespoon olive oil *or*
    cooking oil**
1¼ **cups chicken broth**
1 **cup frozen peas**
2 **tablespoons coarsely
    chopped raisins**
⅛ **teaspoon ground
    cinnamon**
    Dash salt
¾ **cup couscous
    (about 4½ ounces)**

In a medium saucepan cook sweet pepper, onion, and carrots in hot oil over medium heat about 10 minutes or till tender. Stir in chicken broth, peas, raisins, cinnamon, and salt. Bring to boiling. Stir in couscous. Cover saucepan and remove from heat. Let stand for 5 minutes. Makes 4 to 6 side-dish servings.

Per serving: 234 calories, 8 g protein, 41 g carbohydrate, 4 g total fat (1 g saturated), 0 mg cholesterol, 320 mg sodium, 320 mg potassium.

Barley-Vegetable Medley

1½ **cups water**
 1 **cup fresh or frozen whole
   kernel corn**
 ½ **cup quick-cooking barley**
 ½ **cup chopped onion**
 ½ **cup chopped green sweet
   pepper**
 ½ **cup coarsely shredded
   carrot**
 2 **teaspoons instant beef
   bouillon granules**
 ½ **teaspoon dried basil,
   crushed**
 ¼ **teaspoon dried thyme,
   crushed**
 ¼ **teaspoon dried oregano,
   crushed**
 ⅛ **teaspoon pepper**
 1 **large tomato, chopped**

In a medium saucepan bring water to boiling. Stir in corn, barley, onion, sweet pepper, carrot, bouillon granules, basil, thyme, oregano, and pepper; return to boiling. Reduce heat and simmer, covered, about 10 minutes or till barley is tender, stirring occasionally. Drain barley mixture. Stir in chopped tomato. Cook and stir about 1 minute more or till heated through. Makes 6 side-dish servings.

Per serving: 110 calories, 3 g protein, 24 g carbohydrate, 1 g total fat (0 g saturated), 0 mg cholesterol, 306 mg sodium, 245 mg potassium.

Cinnamon-Raisin Oatmeal

1½ **cups quick-cooking rolled
   oats**
 1 **cup raisins *or* mixed dried
   fruit bits**
 ¼ **cup chopped nuts**
 ¼ **cup packed brown sugar**
 ½ **teaspoon ground
   cinnamon**
 ¼ **teaspoon salt**
 ¼ **teaspoon ground nutmeg**
 3 **cups water**
   Milk (optional)

Stir together quick-cooking rolled oats, raisins or dried fruit bits, nuts, brown sugar, cinnamon, salt, and nutmeg. Store in an airtight container at room temperature.

In a medium saucepan bring water to boiling. Slowly add oat mixture to water, stirring constantly. Cook, stirring constantly, for 1 minute. Cover; remove from heat. Let stand for 1 to 3 minutes or till of desired consistency. Serve with milk, if desired. Makes 4 servings.

Note: For 1 serving, use ¾ cup water and ⅔ cup oat mixture.

Micro-cooking: For one serving, in a 2-cup measure, micro-cook ¾ cup water on 100% power (high) for 1¾ to 2¾ minutes or till boiling. Slowly stir in ⅔ cup oat mixture. Cook, uncovered, on high for 30 seconds, stirring once. Let stand 1 minute.

Per serving: 323 calories, 7 g protein, 64 g carbohydrate, 6 g total fat (1 g saturated), 0 mg cholesterol, 149 mg sodium, 447 mg potassium.

EGGS AND CHEESE

Fiesta Egg Salad Pockets

Fiesta Egg Salad Pockets

6 **hard-cooked eggs, chopped**
1 **small tomato, seeded and chopped**
¼ **cup finely chopped onion**
¼ **cup finely chopped green sweet pepper**
¼ **cup chopped pitted ripe olives**
2 **tablespoons snipped fresh cilantro**
½ **cup mayonnaise *or* salad dressing**
¼ **teaspoon garlic salt**
⅛ **teaspoon ground red pepper**
2 **whole wheat pita bread rounds, halved crosswise**
  Leaf lettuce
1 **small avocado, seeded, peeled, and sliced**

In a medium mixing bowl combine eggs, chopped tomato, onion, sweet pepper, olives, and cilantro. Combine mayonnaise or salad dressing, garlic salt, and red pepper; add to egg mixture, mixing well. Cover and refrigerate for 2 to 4 hours.

To serve, line each pita half with lettuce; fill with avocado slices and egg salad mixture. Makes 4 servings.

Per serving: 559 calories, 18 g protein, 37 g carbohydrate, 40 g total fat (6 g saturated), 336 mg cholesterol, 639 mg sodium, 786 mg potassium.

Creamed Eggs in Patty Shells

1 **10-ounce package (6) frozen patty shells**
½ **cup fresh asparagus, cut into 1-inch pieces**
2 **tablespoons margarine *or* butter**
1 **cup sliced fresh mushrooms**
2 **tablespoons finely chopped onion**
¼ **cup margarine *or* butter**
3 **tablespoons all-purpose flour**
1⅔ **cups milk**
½ **cup shredded Muenster *or* Swiss cheese**
1 **tablespoon Dijon-style mustard**
½ **teaspoon salt**
¼ **teaspoon pepper**
5 **hard-cooked eggs, chopped**

Bake frozen patty shells according to package directions; set aside. In a small saucepan cook and stir asparagus in the 2 tablespoons margarine or butter till crisp-tender. Add mushrooms and onion; cook and stir till tender. Set aside.

In another saucepan melt the ¼ cup margarine or butter; stir in flour. Add milk all at once. Cook and stir over medium heat till thickened and bubbly. Cook and stir 1 minute more. Remove from heat. Add cheese, mustard, salt, and pepper. Stir till cheese melts. Stir in reserved mushroom mixture and eggs. Cook and stir till heated through. Spoon into patty shells. Makes 6 servings.

Per serving: 468 calories, 13 g protein, 25 g carbohydrate, 35 g total fat (6 g saturated), 192 mg cholesterol, 701 mg sodium, 251 mg potassium.

Tomato, Bacon, and Chive French Omelet

2 eggs
1 tablespoon water
   Dash salt
   Dash pepper
1 tablespoon margarine *or*
   butter
1 small tomato, chopped
   (⅓ cup)
¼ cup shredded Monterey
   Jack cheese (1 ounce)
2 slices bacon, crisp-cooked,
   drained, and crumbled
1 tablespoon snipped fresh
   chives

In a bowl combine eggs, water, salt, and pepper. Using a fork, beat till combined but not frothy. In an 8- or 10-inch skillet with flared sides, heat margarine or butter till a drop of water sizzles. Lift and tilt the pan to coat the sides.

Add egg mixture to skillet; cook over medium heat. **1** As eggs set, run a spatula around the edge of the skillet, lifting eggs and letting uncooked portion flow underneath. **2** When eggs are set but still shiny, remove from the heat. Sprinkle cheese, tomato, bacon, and chives across center of omelet. **3** Fold sides over. **4** Invert omelet onto serving plate. Makes 1 serving.

Per serving: 451 calories, 24 g protein, 6 g carbohydrate, 37 g total fat (13 g saturated), 462 mg cholesterol, 757 mg sodium, 424 mg potassium.

1 To allow the uncooked portion of the eggs to flow underneath to cook, run spatula around edge of skillet.

2 When eggs are set but still shiny, remove from heat and sprinkle filling atop.

3 Using a spatula, carefully lift one-third of the cooked omelet and fold over center. Repeat with remaining one-third to overlap.

4 Tilt skillet, then invert so omelet rolls out onto plate.

Zucchini and Dried Tomato Frittata

8 **beaten eggs**
2 **tablespoons snipped fresh parsley**
½ **teaspoon dried Italian seasoning, crushed**
¼ **teaspoon pepper**
   Dash garlic powder
½ **cup thinly sliced zucchini**
½ **cup oil-packed dried tomatoes, drained and chopped**
½ **cup sliced fresh mushrooms**
¼ **cup finely chopped onion**
2 **tablespoons margarine *or* butter**
3 **tablespoons grated Romano cheese**
½ **cup shredded mozzarella cheese (2 ounces)**

In a bowl combine eggs, parsley, Italian seasoning, pepper, and garlic powder; set aside. In a 10-inch broiler-proof skillet cook zucchini, tomatoes, mushrooms, and onion in margarine or butter about 4 minutes or till tender. Sprinkle with Romano cheese.

Pour egg mixture into skillet over vegetables. Cook over medium heat. As mixture sets, run a spatula around edge of skillet, lifting egg mixture to allow uncooked portions to flow underneath. Continue cooking and lifting edges about 3 minutes or till egg mixture is almost set (surface will be moist).

Sprinkle mozzarella cheese atop egg mixture. Place skillet under the broiler 4 to 5 inches from the heat. Broil for 1 to 2 minutes or till cheese melts and top is almost set. Cut into wedges. Makes 4 servings.

Per serving: 297 calories, 19 g protein, 7 g carbohydrate, 21 g total fat (7 g saturated), 439 mg cholesterol, 361 mg sodium, 447 mg potassium.

Sausage-Spinach Scramble

¾ **pound bulk pork sausage**
1 **cup chopped onion**
1 **cup sliced fresh mushrooms**
½ **cup chopped red sweet pepper**
2 **cloves garlic, minced**
1 **10-ounce package frozen chopped spinach, thawed and well drained**
½ **teaspoon dried oregano, crushed**
¼ **teaspoon dried basil, crushed**
5 **beaten eggs**
2 **tablespoons grated Parmesan cheese**

In a large skillet cook sausage, onion, mushrooms, sweet pepper, and garlic over medium-high heat till meat is browned and no longer pink and vegetables are tender. Drain fat well.

Stir in spinach, oregano, and basil; cook and stir for 3 minutes. Reduce heat to medium; add eggs. Cook till eggs are cooked throughout but still glossy and moist, stirring frequently. Sprinkle with Parmesan cheese. Makes 6 servings.

Per serving: 202 calories, 14 g protein, 8 g carbohydrate, 13 g total fat (5 g saturated), 201 mg cholesterol, 474 mg sodium, 399 mg potassium.

Deviled Eggs

6 eggs
**¼ cup mayonnaise *or* salad
   dressing**
**1 teaspoon prepared
   mustard**
**1 teaspoon vinegar
   Salt and pepper (optional)**

To hard-cook eggs, place eggs in a saucepan with enough *cold* water to cover. Bring to boiling over high heat. Reduce heat so water is just below simmering. Cook, covered, for 15 minutes. Drain.

Fill saucepan with cold water and let stand 2 minutes. (*Or*, to quickly cool, add a few ice cubes.) Drain. Gently tap each egg on the countertop. Roll egg between palms of hands. Peel off eggshell, starting at the large end.

1 2 Halve hard-cooked eggs lengthwise and remove yolks. Place yolks in a bowl; mash with a fork. Add mayonnaise or salad dressing, mustard, and vinegar; mix well. Season with salt and pepper, if desired. **3 4** Stuff egg white halves with yolk mixture. Makes 12 servings.

Per serving: 72 calories, 3 g protein, 0 g carbohydrate, 6 g total fat (1 g saturated), 109 mg cholesterol, 62 mg sodium, 34 mg potassium.

1 Cut hard-cooked eggs in half lengthwise.

2 With a small spoon, remove yolks and set egg whites aside.

3 Refill egg whites with yolk mixture. Using 2 spoons, fill the egg white cavities with yolk mixture.

4 *Or*, pipe the yolk mixture into the cavities with a large star tip and decorating bag.

Pepper-Cheese Egg Bake

½ cup chopped red sweet pepper
½ cup chopped green sweet pepper
¼ cup chopped onion
1 teaspoon cooking oil
5 eggs
⅓ cup milk
1 cup shredded cheddar cheese
1 cup shredded Monterey Jack cheese with jalapeño peppers
¾ cup small-curd cottage cheese

In a medium skillet cook sweet peppers and onion in hot oil about 5 minutes or till tender. In a bowl beat together eggs and milk. Stir in cheddar cheese, Monterey Jack cheese, *undrained* cottage cheese, and pepper mixture.

Divide cheese mixture evenly among six 10-ounce custard cups or individual casseroles. Place custard cups or casseroles in a 13x9x2-inch baking pan. Pour hot water into baking pan around custard cups or casseroles to a depth of 1 inch.

Bake, uncovered, in a 350° oven about 40 minutes or till just set. Remove custard cups or casseroles from baking pan. Let stand 5 minutes before serving. Makes 6 servings.

Per serving: 263 calories, 19 g protein, 5 g carbohydrate, 18 g total fat (10 g saturated), 219 mg cholesterol, 385 mg sodium, 203 mg potassium.

Cheese and Sausage-Apple Bake

½ pound bulk pork sausage
2 small apples, peeled, cored, and chopped (1½ cups)
½ cup finely chopped onion
1 tablespoon all-purpose flour
Nonstick spray coating
12 slices white bread
1½ cups shredded cheddar cheese
6 eggs
2 cups milk
¼ teaspoon apple pie spice
Dash ground ginger

In a large skillet cook sausage, chopped apple, and onion till meat is browned and no longer pink and onion is tender. Drain fat well. Stir in flour.

Spray a 2-quart rectangular baking dish with nonstick spray coating. Trim crusts from bread. Arrange six bread slices in the bottom of the prepared dish. Spoon sausage mixture over bread. Sprinkle with cheese. Top with remaining bread slices.

Combine eggs, milk, apple pie spice, and ginger; beat well. Pour over bread slices. Cover and chill for 2 to 24 hours. Bake, uncovered, in a 325° oven for 45 to 50 minutes or till set. Let stand 10 minutes before serving. Makes 6 servings.

Per serving: 462 calories, 24 g protein, 38 g carbohydrate, 24 g total fat (11 g saturated), 264 mg cholesterol, 765 mg sodium, 404 mg potassium.

Artichoke Quiche

**Pastry for Single-Crust Pie
(see recipe, page 199)**
½ **cup chopped onion**
¼ **cup thinly sliced celery**
1 **clove garlic, minced**
1 **tablespoon cooking oil**
1 **14-ounce can artichoke
hearts, drained and
chopped**
1½ **cups shredded mozzarella
cheese (6 ounces)**
3 **beaten eggs**
1½ **cups milk**
¼ **teaspoon salt**
¼ **teaspoon dried oregano,
crushed**
⅛ **teaspoon pepper**

Prepare Pastry for Single-Crust Pie, crimping edges high. Line the unpricked pastry shell with a double thickness of heavy-duty foil. Bake in a 450° oven for 8 minutes. Remove foil. Bake for 5 to 6 minutes more or till pastry is golden. Remove from oven. Reduce oven temperature to 325°.

In a large skillet cook onion, celery, and garlic in hot oil till tender. Remove from heat. Stir in artichokes. Spread artichoke mixture over bottom of hot pastry shell. Sprinkle mozzarella cheese evenly over artichoke mixture.

Combine eggs, milk, salt, oregano, and pepper; pour over cheese. Bake in a 325° oven for 45 to 50 minutes or till a knife inserted in center comes out clean. Let stand 10 minutes before serving. Makes 6 servings.

Per serving: 372 calories, 16 g protein, 28 g carbohydrate, 22 g total fat (8 g saturated), 127 mg cholesterol, 432 mg sodium, 335 mg potassium.

Cheddar Cheese-Hash Brown Bake

1 **cup chopped onion**
½ **cup chopped celery**
2 **tablespoons margarine *or***
    butter
2 **8-ounce cartons plain**
    low-fat yogurt
1 **11-ounce can condensed**
    cheddar cheese soup
1 **cup shredded cheddar**
    cheese (4 ounces)
1 **32-ounce package loose-**
    pack frozen hash brown
    potatoes
1½ **cups cornflakes, crushed**

In a small skillet cook onion and celery in margarine or butter till tender. In a large mixing bowl combine yogurt, soup, shredded cheese, and onion mixture; stir in potatoes. Spoon potato mixture into a lightly greased 2-quart rectangular baking dish. Top with crushed cornflakes. Bake in a 350° oven about 1 hour or till golden brown. Makes 10 to 12 servings.

Per serving: 281 calories, 11 g protein, 35 g carbohydrate, 11 g total fat (6 g saturated), 25 mg cholesterol, 532 mg sodium, 589 mg potassium.

Ham and Cheese Soufflé

¼ **cup margarine *or* butter**
¼ **cup all-purpose flour**
¼ **teaspoon dry mustard**
    Dash ground red pepper
1½ **cups milk**
2 **cups shredded cheddar**
    cheese
6 **egg yolks**
1 **cup diced fully cooked**
    ham
3 **tablespoons snipped fresh**
    parsley
6 **egg whites**

Measure enough foil to wrap around a 2-quart soufflé dish with 6 inches to spare. Fold foil into thirds lengthwise. Lightly butter one side. With buttered side in, position foil around outside of dish, letting it extend 2 inches above the top. Fasten the foil.

For cheese sauce, in a medium saucepan melt margarine or butter; stir in flour, mustard, and red pepper. Add milk all at once. Cook and stir till thickened and bubbly. Remove from heat. Add cheese, *1 cup* at a time, stirring till melted.

In a bowl beat egg yolks with a fork till combined. Slowly add cheese sauce to yolks, stirring constantly. Add ham and parsley; mix well.

In a clean bowl beat egg whites with electric mixer till stiff peaks form (tips stand straight). Gently fold about *2 cups* of the stiffly-beaten whites into cheese sauce. Gradually pour cheese sauce mixture over remaining stiffly-beaten whites, folding to combine. Pour into the ungreased soufflé dish.

Bake in a 350° oven for 45 to 50 minutes or till a knife inserted near the center comes out clean. Gently peel off the foil; serve soufflé immediately. Makes 6 servings.

Per serving: 381 calories, 24 g protein, 8 g carbohydrate, 28 g total fat (12 g saturated), 270 mg cholesterol, 727 mg sodium, 290 mg potassium.

SALADS

Chicken Salad in Melon Boats

Chicken Salad in Melon Boats

2 **cups cubed cooked chicken (about 10 ounces)**
½ **cup halved red grapes**
¼ **cup sliced celery**
¼ **cup chopped green onion**
½ **cup plain yogurt**
¼ **cup chutney, chopped**
½ **cup cashews, coarsely chopped**
1 **small cantaloupe, cut into 4 wedges**
   Red grapes (optional)

Combine chicken, ½ cup grapes, celery, and green onion; set aside.

For dressing, combine yogurt and chutney. Add dressing to chicken mixture; toss to coat. Cover and chill for 2 to 24 hours.

To serve, stir cashews into chicken mixture. Place melon wedges on salad plates. Spoon chicken mixture onto melon wedges. Garnish with additional red grapes, if desired. Makes 4 main-dish servings.

Per serving: 372 calories, 28 g protein, 34 g carbohydrate, 15 g total fat (4 g saturated), 70 mg cholesterol, 212 mg sodium, 920 mg potassium.

Spicy Rice, Black Bean, and Chicken Salad

1 **15-ounce can black beans, rinsed and drained**
1 **cup cooked rice, chilled**
1 **cup quartered cherry tomatoes**
1 **8-ounce can whole kernel corn, drained**
½ **cup finely chopped red onion**
¼ **cup finely chopped green sweet pepper**
1 **jalapeño pepper, seeded and finely chopped**
⅓ **cup salad oil**
⅓ **cup red wine vinegar**
2 **tablespoons snipped fresh cilantro**
2 **cloves garlic, minced**
½ **teaspoon ground cumin**
¼ **teaspoon salt**
¼ **teaspoon ground red pepper**
   Leaf lettuce
8 **ounces cooked chicken, cut into bite-size strips (about 1½ cups)**

In a large bowl combine black beans, rice, cherry tomatoes, corn, red onion, sweet pepper, and jalapeño pepper(see Note page 63); set aside.

For dressing, in a screw-top jar combine oil, vinegar, cilantro, garlic, cumin, salt, and red pepper. Cover and shake well. Pour two-thirds of the dressing over the rice mixture. Toss to coat.

Divide the rice mixture among 4 lettuce-lined salad plates. Arrange chicken strips on top. Drizzle remaining dressing over chicken. Makes 4 main-dish servings.

Per serving: 432 calories, 24 g protein, 44 g carbohydrate, 21 g total fat (3 g saturated), 37 mg cholesterol, 572 mg sodium, 679 mg potassium.

Broccoli-Pepper Salad with Ginger Dressing

2 tablespoons white wine
    vinegar
1 tablespoon salad oil
2 teaspoons minced fresh
    gingerroot
1 clove garlic, minced
    Dash salt
    Dash pepper
3 cups broccoli flowerets
1 cup sliced fresh
    mushrooms
½ cup sliced green onion
1 medium red sweetpepper,
    cut into thin strips
1 medium yellow sweet
    pepper, cut into thin
    strips

Cook broccoli in a small amount of boiling water for 3 minutes or till crisp-tender. Drain broccoli. Rinse with cold water; drain again.

Combine broccoli, mushrooms, green onion, and red and yellow sweet peppers. Toss with Ginger Dressing. Makes 6 servings.

Ginger Dressing: In a screw-top jar, combine vinegar, oil, ginger, garlic, salt, and pepper. Cover and shake well.

Per serving: 54 calories, 3 g protein, 7 g carbohydrate, 3 g total fat (0 g saturated), 0 mg cholesterol, 44 mg sodium, 337 mg potassium.

Fruited Rice and Ham Salad

2 cups cooked long grain
    white *and/or* brown rice
2 cups cubed fully cooked
    ham (about 10 ounces)
2 apples, cored and diced
⅓ cup chopped dates
¼ cup sliced green onion
¼ cup chopped celery
½ cup frozen apple juice
    concentrate, thawed
¼ cup cider vinegar
¼ teaspoon ground allspice
    Leaf lettuce
2 tablespoons chopped
    peanuts

In a large bowl, combine rice, ham, apples, dates, green onion, and celery.

For dressing, in a small bowl combine apple juice concentrate, vinegar, and allspice. Pour over rice mixture. Toss to coat. Cover and chill for 4 to 24 hours. Serve on lettuce-lined salad plates. Sprinkle with peanuts. Makes 4 main-dish servings.

Per serving: 398 calories, 20 g protein, 68 g carbohydrate, 6 g total fat (2 g saturated), 21 mg cholesterol, 816 mg sodium, 730 mg potassium.

Oriental Pork Salad

1 11-ounce can mandarin
    orange sections
12 ounces cooked pork, cut
    into bite-size strips
1 10-ounce package frozen
    sugar snap peas, thawed
    and drained
1 small onion, sliced
½ of a medium red sweet
    pepper, cut into bite-size
    strips
⅓ cup toasted sliced almonds
3 tablespoons salad oil
2 teaspoons soy sauce
1 teaspoon Dijon-style
    mustard
¼ teaspoon crushed red
    pepper

Drain mandarin orange sections, reserving juice. In a large bowl combine orange sections, pork, sugar snap peas, onion, sweet pepper, and almonds.

For dressing, in a screw-top jar combine reserved juice from orange sections, oil, soy sauce, mustard, and crushed red pepper. Cover and shake well. Pour dressing over pork mixture; toss to coat. Let salad stand at room temperature for 15 minutes. Serve with slotted spoon. Makes 4 main-dish servings.

Per serving: 421 calories, 29 g protein, 16 g carbohydrate, 27 g total fat (6 g saturated), 77 mg cholesterol, 269 mg sodium, 655 mg potassium.

Greens with Maple Vinaigrette

6 cups torn mixed greens*
1 medium apple, cored and cut into bite-size pieces
1 cup toasted walnut pieces
½ cup raisins
¼ cup olive oil *or* salad oil
2 tablespoons apple cider *or* apple juice
2 tablespoons cider vinegar
1 tablespoon maple-flavored syrup *or* maple syrup
1 tablespoon finely chopped onion
¼ teaspoon salt
⅛ teaspoon pepper

1 2 To prepare lettuce, remove core, rinse, and drain. **3**Remove core and center vein from romaine. **4**Rinse greens and pat dry with paper towels.

For salad, place torn salad greens in a large salad bowl. Add apple, walnuts, and raisins. Set aside.

For vinaigrette, in a screw-top jar combine oil, apple cider or juice, vinegar, maple syrup, onion, salt, and pepper. Cover and shake well.

5Drizzle vinaigrette over salad; toss to coat. Makes 6 side-dish servings.

*Iceberg, romaine, or Bibb (Boston) lettuce may be used.

Per serving: 278 calories, 4 g protein, 21 g carbohydrate, 22 g total fat (2 g saturated), 0 mg cholesterol, 111 mg sodium, 412 mg potassium.

1After removing wilted and discolored leaves, loosen the lettuce core by hitting the stem end sharply on the kitchen countertop. Twist the core to remove it.

2Rinse the head of lettuce, bottom side up, under cold running water. Invert the head to drain thoroughly in a colander set in the sink or on a draining board.

3Cut the bottom core from romaine or Bibb (Boston) lettuce. Remove center vein from romaine by cutting along both sides.

4Rinse greens and place on several layers of paper towels. Place another paper towel atop greens. Pat gently to remove water clinging to leaves.

5Add dressing to salad and toss salad mixture, using two salad servers or spoons.

SALADS

Tarragon Shrimp Salad

1 **pound shrimp, peeled and deveined**
1 **cup frozen peas, thawed**
1 **cup thinly sliced carrots**
½ **cup thinly sliced celery**
¼ **cup thinly sliced green onion**
½ **cup mayonnaise *or* salad dressing**
¼ **cup Dijon-style mustard**
2 **tablespoons tarragon vinegar *or* cider vinegar**
1 **teaspoon dried tarragon, crushed**
¼ **teaspoon pepper**
  Spinach *or* leaf lettuce

Cook shrimp in boiling water for 2 to 3 minutes or till shrimp turn pink. Drain shrimp. Cover and chill for at least 3 hours.

In a large bowl combine chilled shrimp, peas, carrots, celery, and onion; set aside.

For dressing, in a small bowl stir together mayonnaise or salad dressing, mustard, vinegar, tarragon, and pepper. Pour dressing over shrimp mixture; toss gently to coat. Cover and chill for up to 6 hours.

To serve, arrange shrimp mixture atop spinach or lettuce leaves. Makes 4 main-dish servings.

Per serving: 355 calories, 23 g protein, 12 g carbohydrate, 24 g total fat (4 g saturated), 190 mg cholesterol, 822 mg sodium, 558 mg potassium.

Italian Salad with Dried Tomato Vinaigrette

2 **cups broccoli flowerets**
2 **cups cauliflower flowerets**
1 **small red onion, thinly sliced**
½ **cup sliced pitted ripe olives**
½ **cup chopped red sweet pepper**
¼ **cup vinegar**
¼ **cup snipped oil-packed dried tomatoes, drained**
2 **tablespoons olive oil *or* salad oil**
2 **tablespoons water**
1 **tablespoon snipped fresh oregano *or* 1 teaspoon dried oregano, crushed**
1 **tablespoon Dijon-style mustard**
1½ **teaspoons sugar**

In a large mixing bowl combine the broccoli, cauliflower, onion, olives, and sweet pepper.

For vinaigrette, in a screw-top jar combine vinegar, dried tomatoes, oil, water, oregano, mustard, and sugar. Cover and shake well. Pour over vegetable mixture. Toss to coat. Cover and chill for 2 to 24 hours. Toss again before serving. Makes 6 side-dish servings.

Per serving: 87 calories, 2 g protein, 8 g carbohydrate, 6 g total fat (1 g saturated), 0 mg cholesterol, 114 mg sodium, 331 mg potassium.

Summer Pasta Salad

6 ounces tiny shell macaroni
   (1½ cups)
½ cup chopped onion
½ cup chopped green sweet
   pepper
2 garlic cloves, minced
1 tablespoon cooking oil
1 cup cubed Monterey Jack
   cheese (4 ounces)
½ cup frozen whole kernel
   corn
2 tablespoons snipped fresh
   parsley
¾ cup bottled Honey-Dijon
   Salad Dressing
1 cup halved cherry
   tomatoes
   Parmesan cheese (optional)

Cook pasta according to package directions. Drain pasta. Rinse with cold water; drain again. Set pasta aside. In a small skillet cook onion, sweet pepper, and garlic in hot oil about 5 minutes or till tender; set aside.

In a large mixing bowl combine Monterey Jack cheese, corn, parsley, cooked pasta, and onion mixture.

Pour Honey-Dijon dressing over pasta mixture and toss to coat. Cover and chill up to 24 hours. Just before serving, stir in tomatoes. Sprinkle with Parmesan cheese, if desired. Makes 6 side-dish servings.

Per serving: 330 calories, 9 g protein, 35 g carbohydrate, 18 g total fat (5 g saturated), 17 mg cholesterol, 195 mg sodium, 190 mg potassium.

Herbed Baby Corn and Garbanzo Beans

1 15-ounce can garbanzo
   beans, rinsed and
   drained
1 14-ounce can baby corn,
   drained
1 medium tomato, seeded
   and chopped
⅓ cup sliced pitted ripe
   olives
¼ cup thinly sliced green
   onion
3 tablespoons olive oil *or*
   salad oil
3 tablespoons red wine
   vinegar
1 tablespoon snipped fresh
   parsley
1 clove garlic, minced
1 teaspoon ground cumin
1 teaspoon dried oregano,
   crushed
¼ teaspoon crushed red
   pepper

In a large bowl combine garbanzo beans, baby corn, tomato, olives, and green onion; set aside.

For dressing, in a screw-top jar combine oil, vinegar, parsley, garlic, cumin, oregano, and crushed red pepper. Cover and shake well. Pour over bean mixture; toss to coat. Cover and chill for 2 to 24 hours. Makes 6 side-dish servings.

Per serving: 173 calories, 5 g protein, 21 g carbohydrate, 8 g total fat (1 g saturated), 0 mg cholesterol, 265 mg sodium, 463 mg potassium.

Calico Coleslaw

¾ cup mayonnaise *or* salad
   dressing
2 tablespoons sugar
2 tablespoons white wine
   vinegar
½ teaspoon celery seed
1½ cups shredded green
   cabbage
1½ cups shredded red cabbage
½ cup shredded carrot
½ cup finely chopped green
   sweet pepper
½ cup finely chopped celery
¼ cup finely chopped onion
3 tablespoons snipped fresh
   parsley
1 cup diced tomato

For dressing, stir together the mayonnaise or salad dressing, sugar, vinegar, and celery seed.

In a large mixing bowl combine green cabbage, red cabbage, carrot, sweet pepper, celery, onion, and parsley. Pour the dressing over the cabbage mixture; toss to coat. Cover and chill for 1 to 8 hours. Just before serving, stir in tomato. Makes 6 side-dish servings.

Note: If you want to prepare the salad up to 24 hours in advance, make the dressing and toss together the vegetable mixture (except the tomato) and chill in separate containers. Just before serving, toss the vegetable mixture with the dressing and stir in the tomato.

Per serving: 244 calories, 2 g protein, 12 g carbohydrate, 22 g total fat (3 g saturated), 16 mg cholesterol, 180 mg sodium, 289 mg potassium.

New-Style Slaw

2 cups shredded red cabbage
1 cup shredded jicama
1 cup shredded carrots
1 medium apple, peeled and
   chopped
½ cup toasted pecan pieces
¼ cup salad oil
2 tablespoons cider vinegar
1 tablespoon honey
2 teaspoons Dijon-style
   mustard
¼ teaspoon salt
¼ teaspoon pepper

1 Shred cabbage with a knife. **2 3** Peel and shred jicama. In a large bowl combine cabbage, jicama, carrots, apple, and nuts; set aside.

4 For dressing, in a screw-top jar combine oil, vinegar, honey, mustard, salt, and pepper. Cover and shake well. Pour over cabbage mixture; toss to coat. Serve immediately or cover and chill for up to 2 hours. Makes 6 side-dish servings.

Per serving: 199 calories, 2 g protein, 16 g carbohydrate, 16 g total fat (2 g saturated), 0 mg cholesterol, 140 mg sodium, 191 mg potassium.

1 For coarse shreds, hold a quarter head of cabbage firmly against the cutting board. Using a knife, slice the cabbage into long, coarse shreds.

2 Carefully peel jicama and cut into pieces that are easy to handle.

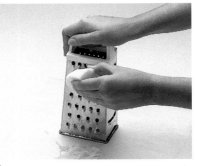

3 To shred jicama, hold a piece at an angle to the surface of a coarse shredder. Rub jicama along surface from top to bottom.

4 Combine the dressing ingredients in a screw-top jar. Shake the jar well to combine thoroughly.

SALADS

New Potato and Green Bean Salad

½ **pound small new potatoes, quartered**
½ **pound green beans, cut diagonally into 1-inch pieces**
½ **cup thinly sliced radishes**
⅓ **cup thinly sliced celery**
⅓ **cup chopped onion**
3 **tablespoons olive oil *or* salad oil**
3 **tablespoons white wine vinegar**
1 **tablespoon water**
2 **teaspoons Dijon-style mustard**
1 **tablespoon snipped fresh parsley**
1 **teaspoon snipped fresh thyme**
1 **teaspoon snipped fresh rosemary**
1 **clove garlic, minced**
¼ **teaspoon salt**

In a covered saucepan cook potatoes in boiling water for 12 to 15 minutes or till nearly tender. Add green beans; cook 5 minutes more or till crisp-tender. Drain well.

In a large bowl combine potatoes, green beans, radishes, celery, and onion; set aside.

For dressing, in a screw-top jar combine oil, vinegar, water, mustard, parsley, thyme, rosemary, garlic, and salt. Cover and shake well. Pour dressing over vegetable mixture; toss gently to coat. Cover and chill for 4 to 6 hours, stirring occasionally. Makes 6 side-dish servings.

Note: When using dried thyme or rosemary reduce 1 teaspoon to ¼ teaspoon.

Per serving: 120 calories, 2 g protein, 14 g carbohydrate, 7 g total fat (1 g saturated), 0 mg cholesterol, 152 mg sodium, 372 mg potassium.

Grilled Beef, Potato, and Onion Salad

⅓ **cup mayonnaise *or* salad dressing**
¼ **cup plain yogurt**
¼ **cup finely chopped onion**
2 **teaspoons white wine vinegar**
¼ **teaspoon salt**
¼ **teaspoon pepper**
1 **pound tiny new red potatoes**
1 **pound boneless beef sirloin steak, cut 1 inch thick**
4 **cups torn mixed greens**
1 **cup sliced fresh mushrooms**
1 **small onion, thinly sliced (optional)**
½ **cup sliced radishes**

For dressing, in a small bowl stir together mayonnaise or salad dressing, yogurt, finely chopped onion, vinegar, salt, and pepper. Cover and chill till serving time.

In a large saucepan cook potatoes in a small amount of lightly salted boiling water for 20 to 25 minutes. Drain; cool slightly. Cut into ¼-inch-thick slices.

Meanwhile, slash fat on edge of steak at 1-inch intervals, being careful not to cut into meat. Grill steak directly over medium coals for 6 minutes. Turn steak and grill for 7 to 8 minutes more for medium doneness. Cut into thin slices.

Line four salad plates with mixed greens. Combine potatoes, mushrooms, sliced onion (if desired), and radishes. Arrange potato mixture and steak on the greens. Drizzle dressing over each salad. Makes 4 main-dish servings.

Per serving: 449 calories, 30 g protein, 30 g carbohydrate, 23 g total fat (5 g saturated), 89 mg cholesterol, 438 mg sodium, 976 mg potassium.

Creamy Potato Salad

6 **medium potatoes
(2 pounds)**
1¼ **cups mayonnaise *or* salad
dressing**
1 **cup thinly sliced celery**
¾ **cup chopped greenpepper**
⅓ **cup chopped onion**
1 **tablespoon vinegar**
2 **teaspoons Dijon-style
mustard *or* prepared
mustard**
1 **teaspoon salt**
½ **teaspoon pepper**
6 **hard-cooked eggs, coarsely
chopped**

1 In a covered saucepan cook potatoes in boiling water for 20 to 25 minutes or till just tender; drain well. **2 3** Peel and cube potatoes.
4 In a very large bowl combine mayonnaise or salad dressing, celery, green pepper, onion, vinegar, mustard, salt, and pepper. Add potatoes and eggs. Toss lightly to mix. Cover and chill for 6 to 24 hours. Makes 12 side-dish servings.

Per serving: 277 calories, 5 g protein, 18 g carbohydrate, 21 g total fat (4 g saturated), 120 mg cholesterol, 375 mg sodium, 357 mg potassium.

1 To check doneness, carefully insert fork into one of the potatoes. If fork can be inserted and removed easily, potatoes are done.

2 Drain potatoes and cool slightly. Carefully scrape and pull away peel with a sharp paring knife.

3 Cut each potato into bite-size pieces.

4 Combine all ingredients except potatoes and eggs in a large bowl. Add potatoes and chopped eggs. Toss lightly to mix.

SALADS

Spinach-Orange Toss

4 **cups torn fresh spinach**
2 **oranges, peeled and sectioned**
1 **cup peel jicama cut into julienne strips**
1 **small red onion, thinly sliced**
¼ **cup sliced pitted ripe olives**
3 **tablespoons salad oil**
1 **tablespoon red wine vinegar**
1 **tablespoon orange juice**
½ **teaspoon ground cumin**
3 **tablespoons toasted pine nuts *or* slivered almonds**

Place spinach in a large salad bowl. Add orange sections, jicama, onion, and olives. Set aside.

For dressing, in a screw-top jar combine salad oil, vinegar, orange juice, and cumin. Cover and shake well. Pour the dressing over salad. Toss lightly to coat. Sprinkle with toasted pine nuts or almonds. Makes 4 to 6 side-dish servings.

Per serving: 582 calories, 5 g protein, 13 g carbohydrate, 60 g total fat (9 g saturated), 0 mg cholesterol, 84 mg sodium, 455 mg potassium.

Frosty Banana-Berry Squares

½ **of an 8-ounce container soft-style cream cheese with strawberries**
¼ **cup sugar**
1 **8-ounce carton strawberry yogurt**
2 **teaspoons finely shredded orange peel**
2 **tablespoons orange juice**
1 **teaspoon vanilla**
1 **cup whipping cream**
2 **medium bananas, sliced**
1 **cup fresh blueberries**
1 **cup thinly sliced fresh strawberries**

In a large mixing bowl stir together cream cheese and sugar. Stir in yogurt, orange peel, orange juice, and vanilla. Set aside.

In a medium mixing bowl beat whipping cream with an electric mixer on medium speed till soft peaks form. Fold whipped cream, bananas, blueberries, and strawberries into the cream cheese mixture. Pour into a 2-quart square baking dish. Cover; freeze for 8 to 24 hours or till firm.

To serve, let stand at room temperature for 20 minutes to thaw slightly. Cut into squares. Makes 9 side-dish servings.

Per serving: 218 calories, 3 g protein, 23 g carbohydrate, 14 g total fat (9 g saturated), 48 mg cholesterol, 53 mg sodium, 241 mg potassium.

Citrus Melon Bowl

4 oranges
2 large pink grapefruit
1 tablespoon sugar
1 teaspoon finely chopped crystallized ginger
2 cups cubed honeydew melon *or* cantaloupe
2 kiwi fruit, peeled and sliced *or* 1 cup halved strawberries

Finely shred enough orange peel from 1 of the oranges to equal *½ teaspoon*; set orange peel aside. Working over a large bowl to catch the juices, peel and section oranges; reserve *¼ cup* of the orange juice. (Add prepared orange juice to equal *¼ cup juice*, if necessary.) Peel and section grapefruit, reserving juices for another use; add grapefruit sections to orange sections.

For dressing, in a small bowl combine reserved orange juice, sugar, ginger, and orange peel. Add melon and kiwi fruit or strawberries to orange and grapefruit sections. Pour dressing over fruit; toss gently to coat. Cover and chill for 2 to 4 hours. Makes 6 side-dish servings.

Per serving: 98 calories, 1 g protein, 24 g carbohydrate, 0 g total fat (0 g saturated), 0 mg cholesterol, 7 mg sodium, 450 mg potassium.

Sparkling Melon-Grape Mold

1 **6-ounce package lemon flavored gelatin**
1½ **cups boiling water**
1 **12-ounce can ginger ale**
1 **tablespoon finely shredded lemon peel**
2 **tablespoons lemon juice**
1½ **cups seedless red grapes**
1 **cup cubed cantaloupe**
1 **cup cubed honeydew melon**

In a large bowl dissolve gelatin in boiling water. Stir in ginger ale, lemon peel, and lemon juice. Chill till mixture is partially set (the consistency of unbeaten egg whites).

Meanwhile, cut grapes in half, if desired.

Pour *1 cup* of the partially set gelatin mixture into a 6-cup mold. Layer *half* of the red grapes on the gelatin mixture in the mold; chill for 15 minutes. Arrange cantaloupe and honeydew cubes atop grapes in mold. Spoon enough remaining gelatin mixture over the melon cubes to cover. Arrange the remaining grapes atop the gelatin layer. Add remaining gelatin. Cover and chill for 6 to 24 hours or till firm. Unmold onto serving plate. Makes 10 to 12 side-dish servings.

Per serving: 98 calories, 2 g protein, 24 g carbohydrate, 0 g total fat (0 g saturated), 0 mg cholesterol, 50 mg sodium, 145 mg potassium.

Holiday Raspberry Mold

2 **cups boiling water**
1 **6-ounce package raspberry flavored gelatin**
1 **10-ounce package frozen red raspberries**
1 **8-ounce can crushed pineapple**
1 **teaspoon lemon juice**
¼ **teaspoon ground allspice**
1 **8-ounce can pear halves (juice pack)**
⅓ **cup toasted chopped pecans**

In a medium saucepan heat water to boiling. Add gelatin, stirring to dissolve. Stir in raspberries till thawed. Stir in *undrained* pineapple, lemon juice, and allspice.

Drain pears, reserving juice; chop pears. Stir chopped pears and reserved pear juice into saucepan. Chill till partially set (the consistency of unbeaten egg whites). Fold pecans into partially set gelatin. Pour gelatin mixture into a 6-cup mold. Cover and chill at least 5 hours or till firm. Unmold onto a serving plate. Makes 10 to 12 side-dish servings.

Per serving: 135 calories, 2 g protein, 28 g carbohydrate, 2 g total fat (0 g saturated), 0 mg cholesterol, 73 mg sodium, 96 mg potassium.

Pineapple-Orange Gazpacho Mold

1½ cups tomato juice
 1 envelope unflavored
    gelatin
 ½ cup pineapple-orange juice
 1 tablespoon lime juice
    Dash bottled hot pepper
      sauce
 ¼ cup finely chopped seeded
      cucumber
 ¼ cup finely chopped red
      sweet pepper
 ¼ cup finely chopped celery
 ¼ cup finely chopped onion
 ¼ cup finely chopped
      Anaheim pepper *or*
    1 tablespoon finely
      chopped jalapeño pepper
    Leaf lettuce

In a medium saucepan stir together *1 cup* of the tomato juice and the gelatin. Let stand for 5 minutes. Cook over medium heat for 3 to 5 minutes or till gelatin dissolves. Add remaining tomato juice, pineapple-orange juice, lime juice, and hot pepper sauce. **1** Chill till partially set (the consistency of unbeaten egg whites).

Stir cucumber, sweet pepper, celery, onion, and Anaheim or jalapeño pepper (see Note, page 63) into partially set gelatin mixture. Pour into a 3- or 3½-cup mold. Cover and chill for 6 to 24 hours or till firm. **2 3** To unmold, place the salad in a bowl of warm water; loosen edges with a knife. **4 5** Invert onto a lettuce-lined plate. Makes 4 to 6 side-dish servings.

Per serving: 51 calories, 3 g protein, 11 g carbohydrate, 0 g total fat (0 g saturated), 0 mg cholesterol, 332 mg sodium, 402 mg potassium.

1 Chill tomato-gelatin mixture until the mixture has the consistency of unbeaten egg whites.

2 To unmold, place the salad in a bowl or sink of warm water for about 30 seconds.

3 Run a knife or small metal spatula around the edge to loosen edges.

4 Center a plate upside down over the mold. Holding the plate and mold together, invert them.

5 Shake the mold gently and carefully lift it off.

Bacon-Tomato Dressing

3 slices bacon
½ cup tomato juice
3 tablespoons red wine vinegar
3 tablespoons olive oil *or* salad oil
2 tablespoons snipped fresh basil
¼ teaspoon garlic powder
¼ teaspoon pepper
Dash hot pepper sauce

Place bacon in a cold skillet. Cook over medium heat for 4 minutes. Turn bacon over and cook for 4 to 6 minutes more or till crisp. Remove bacon from skillet; drain on paper towels. Cool; crumble into bite-size pieces.

In a small saucepan combine bacon, tomato juice, vinegar, oil, basil, garlic powder, pepper, and hot pepper sauce. Cook over medium-low heat till warm. Serve over tossed spinach, mixed greens, or mixed vegetables. Makes about 1 cup.

Per tablespoon: 31 calories, 0 g protein, 1 g carbohydrate, 3 g total fat (1 g saturated), 1 mg cholesterol, 47 mg sodium, 28 mg potassium.

Creamy Orange Spiced Dressing

1 8-ounce carton plain low fat yogurt
3 tablespoons orange juice
1 tablespoon orange marmalade
¼ teaspoon ground cinnamon
⅛ teaspoon ground ginger
⅛ teaspoon ground nutmeg

In a small bowl combine yogurt, orange juice, orange marmalade, cinnamon, ginger, and nutmeg. Stir till smooth. Cover and chill thoroughly. Serve with fresh fruit. Makes about 1 cup.

Per tablespoon: 15 calories, 1 g protein, 2 g carbohydrate, 0 g total fat (0 g saturated), 1 mg cholesterol, 9 mg sodium, 39 mg potassium.

Strawberry Vinaigrette

¾ cup sliced fresh strawberries
¼ cup red wine vinegar
1 tablespoon salad oil
1½ teaspoons sugar
1 teaspoon water
½ teaspoon snipped fresh rosemary *or* ⅛ teaspoon dried rosemary, crushed
½ teaspoon soy sauce
⅛ teaspoon pepper

In a blender container or food processor bowl combine strawberries, vinegar, oil, sugar, water, rosemary, soy sauce, and pepper. Cover and blend or process till smooth. Transfer to covered container and chill thoroughly. Serve over salad greens. Makes about ¾ cup.

Per tablespoon: 15 calories, 0 g protein, 1 g carbohydrate, 1 g total fat (0 g saturated), 0 mg cholesterol, 14 mg sodium, 18 mg potassium.

VEGETABLES

Cauliflower and Snap Pea Stir-Fry

Cauliflower and Snap Pea Stir-Fry

¼ **cup orange juice**
1 **tablespoon soy sauce**
1 **teaspoon toasted sesame oil**
½ **teaspoon cornstarch**
1 **tablespoon cooking oil**
2 **cloves garlic, minced**
2 **cups sliced cauliflower flowerets**
1 **10-ounce package sugar snap peas, thawed**
1 **small red sweet pepper, cut into julienne strips**
2 **teaspoons toasted sesame seed**

For sauce, in a small bowl stir together orange juice, soy sauce, sesame oil, and cornstarch. Set aside.

Pour cooking oil into a wok or large skillet. Preheat over medium-high heat. Stir-fry garlic in hot oil for 30 seconds. Add cauliflower; stir-fry for 2 minutes. Add sugar snap peas and sweet pepper; stir-fry for 1 to 2 minutes more or till vegetables are crisp-tender. Push vegetables from the center of the wok or skillet.

Stir sauce. Add sauce to center of wok. Cook and stir till thickened and bubbly. Stir vegetables into sauce. Sprinkle with sesame seed. Serve immediately. Makes 4 servings.

Per serving: 113 calories, 4 g protein, 12 g carbohydrate, 6 g total fat (1 g saturated), 0 mg cholesterol, 266 mg sodium, 412 mg potassium.

Baked Artichokes and Tomatoes

1 **cup soft bread crumbs**
3 **tablespoons grated Parmesan cheese**
2 **tablespoons snipped fresh parsley**
¼ **cup Italian salad dressing**
1 **14-ounce can artichoke hearts, drained and cut in half**
2 **medium tomatoes, peeled, seeded, and cut into wedges**
1 **4½-ounce can sliced mushrooms, drained**

In a small mixing bowl combine bread crumbs, Parmesan cheese, parsley, and *3 tablespoons* of the salad dressing. Toss to coat; set aside.

Stir together artichokes, tomatoes, mushrooms, and remaining salad dressing. Spoon artichoke mixture into a 1½-quart casserole. Sprinkle with bread crumb mixture.

Bake in a 350° oven for 30 to 35 minutes or till crumbs are lightly browned. Makes 4 servings.

Per serving: 177 calories, 7 g protein, 20 g carbohydrate, 10 g total fat (2 g saturated), 4 mg cholesterol, 665 mg sodium, 452 mg potassium.

Dilly Green Beans

1 **pound green beans**
1 **cup chopped onion**
1 **cup chopped red sweet pepper**
2 **teaspoons cooking oil**
½ **cup water**
¾ **teaspoon dried dillweed**
½ **teaspoon garlic salt**
¼ **teaspoon pepper**

Wash beans; remove ends and strings. Cut into 2-inch pieces.

In a large saucepan cook onion and sweet pepper in hot oil for 4 to 5 minutes or till crisp-tender. Stir in green beans, water, dillweed, garlic salt, and pepper. Bring to boiling. Reduce heat and simmer, covered, for 12 to 15 minutes or till beans are tender. Makes 6 servings.

Per serving: 57 calories, 2 g protein, 10 g carbohydrate, 2 g total fat (0 g saturated), 0 mg cholesterol, 175 mg sodium, 298 mg potassium.

Roasted Asparagus with Celery-Almond Sauce

1 **pound asparagus spears**
1 **tablespoon olive oil *or* cooking oil**
2 **tablespoons slivered almonds**
2 **tablespoons finely chopped celery**
1 **tablespoon margarine *or* butter**
1 **tablespoon lemon juice**
½ **teaspoon soy sauce**
¼ **teaspoon lemon-pepper seasoning**

1 Break off woody asparagus where spears snap easily; scrape off scales. Wash asparagus. **2** Arrange asparagus spears in a shallow baking pan. Drizzle with oil. **3** Bake in a 425° oven for 10 to 15 minutes or till asparagus is crisp-tender and beginning to brown. Transfer asparagus to a serving dish.

Meanwhile, for sauce, in a small saucepan cook almonds and celery in margarine or butter till almonds are toasted and celery is crisp-tender. Stir in lemon juice, soy sauce, and lemon-pepper seasoning. Pour over asparagus. Makes 3 or 4 servings.

Per serving: 124 calories, 4 g protein, 6 g carbohydrate, 11 g total fat (2 g saturated), 0 mg cholesterol, 200 mg sodium, 331 mg potassium.

1 Break off woody end of each asparagus spear where it snaps easily.

2 Arrange asparagus spears in a single layer in a shallow baking pan. Drizzle evenly with olive oil.

3 When done, asparagus spears will be tender and begin to brown.

Picnic Baked Beans

½ **cup chopped onion**
2 **cloves garlic, minced**
1 **tablespoon cooking oil**
1 **16-ounce can pork and beans with tomato sauce**
2 **15-ounce cans pinto beans, rinsed and drained**
½ **cup chili sauce**
½ **cup diced fully cooked ham**
¼ **cup maple syrup *or* maple-flavored syrup**
1 **tablespoon brown mustard**
¼ **teaspoon ground allspice**
¼ **teaspoon crushed red pepper**
¼ **teaspoon ground cinnamon**
⅛ **teaspoon ground ginger**

In a small skillet cook onion and garlic in hot oil till tender; drain. In a medium mixing bowl combine pork and beans, pinto beans, chili sauce, ham, maple syrup or maple-flavored syrup, mustard, allspice, red pepper, cinnamon, ginger, and onion mixture.

Transfer bean mixture to a 2-quart casserole. Bake, covered, in a 375° oven for 30 minutes. Uncover and continue baking for 15 to 20 minutes more or till hot and bubbly. Makes 6 servings.

Per serving: 283 calories, 14 g protein, 51 g carbohydrate, 4 g total fat (1 g saturated), 9 mg cholesterol, 1351 mg sodium, 818 mg potassium.

Broccoli with Lemon-Butter Sauce

1½ **pounds broccoli**
2 **tablespoons chopped green onion**
1 **small clove garlic, minced**
¼ **cup margarine *or* butter**
1 **2-ounce jar sliced pimiento, drained**
¼ **teaspoon finely shredded lemon peel**
2 **tablespoons lemon juice**
2 **teaspoons Dijon-style mustard**
¼ **teaspoon pepper**

Wash broccoli; remove outer leaves and tough parts of broccoli stalks. Cut broccoli lengthwise into spears. Cook broccoli, covered, in a small amount of boiling water for 9 to 11 minutes or till crisp-tender. Drain and keep warm.

Meanwhile, in a small saucepan cook onion and garlic in margarine or butter till tender. Stir in pimiento, lemon peel, lemon juice, mustard, and pepper. Cook and stir till heated through. Transfer broccoli to a serving dish. Stir sauce and pour over broccoli. Makes 4 or 5 servings.

Per serving: 160 calories, 6 g protein, 11 g carbohydrate, 12 g total fat (2 g saturated), 0 mg cholesterol, 314 mg sodium, 562 mg potassium.

Fennel and Carrot Duo

1 **head fennel (about 1 pound)**
2 **cups thinly sliced carrots**
½ **cup chopped onion**
1 **teaspoon fennel seed, crushed**
1 **tablespoon snipped fresh basil** *or* ½ **teaspoon dried basil, crushed**
⅛ **teaspoon pepper**
1 **tablespoon cooking oil**
⅓ **cup chicken broth**

Rinse fennel thoroughly. **1** Cut off and discard upper stalks of fennel. Remove any wilted outer layer of stalks; cut off a thin slice from the base. **2** Chop fennel. (You should have about 1 cup.)

3 In a medium saucepan cook and stir chopped fennel, carrots, onion, crushed fennel seed, basil, and pepper in hot oil for 5 minutes. Stir in chicken broth. Bring to boiling. Reduce heat and simmer, covered, for 15 to 20 minutes or till tender. Makes 4 servings.

Per serving: 81 calories, 2 g protein, 11 g carbohydrate, 4 g total fat (1 g saturated), 0 mg cholesterol, 123 mg sodium, 309 mg potassium.

1 Rinse fennel thoroughly. Trim away base of bulb and stalks. Discard hard outside stalks.

2 To chop fennel bulb, cut in half lengthwise. Cut halves into ¼-inch-wide strips. Pile strips together and cut crosswise into even pieces.

3 Crush fennel seeds with a mortar and pestle or spread seeds between sheets of waxed paper and crush with a rolling pin.

VEGETABLES

Brussels Sprouts with Mustard

1 **pound Brussels sprouts**
1½ **cups water**
1 **teaspoon instant chicken bouillon granules**
2 **tablespoons Dijon-style mustard**
1 **tablespoon brown mustard**
1 **teaspoon honey**
½ **teaspoon finely shredded lemon peel**
1 **teaspoon lemon juice**

Trim stems and remove any wilted outer leaves from Brussels sprouts; wash. In a medium saucepan combine sprouts, water, and bouillon granules. Bring to boiling. Reduce heat and simmer, covered, for 10 to 12 minutes or till crisp-tender. Drain.

Meanwhile, combine Dijon-style mustard, brown mustard, honey, lemon peel, and lemon juice; pour over cooked Brussels sprouts. Toss lightly to coat. Serve immediately. Makes 4 servings.

Per serving: 69 calories, 4 g protein, 13 g carbohydrate, 1 g total fat (0 g saturated), 0 mg cholesterol, 481 mg sodium, 415 mg potassium.

Gingered Carrots

¾ **pound medium carrots, washed, trimmed and peeled *or* scrubbed**
2 **tablespoons margarine *or* butter**
2 **tablespoons brown sugar**
1½ **teaspoons finely chopped crystallized ginger**

Cut carrots in half crosswise and lengthwise. In a medium saucepan cook carrots in a small amount of boiling water for 7 to 9 minutes or till crisp-tender. Drain carrots; remove from pan.

In the same saucepan combine margarine or butter, brown sugar, and ginger. Stir over medium heat till combined. Stir in carrots. Cook and stir about 2 minutes or till glazed, stirring frequently. Makes 4 servings.

Per serving: 117 calories, 1 g protein, 16 g carbohydrate, 6 g total fat (1 g saturated), 0 mg cholesterol, 121 mg sodium, 204 mg potassium.

Mexicali Corn Bake

1 **17-ounce can whole kernel corn, drained**
1 **16½-ounce can cream-style corn**
1 **8-ounce carton dairy sour cream**
1 **7½-ounce package corn muffin mix**
1 **4-ounce can diced green chili peppers, drained**
1 **2-ounce jar sliced pimiento, drained**
1 **beaten egg**
2 **tablespoons margarine *or* butter, melted**
2 **tablespoons snipped fresh parsley**

In a medium mixing bowl combine whole kernel corn, cream-style corn, sour cream, corn muffin mix, chili peppers, pimiento, egg, and margarine or butter. Pour into a lightly greased 1½-quart casserole. Bake in a 350° oven about 45 minutes or till set. Sprinkle with parsley. Makes 8 servings.

Per serving: 283 calories, 6 g protein, 39 g carbohydrate, 13 g total fat (5 g saturated), 39 mg cholesterol, 557 mg sodium, 244 mg potassium.

Oven-Fried Eggplant with Fresh Tomato Sauce

4 **medium tomatoes**
⅓ **cup chopped onion**
½ **teaspoon sugar**
½ **teaspoon dried basil, crushed**
¼ **teaspoon dried marjoram, crushed**
¼ **teaspoon salt**
⅛ **teaspoon pepper**
1 **clove garlic, minced**
2 **teaspoons olive oil**
1 **medium eggplant**
½ **cup finely crushed cheese crackers**
¼ **cup all-purpose flour**
1 **beaten egg**
1 **tablespoon water**
3 **tablespoons margarine or butter, melted**

For sauce, cut each tomato into 6 wedges. In a skillet cook tomatoes, onion, sugar, basil, marjoram, salt, pepper, and garlic in hot oil for 15 to 20 minutes or till tomatoes are tender. Pour tomato mixture into a blender container or food processor bowl. Cover and blend or process till smooth. Set sauce aside and keep warm.

Wash and peel eggplant; cut crosswise into ½-inch-thick slices. In a shallow dish combine crushed crackers and flour. In another shallow dish combine egg and water. Dip eggplant slices in egg mixture, then into flour mixture, turning to coat both sides. Place eggplant slices in a single layer on a lightly greased 15x10x1-inch baking pan. Drizzle with melted margarine.

Bake in a 400° oven for 10 to 12 minutes or till hot and lightly browned. Serve with sauce. Makes 4 to 6 servings.

Per serving: 444 calories, 8 g protein, 42 g carbohydrate, 28 g total fat (7 g saturated), 74 mg cholesterol, 817 mg sodium, 620 mg potassium.

Autumn Vegetable Combo

1 **cup chopped peeled carrots**
1 **cup chopped peeled parsnips**
1 **cup chopped peeled rutabaga**
1 **cup chopped peeled celeriac**
¾ **cup water**
½ **cup chopped onion**
1 **teaspoon instant chicken bouillon granules**
1 **teaspoon dried tarragon, crushed**
½ **teaspoon finely shredded lemon peel**
   Dash pepper
   Snipped fresh chives (optional)

In a large saucepan combine carrots, parsnips, rutabaga, celeriac, water, onion, bouillon granules, tarragon, lemon peel, and pepper. Bring to boiling. Reduce heat and simmer, covered, for 15 to 20 minutes or till vegetables are tender. Drain. Sprinkle with chives, if desired. Makes 6 servings.

Per serving: 52 calories, 1 g protein, 12 g carbohydrate, 0 g total fat (0 g saturated), 0 mg cholesterol, 188 mg sodium, 329 mg potassium.

Sherried Peas and Carrots with Mushrooms

½ **cup sliced fresh mushrooms**
¼ **cup chopped green onion**
1 **tablespoon margarine *or* butter**
1 **cup shelled peas and 1 cup sliced carrots *or* one 10-ounce package frozen peas and carrots, thawed**
2 **tablespoons dry sherry**
¼ **teaspoon dried thyme, crushed**
¼ **teaspoon salt**
⅛ **teaspoon pepper**

In a saucepan cook mushrooms and onion in margarine or butter till tender. Stir in peas and carrots, sherry, thyme, salt, and pepper. Cook fresh vegetables, covered, for 10 to 12 minutes or till crisp-tender. Cook frozen vegetables, covered, for 3 to 4 minutes or till crisp-tender. Makes 4 servings.

Per serving: 83 calories, 2 g protein, 10 g carbohydrate, 3 g total fat (1 g saturated), 0 mg cholesterol, 191 mg sodium, 217 mg potassium.

Summer Squash with Cheese and Basil

3 small zucchini
3 small yellow summer squash
1 clove garlic, sliced
1 tablespoon olive oil
¼ cup grated Parmesan cheese
¼ cup toasted almonds *or* pistachios
1 tablespoon fresh basil *or* 1 teaspoon dried basil, crushed

1 Wash zucchini and yellow summer squash. Cut diagonally into ¼-inch-thick slices; set aside.

In a large skillet on medium-high heat stir-fry garlic in oil for 1 minute. Add zucchini and squash slices and stir-fry for 5 minutes or till crisp-tender. **2** Toss with Parmesan cheese, toasted almonds or pistachios, and basil. Makes 6 servings.

Per serving: 81 calories, 4 g protein, 5 g carbohydrate, 6 g total fat (1 g saturated), 3 mg cholesterol, 80 mg sodium, 246 mg potassium.

1 To slice squash diagonally, hold squash firmly against cutting board. Place a thin sharp knife atop squash at a 45° angle. Cut down and out.

2 Add parmesan cheese, toasted almonds, and basil to cooked squash, stirring to coat evenly.

Stuffed Yellow Summer Squash

3 **medium yellow summer squash, about 6 inches long (1 pound)**
1 **cup frozen whole kernel corn, thawed**
¼ **cup chopped green onion**
¼ **cup finely chopped sweet red pepper**
2 **ounces semi-soft goat cheese (chevre)**
3 **slices bacon, crisp-cooked, drained, and crumbled**
2 **teaspoons snipped fresh parsley**
¼ **teaspoon dried thyme, crushed**
⅛ **teaspoon pepper**

Wash squash; cut in half lengthwise. Scoop out pulp and seeds, leaving a ¼-inch-thick shell; discard pulp and seeds.

For stuffing, in a medium mixing bowl combine corn, green onion, sweet pepper, cheese, bacon, parsley, thyme, and pepper. Divide stuffing evenly among squash halves. Place filled squash halves in a 3-quart rectangular baking dish.

Bake, covered, in a 350° oven for 30 to 35 minutes or till squash is tender and stuffing is heated through. Makes 6 servings.

Per serving: 84 calories, 4 g protein, 8 g carbohydrate, 5 g total fat (2 g saturated), 11 mg cholesterol, 107 mg sodium, 210 mg potassium.

Waldorf Acorn Squash

2 **medium acorn squash**
1 **cup finely chopped apple**
½ **cup finely chopped celery**
½ **cup toasted chopped walnuts**
2 **tablespoons honey**
1 **teaspoon finely shredded orange peel**
¼ **teaspoon ground cinnamon**
¼ **cup margarine *or* butter, melted**

Wash squash; halve lengthwise and remove seeds. Place squash, cut side down, in a large baking pan. Bake, covered, in a 350° oven for 30 minutes.

Meanwhile, combine chopped apple, celery, walnuts, honey, orange peel, and cinnamon. Remove squash from oven. Turn cut side up. Divide apple mixture evenly among squash halves. Drizzle with melted margarine or butter. Bake, covered, for 20 to 25 minutes more or till squash is tender. Makes 4 servings.

Per serving: 320 calories, 4 g protein, 37 g carbohydrate, 19 g total fat (3 g saturated), 0 mg cholesterol, 158 mg sodium, 676 mg potassium.

Mexican-Stuffed Baked Potatoes

4 **medium baking potatoes**
⅓ **cup milk**
1 **4-ounce can diced green chili peppers, drained**
1 **2-ounce jar sliced pimiento, drained**
½ **teaspoon garlic salt**
⅛ **teaspoon ground cumin**
¾ **cup shredded sharp cheddar cheese (3 ounces)**
¼ **cup dairy sour cream**
   Snipped fresh cilantro *or* parsley (optional)

Scrub potatoes thoroughly with a brush. Pat dry. **1** Prick potatoes with a fork; wrap each potato in foil. Bake in a 425° oven for 40 to 60 minutes or till tender.

2 Remove foil; cut a lengthwise slice from the top of each potato. Discard skin from slice and place potato pulp in a bowl. **3** Gently scoop out each potato, leaving a thin shell. Add pulp to the bowl.

4 With an electric mixer on low speed beat potato pulp. Add milk, chili peppers, pimiento, garlic salt, and cumin; beat till smooth. Stir in *½ cup* of the shredded cheese. **5** Pile mashed potato mixture into potato shells. Place in a 2-quart rectangular baking dish.

Bake in a 425° oven for 25 to 30 minutes or till lightly browned and heated through. Top with remaining cheese and bake 2 to 3 minutes more or till cheese melts. Top with sour cream and sprinkle with cilantro or parsley, if desired. Makes 4 servings.

Per serving: 294 calories, 11 g protein, 40 g carbohydrate, 11 g total fat (7 g saturated), 30 mg cholesterol, 501 mg sodium, 783 mg potassium.

1 Prick potato skins with a fork before baking.

2 Let potatoes cool slightly. Cut a lengthwise slice from the top of each potato.

3 Using a spoon, scoop potato pulp from lengthwise slice and inside of potato, leaving a ¼-inch thick shell. Place potato pulp in bowl.

4 Using an electric mixer, beat the potato pulp on low speed till almost smooth.

5 Spoon potato mixture into the reserved potato shells. Top with remaining ¼ cup cheese.

Swiss Scalloped Potatoes

½ **cup chopped green onion**
2 **tablespoons margarine *or* butter**
2 **tablespoons all-purpose flour**
¼ **teaspoon salt**
⅛ **teaspoon ground nutmeg**
⅛ **teaspoon white pepper**
1¼ **cups milk**
¾ **cup shredded Swiss cheese**
2 **tablespoons snipped fresh parsley**
3 **medium potatoes, peeled and thinly sliced (3 cups)**
Paprika

For sauce, cook green onion in margarine or butter till tender. Stir in flour, salt, nutmeg, and pepper. Add milk all at once. Cook and stir till thickened and bubbly. Remove from heat; add Swiss cheese and parsley, stirring till cheese melts. Place *half* of the sliced potatoes in a greased 1-quart casserole. Cover with *half* the sauce. Repeat layers.

Bake, covered, in a 350° oven for 45 minutes. Uncover; bake about 20 minutes more or till potatoes are tender. Sprinkle with paprika. Let stand 5 minutes. Makes 4 servings.

Per serving: 291 calories, 11 g protein, 30 g carbohydrate, 14 g total fat (6 g saturated), 25 mg cholesterol, 300 mg sodium, 541 mg potassium.

Hawaiian Sweet Potato Casserole

2 **cups shredded, peeled sweet potato**
1 **8-ounce can crushed pineapple**
1 **3½-ounce jar macadamia nuts, chopped *or* ¾ cup chopped almonds**
¼ **cup milk**
¼ **cup packed brown sugar**
2 **tablespoons margarine *or* butter, melted**
2 **tablespoons all-purpose flour**
2 **beaten eggs**
¼ **teaspoon ground cinnamon**
⅛ **teaspoon ground ginger**

In a medium mixing bowl combine shredded sweet potato, *undrained* pineapple, chopped nuts, milk, brown sugar, melted margarine or butter, flour, eggs, cinnamon, and ginger; stir till well combined.

Spoon sweet potato mixture into a 1½-quart casserole. Bake, covered, in a 350° oven for 45 minutes. Uncover and bake for 20 to 25 minutes more or till a knife inserted in center comes out clean. Makes 6 servings.

Per serving: 270 calories, 5 g protein, 26 g carbohydrate, 16 g total fat (3 g saturated), 72 mg cholesterol, 159 mg sodium, 270 mg potassium.

Roasted Corn and Zucchini Kabobs

2 fresh ears of corn
2 medium zucchini, cut into 1-inch-thick slices
¼ cup margarine *or* butter
½ teaspoon dried thyme, crushed
¼ teaspoon dried marjoram *or* basil, crushed
¼ teaspoon onion salt
¼ teaspoon pepper
2 medium red sweet peppers, cut into 1½-inch pieces

Remove the husks from fresh ears of corn; scrub with a stiff brush to remove silks. Rinse. Cut each ear of corn into 2-inch pieces. Cook corn, covered, in a small amount of boiling water for 3 minutes. Add zucchini; cook for 1 minute more. Drain and cool.

Meanwhile, in a small saucepan melt margarine or butter. Stir in thyme, marjoram or basil, onion salt, and pepper.

Alternately thread corn, zucchini, and sweet pepper onto four 12-inch skewers. Brush with margarine or butter mixture. Grill kabobs on the grill rack of an uncovered grill directly over medium coals for 10 to 15 minutes or till done, turning occasionally and brushing with margarine or butter mixture. Makes 4 servings.

Per serving: 163 calories, 2 g protein, 14 g carbohydrate, 12 g total fat (2 g saturated), 0 mg cholesterol, 243 mg sodium, 296 mg potassium.

Spinach and Sweet Pepper Sauté

1 pound fresh spinach
1 cup chopped onion
1 cup chopped yellow sweet
  pepper
1 tablespoon olive oil *or*
  cooking oil
½ teaspoon salt
½ teaspoon dried basil *or*
  thyme, crushed
⅛ teaspoon pepper
1 medium tomato, chopped
¼ cup chopped peanuts

Wash spinach; pat dry with paper towels. Remove and discard stems from spinach; set aside.

In a Dutch oven cook onion and sweet pepper in hot oil till tender. Stir in salt, basil or thyme, pepper, and spinach. Cook and stir for 1 to 2 minutes or till spinach just wilts. Stir in chopped tomato and peanuts. Serve immediately with a slotted spoon. Makes 4 servings.

Per serving: 136 calories, 7 g protein, 12 g carbohydrate, 8 g total fat (1 g saturated), 0 mg cholesterol, 361 mg sodium, 879 mg potassium.

Scalloped Tomatoes

3 slices bread, toasted
2 tablespoons margarine *or*
  butter
½ cup chopped celery
½ cup chopped onion
3 medium tomatoes, peeled
  and cut up (about
  2 cups) *or* one 16-ounce
  can tomatoes, cut up
2 tablespoons water
1 tablespoon all-purpose
  flour
1 teaspoon sugar
½ teaspoon dried marjoram
  ***or* basil, crushed**
¼ teaspoon salt
⅛ teaspoon pepper
  Grated Parmesan cheese
  (optional)

Spread toast with *1 tablespoon* of the margarine or butter. Cut toast into cubes; set aside.

Cook celery and onion in remaining margarine or butter till crisp-tender. Add fresh tomatoes or *undrained* canned tomatoes. Bring to boiling. Reduce heat and simmer, covered, for 8 minutes.

Meanwhile, combine water, flour, sugar, marjoram or basil, salt, and pepper; stir into tomato mixture. Cook and stir till bubbly. Stir *two-thirds* of the toast cubes into the tomato mixture. Pour into a 1-quart casserole. Top tomato mixture with remaining toast cubes. Sprinkle with grated Parmesan cheese, if desired. Bake, uncovered, in a 350° oven about 20 minutes or till bubbly. Makes 4 servings.

Per serving: 149 calories, 3 g protein, 20 g carbohydrate, 7 g total fat (1 g saturated), 0 mg cholesterol, 201 mg sodium, 392 mg potassium.

Spaghetti Squash Provençale

1 **3-pound spaghetti squash**
¼ **cup chopped onion**
¼ **cup sliced fresh mushrooms**
¼ **teaspoon salt**
⅛ **teaspoon dried thyme, crushed**
   Dash dried rosemary, crushed
1 **clove garlic, minced**
1 **tablespoon olive oil *or* cooking oil**
1 **tablespoon margarine *or* butter**
1 **small tomato, seeded and chopped**
1 **tablespoon chopped pitted ripe olives**
1 **tablespoon snipped fresh parsley**
1 **tablespoon grated Parmesan cheese**

1 Wash squash; cut in half lengthwise and discard seeds. Reserve *half* the squash for another use. Place remaining squash half, cut side down, in a large saucepan or Dutch oven; add water to a depth of 2 inches. Bring to boiling. Reduce heat and simmer, covered, for 20 to 25 minutes or till tender.

Meanwhile, for sauce, in a medium saucepan cook onion, mushrooms, salt, thyme, rosemary, and garlic in hot oil and margarine or butter till tender. Stir in chopped tomato and olives. Set sauce aside and keep warm.

Drain squash and cool till easy to handle. **2** Use a fork to scrape the inside of the squash into strands; discard shell. Place squash strands in saucepan with sauce and toss to coat. Cook and stir over medium heat for 2 to 3 minutes or till heated through. Sprinkle with parsley and Parmesan cheese. Makes 4 to 6 servings.

Per serving: 105 calories, 2 g protein, 8 g carbohydrate, 8 g total fat (1 g saturated), 1 mg cholesterol, 233 mg sodium, 223 mg potassium.

1 Remove and discard seeds from squash halves.

2 Twist the fork slightly to separate cooked squash into strands. Rake the squash strands out of the shell.

VEGETABLES

Baked Tomato Casserole

2 14½-ounce cans tomatoes, undrained and coarsely chopped
½ cup finely chopped onion
¼ cup diced celery
¼ cup diced green sweet pepper
4 slices white bread, lightly toasted and cut into ¾-inch cubes
2 tablespoons brown sugar
1 tablespoon margarine *or* butter, melted
½ teaspoon dried basil, crushed
¼ teaspoon salt
¼ teaspoon pepper

Combine tomatoes, onion, celery, sweet pepper, bread cubes, brown sugar, margarine or butter, basil, salt, and pepper and spoon into a lightly greased 1½-quart casserole. Bake in 350° oven for 35 to 40 minutes or till thickened and bubbly. Makes 6 servings.

Per serving: 112 calories, 3 g protein, 20 g carbohydrate, 3 g total fat (1 g saturated), 0 mg cholesterol, 429 mg sodium, 387 mg potassium.

Spinach-Green Bean Casserole

1 10-ounce package frozen chopped spinach
1 9-ounce package frozen French-style green beans
¾ cup chopped onion
1 clove garlic, minced
1 tablespoon margarine *or* butter
1 tablespoon all-purpose flour
⅛ teaspoon ground nutmeg
¾ cup milk
½ of a 3-ounce package cream cheese
½ cup soft bread crumbs
2 tablespoons grated Parmesan cheese
1 tablespoon margarine *or* butter, melted

Thaw spinach and beans; drain well. Cook onion and garlic in 1 tablespoon margarine or butter till tender. Stir in flour, nutmeg, ½ teaspoon *salt,* and dash *pepper.* Add milk. Cook and stir till bubbly. Stir in cream cheese till melted. Stir in spinach and beans. Transfer to a 1-quart casserole. Bake, covered, in a 350° oven for 30 minutes; stir.

Meanwhile, combine bread crumbs, Parmesan cheese, and the melted margarine or butter. Sprinkle crumbs over casserole. Bake, uncovered, 10 to 15 minutes more or till heated through. Makes 4 servings.

Per serving: 201 calories, 8 g protein, 19 g carbohydrate, 12 g total fat (5 g saturated), 18 mg cholesterol, 279 mg sodium, 446 mg potassium.

SAUCES AND RELISHES

Plum-Apple Dessert Sauce

SAUCES AND RELISHES

Plum-Apple Dessert Sauce

¼ cup sugar
2 teaspoons cornstarch
¼ teaspoon ground
    cinnamon
⅛ teaspoon ground allspice
½ cup apple juice
1 cup thinly sliced fresh
    plums
½ teaspoon finely shredded
    orange peel

In a medium saucepan combine sugar, cornstarch, cinnamon, and allspice. Add apple juice all at once, stirring till smooth. Add sliced plums. Cook and stir over medium heat till thickened and bubbly. Cook and stir 2 minutes more.

Remove saucepan from heat. Stir in orange peel. Serve sauce warm over angel cake or sponge cake. Makes about 1¼ cups (twenty 1-tablespoon servings).

Per tablespoon: 87 calories, 0 g protein, 22 g carbohydrate, 0 g total fat (0 g saturated), 0 mg cholesterol, 1 mg sodium, 132 mg potassium.

Chocolate-Nut Sauce

¾ cup sifted powdered sugar
3 tablespoons unsweetened
    cocoa powder
1 tablespoon cornstarch
1 cup evaporated milk
¼ cup toasted chopped nuts
1 tablespoon amaretto
1 teaspoon vanilla

In a small saucepan combine powdered sugar, cocoa powder, and cornstarch. Add evaporated milk all at once. Cook and stir over medium heat till thickened and bubbly. Cook and stir 1 minute more.

Remove saucepan from heat. Stir in nuts, amaretto, and vanilla. Serve sauce warm over ice cream or poached fruit. Makes about 1 cup (sixteen 1-tablespoon servings).

Per tablespoon: 199 calories, 5 g protein, 30 g carbohydrate, 5 g total fat (3 g saturated), 18 mg cholesterol, 67 mg sodium, 192 mg potassium.

Toasted Coconut Sauce

⅓ cup packed brown sugar
1 tablespoon cornstarch
1½ cups half-and-half *or* light
    cream
½ cup toasted flaked coconut
1 teaspoon vanilla

In a small saucepan combine brown sugar and cornstarch. Add half-and-half or light cream all at once. Cook and stir over medium heat till thickened and bubbly. Cook and stir 1 minute more.

Remove saucepan from heat. Stir in coconut and vanilla. Serve sauce over fresh fruit or chocolate ice cream. Makes about 1⅔ cups (twenty-six 1-tablespoon servings).

Per tablespoon: 40 calories, 1 g protein, 4 g carbohydrate, 2 g total fat (1 g saturated), 5 mg cholesterol, 10 mg sodium, 34 mg potassium.

Basic White Sauce

1 tablespoon margarine *or*
    butter
1 tablespoon all-purpose
    flour
⅛ teaspoon salt
    Dash pepper
¾ cup milk

In a small saucepan melt margarine or butter. **1** Stir in flour, salt, and pepper. **2** Add milk all at once. **3** Cook and stir over medium heat till thickened and bubbly. Cook and stir 1 minute more. Makes ¾ cup (twelve 1-tablespoon servings).

Note: 4 Thin White Sauce pours easily. **5** Medium White Sauce is thicker but still pourable. **6** Thick White Sauce does not pour easily.

Per tablespoon: 18 calories, 1 g protein, 1 g carbohydrate, 1 g total fat (0 g saturated), 1 mg cholesterol, 41 mg sodium, 25 mg potassium.

Cheese Sauce: Prepare as above, *except* omit salt. Over low heat, stir ¾ cup shredded process *Swiss, American,* or *Gruyère cheese* or ¼ cup crumbled *blue cheese* into the *cooked* sauce till melted. Serve with vegetables. Makes about 1 cup (sixteen 1-tablespoon servings).

Per tablespoon: 32 calories, 2 g protein, 1 g carbohydrate, 2 g total fat (1 g saturated), 5 mg cholesterol, 87 mg sodium, 30 mg potassium.

1 Blend flour, salt, and pepper into melted margarine or butter with a wooden spoon till no lumps remain.

2 With the saucepan over low heat, add milk all at once to flour mixture, stirring to blend.

3 Cook over medium heat, stirring constantly with a wooden spoon, till mixture bubbles across entire surface. Cook 1 minute more.

4 Thin White Sauce pours easily and can be used as a base for soups and creamed vegetables.

5 Medium White Sauce is thicker but still pourable. Use in scalloped and creamed dishes and as a sauce base.

6 Thick White Sauce does not pour easily. Use it in soufflés or mix with chopped cooked meat when making croquettes.

SAUCES AND RELISHES

Citrus-Pecan Sauce

¾ **cup orange marmalade**
¼ **cup strawberry jam**
¼ **cup orange juice**
¼ **cup finely chopped pecans**

In a small saucepan combine orange marmalade, strawberry jam, and orange juice. Cook and stir over medium-low heat till marmalade and jam melt. Remove saucepan from heat. Stir in pecans.

Serve sauce warm over ice cream, angel cake, or pound cake. Makes about 1½ cups (twenty-four 1-tablespoon servings).

Per tablespoon: 130 calories, 1 g protein, 29 g carbohydrate, 2 g total fat (0 g saturated), 0 mg cholesterol, 5 mg sodium, 47 mg potassium.

Mustard-Chive Sauce

¾ **cup chicken broth**
⅓ **cup half-and-half or light cream**
2 **tablespoons all-purpose flour**
2 **tablespoons snipped fresh chives**
2 **tablespoons Dijon-style mustard**
¼ **to ½ teaspoon coarsely ground pepper**

In a small saucepan stir together chicken broth, half-and-half or light cream, and flour. Cook and stir over medium heat till thickened and bubbly. Add chives, mustard, and coarsely ground pepper. Cook and stir 1 minute more. Serve sauce with beef or lamb. Makes about 1 cup (eight 2-tablespoon servings).

Per 2 tablespoons: 28 calories, 1 g protein, 2 g carbohydrate, 2 g total fat (1 g saturated), 4 mg cholesterol, 171 mg sodium, 43 mg potassium.

Parsley-Almond Sauce

½ **cup small-curd cottage cheese**
3 **tablespoons snipped fresh parsley**
2 **tablespoons chopped green onion**
2 **tablespoons toasted slivered almonds**
2 **tablespoons mayonnaise or salad dressing**
2 **tablespoons milk**
1 **tablespoon white wine vinegar**
⅛ **teaspoon salt**
⅛ **teaspoon white pepper**
Dash garlic powder

In a blender container or food processor bowl combine cottage cheese, parsley, green onion, almonds, mayonnaise or salad dressing, milk, vinegar, salt, pepper, and garlic powder. Cover and blend or process till smooth.

Cover and store sauce in the refrigerator for 2 to 3 days. Before serving, allow sauce to stand at room temperature for 15 minutes; stir. Serve sauce with poultry or seafood. Makes about ¾ cup (twelve 1-tablespoon servings).

Per tablespoon: 34 calories, 2 g protein, 1 g carbohydrate, 3 g total fat (1 g saturated), 3 mg cholesterol, 72 mg sodium, 29 mg potassium.

Hollandaise Sauce

½ **cup margarine *or* butter**
3 **beaten egg yolks**
1 **tablespoon water**
1 **tablespoon lemon juice**
  Dash salt
  Dash white pepper

Cut margarine or butter into thirds and bring it to room temperature. **1** In the top of a double boiler combine egg yolks, water, lemon juice, salt, and pepper. Add *one piece* of the margarine or butter. Place over *boiling* water (upper pan should not touch water). **2** Cook, stirring rapidly, till margarine melts and sauce begins to thicken.

3 Add the remaining margarine or butter, a piece at a time, stirring constantly. Cook and stir till sauce thickens (1 to 2 minutes). Immediately remove from heat. If sauce is too thick or curdles, immediately beat in 1 to 2 tablespoons hot water. Serve sauce with vegetables, poultry, fish, or eggs. Makes about ¾ cup (twelve 1-tablespoon servings).

Per tablespoon: 83 calories, 1 g protein, 0 g carbohydrate, 9 g total fat (2 g saturated), 53 mg cholesterol, 91 mg sodium, 9 mg potassium.

1 Place ⅓ of margarine, egg yolks, water, lemon juice, pepper, and salt in top of double boiler. Upper pan should not touch boiling water in the bottom of double boiler.

2 Cook over boiling water, stirring rapidly, till margarine melts and sauce begins to thicken.

3 Add remaining margarine and continue cooking till sauce is thick.

SAUCES AND RELISHES

Herbed Brown Sauce

2 tablespoons butter
2 tablespoons all-purpose flour
1 cup beef broth
½ teaspoon dried parsley flakes
½ teaspoon Worcestershire sauce
¼ teaspoon onion powder
¼ teaspoon dried marjoram, crushed

In a small saucepan heat butter over medium heat till browned. Add flour; mix well. Add broth, parsley flakes, Worcestershire sauce, onion powder, and marjoram. Cook and stir over medium heat till thickened and bubbly. Cook and stir 1 minute more. Serve with beef, pork, poultry, or lamb. Makes about 1 cup (eight 2-tablespoon servings).

Per 2 tablespoons: 34 calories, 1 g protein, 2 g carbohydrate, 3 g total fat (2 g saturated), 8 mg cholesterol, 130 mg sodium, 24 mg potassium.

Madras Curry Sauce

2 tablespoons margarine *or* butter
¼ cup chopped onion
¼ cup chopped celery
1 small clove garlic, minced
1 teaspoon curry powder
¼ teaspoon ground cumin
⅛ teaspoon ground cardamom
Dash ground ginger
2 tablespoons all-purpose flour
¾ cup chicken broth
¼ cup apple juice
2 tablespoons flaked coconut

In a saucepan melt margarine or butter over medium heat. Add onion, celery, garlic, curry powder, cumin, cardamom, and ginger. Cook and stir till vegetables are tender. Stir in flour. Add broth and apple juice. Cook and stir over medium heat till thickened and bubbly. Cook and stir 1 minute more. Remove from heat. Stir in coconut. Serve over pork, poultry, or rice. Makes about 1¼ cups (twenty 1-tablespoon servings).

Per tablespoon: 20 calories, 0 g protein, 2 g carbohydrate, 1 g total fat (0 g saturated), 0 mg cholesterol, 44 mg sodium, 28 mg potassium.

Stir-Fry Sauce

½ cup cornstarch
¼ cup packed brown sugar
1 tablespoon ground ginger
½ teaspoon ground red pepper
¼ teaspoon garlic powder
½ cup soy sauce
¼ cup cider vinegar
2 cups chicken *or* beef broth
½ cup dry sherry
⅓ cup water

In a 1-quart jar combine cornstarch, brown sugar, ginger, red pepper, and garlic powder. Add soy sauce and vinegar; cover tightly and shake vigorously. Add broth, sherry, and water; shake well. Store in refrigerator for up to two weeks. Shake mixture well to combine before using in stir-fry recipes. For stir-fry recipes serving 4, use 1 cup of sauce. Makes 3⅓ cups (thirteen ¼-cup servings).

Per ¼ cup: 57 calories, 1 g protein, 10 g carbohydrate, 0 g total fat (0 g saturated), 0 mg cholesterol, 755 mg sodium, 83 mg potassium.

Caribbean Chutney

2 cups finely chopped
   mango
1 cup pineapple juice
1 cup finely chopped fresh
   pineapple
1 cup finely chopped papaya
½ cup finely chopped onion
¼ cup light raisins
2 tablespoons brown sugar
1 teaspoon finely shredded
   lemon peel
1 teaspoon ground ginger
¼ teaspoon ground allspice
1 clove garlic, minced
1 jalapeño pepper, seeded
   and finely chopped

In a large saucepan combine mango, pineapple juice, pineapple, papaya, onion, raisins, brown sugar, lemon peel, ginger, allspice, garlic, and jalapeño pepper. Bring mixture to boiling. Reduce heat and simmer, uncovered, for 20 to 25 minutes or till thickened, stirring occasionally.

Serve chutney warm or at room temperature with beef, pork, or poultry. (Any remaining chutney may be frozen up to 6 months.) Makes about 3½ cups (fifty-six 1-tablespoon servings).

Note: Fresh jalapeño peppers contain oils that can burn your eyes, lips, and skin. Cover your hands with plastic bags or wear plastic gloves and wash your hands thoroughly before touching your eyes or face.

Per tablespoon: 16 calories, 0 g protein, 4 g carbohydrate, 0 g total fat (0 g saturated), 0 mg cholesterol, 1 mg sodium, 40 mg potassium.

SAUCES AND RELISHES

Cranberry-Jalapeño Relish

2 cups cranberries
1 small pear, peeled and quartered
2 tablespoons chopped onion
1 small jalapeño pepper, seeded and halved
⅓ cup sugar
¼ teaspoon ground cinnamon

In a food processor bowl combine cranberries, pear, onion, and jalapeño pepper (see Note page 63.) Cover and process till finely chopped. Transfer mixture to a bowl. Stir in sugar and cinnamon. Cover and chill for 2 to 24 hours. Serve relish with chicken or pork. Makes about 2 cups (thirty-two 1-tablespoon servings).
*See note on page 142.

Per tablespoon: 14 calories, 0 g protein, 4 g carbohydrate, 0 g total fat (0 g saturated), 0 mg cholesterol, 0 mg sodium, 14 mg potassium.

Raspberry Salsa

1 medium tomato, peeled and finely chopped
1 cup fresh raspberries
½ cup finely chopped green pepper
½ cup finely chopped onion
1 tablespoon sugar
1 tablespoon raspberry vinegar
1 teaspoon salad oil
1 clove garlic, minced
¼ teaspoon dry mustard
¼ teaspoon ground cinnamon
⅛ teaspoon ground ginger

In a medium mixing bowl combine chopped tomato, raspberries, green pepper, onion, sugar, raspberry vinegar, oil, garlic, mustard, cinnamon, and ginger. Mix well. Cover and refrigerate for 4 to 24 hours. Serve salsa with ham, pork, or poultry. Makes about 2 cups (sixteen 2-tablespoon servings).

Per 2 tablespoons: 15 calories, 0 g protein, 3 g carbohydrate, 0 g total fat (0 g saturated), 0 mg cholesterol, 1 mg sodium, 51 mg potassium.

Green Salsa

12 tomatillos, chopped (2⅓ cups) or two 18-ounce cans tomatillos, drained and chopped
1 medium onion, chopped
1 or 2 fresh or canned jalapeño peppers, chopped (1 to 2 tablespoons)
1 tablespoon snipped fresh cilantro
1 tablespoon sugar (optional)

In a small mixing bowl combine tomatillos, onion, jalapeño peppers (see Note page 63), and cilantro. If desired, when using canned tomatillos, add sugar to taste. Stir gently to mix. Cover and chill for 1 hour before serving. Store any leftover salsa in the refrigerator for up to 1 week. Makes about 2¾ cups (forty-four 1-tablespoon servings).

Per tablespoon: 3 calories, 0 g protein, 1 g carbohydrate, 0 g total fat, (0 g saturated), 0 mg cholesterol, 0 mg sodium, 25 mg potassium.

BREADS

Raspberry-Bran Muffins, Herbed-Potato Parker House Rolls, Peppery Corn Sticks, and Special Sweet Potato Biscuits

Cardamom-Nut Loaf

3 to 3½ cups all-purpose flour
1 package active dry yeast
1 cup milk
2 tablespoons sugar
2 tablespoons margarine *or* butter
½ teaspoon salt
1 egg
½ cup chopped walnuts
2 teaspoons margarine *or* butter, melted
2 tablespoons sugar
½ teaspoon ground cardamom
½ teaspoon ground cinnamon
¼ teaspoon ground nutmeg
1 teaspoon margarine *or* butter, melted (optional)

In a large mixing bowl combine *1½ cups* of the flour and the yeast. In a saucepan heat and stir milk, 2 tablespoons sugar, 2 tablespoons margarine or butter, and salt till warm (120° to 130°) and margarine or butter almost melts. Add to flour mixture. Add egg. Beat with an electric mixer on low speed for 30 seconds, scraping bowl constantly. Beat on high speed for 3 minutes. Using a spoon, stir in nuts and as much of the remaining flour as you can.

Turn out onto a lightly floured surface. Knead in enough of the remaining flour to make a moderately stiff dough that is smooth and elastic (6 to 8 minutes total). Shape into a ball. Place in a lightly greased bowl; turn once to grease surface. Cover and let rise in a warm place till double (about 45 minutes).

Punch dough down. Turn out onto a lightly floured surface. Cover and let rest 10 minutes. Lightly grease an 8x4x2-inch loaf pan. Roll dough into a 12x8-inch rectangle. Brush with the 2 teaspoons melted margarine or butter. Combine the 2 tablespoons sugar, cardamom, cinnamon, and nutmeg. Sprinkle over dough. Roll dough up tightly from one of the narrow sides. Seal edges and ends. Tuck ends under. Place dough, seam side down, in prepared pan. Cover and let rise in a warm place till nearly double (30 to 40 minutes).

Bake in a 375° oven about 40 minutes or till bread sounds hollow when tapped. Cover loosely with foil the last 10 minutes of baking to prevent overbrowning, if necessary. Remove from pan immediately. Brush with the 1 teaspoon melted margarine or butter, if desired. Cool on a wire rack. Makes 1 loaf. (16 servings).

Per serving: 143 calories, 4 g protein, 21 g carbohydrate, 5 g total fat (1 g saturated), 14 mg cholesterol, 101 mg sodium, 71 mg potassium.

White Bread

5¾ to 6¼ cups all-purpose flour
1 package active dry yeast
2¼ cups milk
2 tablespoons sugar
1 tablespoon shortening, margarine, *or* butter
1 teaspoon salt

In a large mixing bowl combine *2½ cups* of the flour and the yeast. In a saucepan heat and stir milk, sugar, shortening, margarine or butter, and salt till warm (120° to 130°) and shortening almost melts. Add to flour mixture. Beat with an electric mixer on low speed for 30 seconds, scraping bowl constantly. Beat on high speed for 3 minutes. Using a spoon, stir in as much of the remaining flour as you can.

Turn out onto a lightly floured surface. **1** Knead in enough of the remaining flour to make a moderately stiff dough that is smooth and elastic (6 to 8 minutes total). Shape into a ball. Place in a lightly greased bowl; turn once to grease surface. **2** Cover and let rise in a warm place till double (about 45 minutes). **3** Test dough with fingertips to make sure dough has risen sufficiently.

4 Punch dough down. Turn out onto a lightly floured surface. Divide dough in half. Cover and let rest for 10 minutes. Lightly grease two 8x4x2-inch loaf pans. **5** **6** Shape each half of dough into a loaf. Place shaped dough in prepared loaf pans. Cover and let rise in a warm place till nearly double (30 to 45 minutes).

Bake in a 375° oven about 40 minutes or till bread sounds hollow when tapped. Cover loosely with foil the last 10 minutes of baking to prevent overbrowning. Remove from pans immediately. Cool on wire racks. Makes 2 loaves (32 servings).

Per serving: 91 calories, 3 g protein, 17 g carbohydrate, 1 g total fat (0 g saturated), 1 mg cholesterol, 76 mg sodium, 53 mg potassium.

1 To knead, fold dough over; push down with heel of hand. Turn, fold, and push down again.

2 Place dough in a draft-free place (such as upper oven rack with bowl of hot water on low rack) to rise.

3 Dough is ready to shape when two fingertips pressed lightly ½ inch into dough leave an indentation.

White Bread *(continued)*

4 Punch down dough by pushing your fist into center. Pull edges of dough to center.

5 To shape dough gently pull each half into a loaf shape. Tuck edges under.

6 *Or,* roll each half of dough into a 12x8-inch rectangle. Roll up tightly, starting at narrow edge. Seal edge and end. Tuck ends under. Place seam side down in pans.

Zesty Tomato-Herb Bread

4 to 4½ cups all-purpose flour
2 packages active dry yeast
½ teaspoon salt
1 14½-ounce can tomatoes
2 tablespoons olive oil *or* cooking oil
2 tablespoons honey
¼ cup snipped fresh basil
2 tablespoons snipped fresh parsley
Cornmeal
1 slightly beaten egg white
1 tablespoon water
½ teaspoon garlic pepper

In a large mixing bowl combine *2 cups* of the flour, yeast, and salt; set aside. Drain tomatoes, reserving juice. Finely chop the tomatoes.

In a medium saucepan combine chopped tomatoes, reserved tomato juice, oil, and honey. Cook and stir over medium heat till warm (120° to 130°). Add to flour mixture. Beat with an electric mixer on low speed for 30 seconds, scraping bowl constantly. Beat on high speed for 3 minutes. Using a spoon, stir in basil, parsley, and as much of the remaining flour as you can.

Turn out onto a lightly floured surface. Knead in enough of the remaining flour to make a moderately stiff dough that is smooth and elastic (6 to 8 minutes total). Shape into a ball. Place in a lightly greased bowl; turn once to grease surface. Cover and let rise in a warm place till double (about 45 minutes).

Punch dough down. Turn out onto a lightly floured surface. Divide dough in half. Cover and let rest 10 minutes. Shape into 2 round loaves. Place on a greased baking sheet sprinkled with cornmeal. Flatten each slightly to a 6-inch diameter. Cover and let rise in a warm place till nearly double (about 45 minutes).

Combine egg white and water; brush over loaves. Sprinkle with garlic pepper. Bake in a 375° oven for 40 to 45 minutes or till bread sounds hollow when tapped. Cover loosely with foil the last 10 to 20 minutes of baking to prevent overbrowning, if necessary. Cool on wire racks. To serve, cut into wedges. Makes 2 loaves (24 servings).

Per serving: 118 calories, 4 g protein, 23 g carbohydrate, 2 g total fat (0 g saturated), 0 mg cholesterol, 284 mg sodium, 360 mg potassium.

Shredded Wheat Rolls

1¾ **to 2 cups all-purpose flour**
1 **package active dry yeast**
¾ **teaspoon salt**
⅔ **cup warm water**
¼ **cup cooking oil**
2 **tablespoons honey**
1 **beaten egg**
1 **cup whole wheat flour**
½ **cup crushed shredded
    wheat biscuits**

In a large bowl stir together *1¼ cups* of the all-purpose flour, the yeast, and salt. **1**In a saucepan heat and stir water, oil, and honey till warm (120° to 130°). **2**Add to flour mixture along with egg. Beat with an electric mixer on low speed for 30 seconds, scraping bowl constantly. Beat on high speed for 3 minutes. Using a spoon, stir in whole wheat flour, the shredded wheat biscuits, and as much of the remaining all-purpose flour as you can.

Turn out onto a lightly floured surface. Knead in enough of the remaining all-purpose flour to make a moderately stiff dough that is smooth and elastic (6 to 8 minutes). **3**Shape dough into a ball. Place dough in a lightly greased bowl; turn once to grease surface. Cover and let rise in a warm place till double (about 1½ hours).

Punch dough down. Turn out onto a lightly floured surface. Cover and let rest for 10 minutes. Lightly grease 12 muffin cups. **4**Divide dough into 36 pieces. Shape each piece into a ball, pulling edges under to make a smooth top. Place *three* balls, smooth side up, in *each* muffin cup. Cover and let rise in a warm place till nearly double (about 30 minutes).

Bake in a 400° oven for 12 to 15 minutes or till golden brown. Makes 12 rolls.

Per roll: 161 calories, 4 g protein, 25 g carbohydrate, 5 g total fat (1 g saturated), 18 mg cholesterol, 140 mg sodium, 83 mg potassium.

1In a saucepan heat water, oil, and honey till warm (120° to 130°). Use a thermometer to accurately check the temperature of the liquid. The thermometer should not touch the bottom of the pan when getting a reading.

2Add warm liquid to flour mixture along with egg.

3Shape dough into a ball and place in a large greased bowl. Turn dough over once to grease entire surface.

4Divide dough into 36 pieces. Shape each piece into a 1-inch ball, pulling edges under to make a smooth top. Place 3 balls in each greased muffin cup.

Herbed-Potato Parker House Rolls

3 to 3½ cups all-purpose flour
1 package active dry yeast
3 tablespoons snipped fresh chives
2 teaspoons snipped fresh dill
¾ cup water
¼ cup margarine *or* butter
1 teaspoon sugar
½ teaspoon salt
1 egg
¼ cup mashed potatoes
3 tablespoons margarine *or* butter, melted
Grated Parmesan cheese

In a large mixing bowl combine *1½ cups* of the flour, yeast, chives, and dill. In a saucepan heat and stir water, ¼ cup margarine or butter, sugar, and salt till warm (120° to 130°) and margarine or butter almost melts. Add to flour mixture. Add egg and mashed potatoes. Beat with an electric mixer on low speed for 30 seconds, scraping bowl constantly. Beat on high speed for 3 minutes. Using a spoon, stir in as much of the remaining flour as you can.

Turn out onto a lightly floured surface. Knead in enough of the remaining flour to make a moderately stiff dough that is smooth and elastic (6 to 8 minutes total). Shape into a ball. Place in a lightly greased bowl; turn once to grease surface. Cover and let rise in a warm place till double (about 1 hour).

Punch dough down. Turn out onto a lightly floured surface. Divide dough in half. Cover; let rest 10 minutes. Roll *each half* of dough to ¼-inch thickness. Cut with a floured 2½-inch round biscuit cutter. Brush with some of the melted margarine or butter.

To shape, use a wooden spoon handle to make a slightly off-center crease in each round. Fold large half over small half, slightly overlapping. Press folded edge firmly. Place rolls 3 inches apart on greased baking sheets. Cover; let rise till nearly double (about 20 minutes).

Lightly brush tops of rolls with remaining margarine or butter. Sprinkle with Parmesan cheese. Bake in a 375° oven for 12 to 15 minutes or till golden brown. Makes 30 rolls.

Per roll: 73 calories, 2 g protein, 9 g carbohydrate, 3 g total fat (1 g saturated), 7 mg cholesterol, 73 mg sodium, 30 mg potassium.

Zucchini-Tomato Focaccia

1 package active dry yeast
1½ cups warm water
    (105° to 115°)
¼ cup olive oil *or* cooking oil
1 teaspoon salt
3¾ to 4¼ cups all-purpose
    flour
3 medium tomatoes, sliced
2 medium zucchini, thinly
    sliced
¼ cup grated Parmesan
    cheese
2 tablespoons snipped
    Italian parsley
¼ to ½ teaspoon pepper
¼ teaspoon garlic salt

In large bowl sprinkle yeast over warm water. Let stand 5 minutes. Stir in *2 tablespoons* of oil and salt; add *2 cups* of flour. Beat with an electric mixer on low speed for 30 seconds, scraping bowl. Beat on high speed for 3 minutes. With spoon, stir in as much of remaining flour as you can.

Turn out onto a floured surface. Knead in enough remaining flour to make a moderately stiff dough that is smooth and elastic (6 to 8 minutes). Shape dough into a ball. Place in a lightly greased bowl; turn to grease surface. Cover; let rise in a warm place till double (1 hour).

Punch dough down. Turn out onto a floured surface and knead 5 strokes. Divide dough in half. Shape *each half* into a ball; cover and let rest 10 minutes. Press dough into two lightly greased 12-inch pizza pans. Cover; let rise in a warm place till nearly double (about 45 minutes).

Line a 15x10x1-inch baking pan with foil; grease foil. Place tomatoes and zucchini in the pan. Drizzle vegetables with *1 tablespoon* oil. Bake in a 450° oven for 20 to 25 minutes or till zucchini is just tender.

Brush remaining oil over both doughs. Using a wooden spoon handle press slight indentations in dough. Arrange vegetables evenly over each pan of dough. Sprinkle with Parmesan cheese, parsley, pepper, and garlic salt.

Bake in a 400° oven for 30 to 35 minutes or till crust is golden brown. Makes 2 rounds (12 servings).

Per serving: 198 calories, 5 g protein, 30 g carbohydrate, 6 g total fat (1 g saturated), 2 mg cholesterol, 264 mg sodium, 173 mg potassium.

Raspberry-Cinnamon Rolls

4 **to 4½ cups all-purpose**
  flour
1 **package active dry yeast**
1 **cup milk**
⅓ **cup sugar**
5 **tablespoons margarine *or***
  butter
½ **teaspoon salt**
2 **eggs**
3 **tablespoons margarine *or***
  butter, melted
½ **cup sugar**
2 **teaspoons ground**
  cinnamon
1 **teaspoon finely shredded**
  orange peel
1½ **cups fresh red raspberries**
  Powdered Sugar Icing

In a large mixing bowl combine *2 cups* of the flour and the yeast. In a saucepan heat and stir milk, the ⅓ cup sugar, the 5 tablespoons margarine or butter, and salt till warm (120° to 130°) and margarine or butter almost melts. Add to flour mixture along with eggs. Beat with an electric mixer on low speed for 30 seconds, scraping bowl constantly. Beat on high speed for 3 minutes. Using a spoon, stir in as much of the remaining flour as you can.

Turn out onto a lightly floured surface. Knead in enough of the remaining flour to make a moderately stiff dough that is smooth and elastic (6 to 8 minutes total). Shape dough into a ball. Place in a lightly greased bowl; turn once to grease surface. Cover and let rise in a warm place till double (about 1 hour).

Punch dough down. Turn out onto a lightly floured surface. Divide dough in half. Cover and let rest for 10 minutes. Roll *half* of the dough into a 12x8-inch rectangle. Brush *half* of the 3 tablespoons melted margarine or butter over dough. For filling, combine the ½ cup sugar, cinnamon, and orange peel. Fold in raspberries. Sprinkle *half* of the filling over dough. Roll up from one of the long sides. Seal seams. Slice dough into 12 pieces. Repeat with remaining dough, melted margarine, and filling.

Place rolls into two greased 9x1½-inch round baking pans. Cover; let rise till nearly double (about 30 minutes). Bake in a 375° oven for 20 to 25 minutes or till done. Cool slightly; remove from pans. Drizzle with Powdered Sugar Icing. Makes 24.

Powdered Sugar Icing: In a small bowl combine 1 cup sifted *powdered sugar*, 1 tablespoon *orange juice,* and ¼ teaspoon *vanilla.* Stir in additional *orange juice,* 1 teaspoon at a time, till of drizzling consistency.

Per serving: 163 calories, 3 g protein, 27 g carbohydrate, 5 g total fat (1 g saturated), 19 mg cholesterol, 100 mg sodium, 63 mg potassium.

Honey-Berry Bagels

2½ to 3 cups all-purpose flour
1 package active dry yeast
1½ cups warm water
(120° to 130°)
3 tablespoons honey
1½ teaspoons salt
½ teaspoon ground
cinnamon
1½ cups whole wheat flour
¾ cup dried cranberries *or*
raisins
6 cups water
1 tablespoon sugar

Combine *2 cups* of the all-purpose flour and yeast. Add warm water, honey, salt, and cinnamon. Beat with an electric mixer on low speed for 30 seconds, scraping bowl constantly. Beat on high speed for 3 minutes. Using a spoon, stir in whole wheat flour, dried cranberries, and as much of the remaining all-purpose flour as you can.

Turn out onto a lightly floured surface. Knead in enough remaining all-purpose flour to make a moderately stiff dough that is smooth and elastic (6 to 8 minutes total). Cover; let rest 10 minutes. Working quickly, divide dough into 12 portions. Shape each portion into a smooth ball. Cover and let rest 5 minutes.

Punch a hole in the center of each ball with a floured finger. **1** Pull dough gently to make about a 2-inch hole, keeping bagel uniformly shaped. Place on a greased baking sheet. Cover; let rise 20 minutes (start timing after first bagel is shaped).

2 Broil raised bagels about 5 inches from heat for 3 to 4 minutes or till bagels look set, turning once (tops should not brown). Meanwhile, in a 12-inch skillet or 4½-quart Dutch oven bring water and sugar to boiling. **3** Reduce heat and simmer bagels, 4 or 5 at a time, for 7 minutes, turning once. Drain on paper towels. (Let stand on paper towels only a few seconds or they will stick.)

4 Place drained bagels 2 inches apart on a well-greased baking sheet. Bake in a 375° oven for 25 to 30 minutes or till tops are golden brown. Cool on a wire rack. Makes 12.

Per serving: 183 calories, 5 g protein, 41 g carbohydrate, 1 g total fat (0 g saturated), 0 mg cholesterol, 270 mg sodium, 106 mg potassium.

1 With floured fingers gently pull dough to make a 2-inch hole in center.

2 Broil raised bagels 5 inches from heat for 3 to 4 minutes, turning once. Tops should not brown.

3 In a large kettle of simmering water, cook bagels, 4 or 5 at a time, turning once. Drain bagels on paper towels for a few seconds.

4 Place drained bagels on a well-greased baking sheet and bake till tops are golden.

Peppery Corn Sticks

1 cup all-purpose flour
1 cup yellow cornmeal
2 tablespoons sugar
1 tablespoon baking powder
¼ teaspoon salt
¼ teaspoon ground red
  pepper (optional)
2 beaten eggs
1 cup milk
3 tablespoons cooking oil
½ cup shredded Monterey
  Jack cheese with
  jalapeño peppers
  (2 ounces)
¼ cup finely chopped sweet
  red pepper
¼ cup finely chopped green
  pepper

In a mixing bowl combine flour, cornmeal, sugar, baking powder, salt, and, if desired, ground red pepper. In another bowl combine eggs, milk, and oil; add to flour mixture all at once. Stir just till smooth (do not overbeat). Fold in cheese, chopped sweet red pepper, and green pepper.

Spoon batter into greased corn stick pans; fill ⅔ full. Bake in a 425° oven for 12 to 15 minutes or till brown. Makes about 20.

Per serving: 99 calories, 3 g protein, 12 g carbohydrate, 4 g total fat (1 g saturated), 25 mg cholesterol, 57 mg sodium, 53 mg potassium.

Sweet Pepper-Cheese Batter Bread

1 package active dry yeast
¾ cup warm water
  (105° to 115°)
2 beaten eggs
½ cup shredded cheddar
  cheese
½ cup finely chopped sweet
  red *or* green pepper
¼ cup finely chopped onion
¼ cup shortening
2 tablespoons sugar
½ teaspoon dried thyme,
  crushed
½ teaspoon salt
2⅔ cups all-purpose flour

In a large bowl dissolve yeast in warm water. Stir in eggs, cheese, red or green pepper, onion, shortening, sugar, thyme, and salt. Gradually add *2 cups* of the flour, beating with an electric mixer on medium speed till smooth. Using a spoon, stir in remaining flour (batter will be stiff).

Cover; let rise in a warm place till double (about 60 minutes). Stir down dough. Transfer to a greased 9x5x3-inch loaf pan. Smooth top of dough with floured hands. Cover; let rise in a warm place till nearly double (about 40 minutes).

Bake in a 375° oven for 40 to 45 minutes or till bread sounds hollow when tapped. Remove loaf from pan. Cool on a wire rack. Makes 1 loaf (16 servings).

Per serving: 131 calories, 4 g protein, 17 g carbohydrate, 5 g total fat (2 g saturated), 30 mg cholesterol, 97 mg sodium, 53 mg potassium.

Apricot-Raisin Bread

1 **6-ounce package dried**
   apricots, chopped
½ **cup raisins**
1 **cup boiling water**
2 **cups all-purpose flour**
¾ **cup sugar**
1 **tablespoon baking powder**
½ **teaspoon salt**
1 **beaten egg**
¾ **cup orange juice**
¼ **cup cooking oil**
1 **cup chopped walnuts**

In a small bowl place apricots and raisins. Pour boiling water over fruit and let stand for 5 minutes. Drain well and set aside.

In a mixing bowl combine flour, sugar, baking powder, and salt. In another mixing bowl combine egg, orange juice, and oil; add to flour mixture all at once. **1** Fold in fruit and chopped nuts.

2 Pour batter into a greased 9x5x3-inch loaf pan. Bake in a 350° oven for 60 to 65 minutes or till a toothpick inserted near center comes out clean. Cool in pan for 10 minutes. **3** Remove from pan; cool thoroughly on a wire rack. Wrap and store overnight before slicing. Makes 1 loaf (16 servings).

Per serving: 182 calories, 4 g protein, 25 g carbohydrate, 8 g total fat (1 g saturated), 13 mg cholesterol, 76 mg sodium, 243 mg potassium.

1 Carefully fold drained fruit and walnuts into batter with a rubber spatula. Do not overmix.

2 Grease bottom and half way up sides of loaf pan with folded paper towel, pastry brush, or waxed paper.

3 Turn out bread on its side. Remove pan; turn loaf right side up to cool.

Strawberry Bread

2 cups all-purpose flour
½ cup sugar
1½ teaspoons baking powder
½ teaspoon baking soda
¼ teaspoon salt
1 10-ounce package frozen
    strawberries, thawed
1 beaten egg
⅓ cup cooking oil
½ cup chopped pecans
1 tablespoon sugar
½ teaspoon ground
    cinnamon

In a mixing bowl combine flour, the ½ cup sugar, baking powder, baking soda, and salt. Make a well in the center. Combine strawberries, egg, and oil; add all at once to flour mixture. Stir just till moistened (batter should be lumpy).

Spoon batter into a greased and floured 8x4x2-inch loaf pan. Combine chopped pecans, the 1 tablespoon sugar, and cinnamon; sprinkle over batter.

Bake in a 350° oven for 55 to 60 minutes or till a toothpick inserted near center comes out clean. Cool in the pan for 10 minutes. Remove from pan; cool thoroughly on a wire rack. Wrap and store overnight before slicing. Store in the refrigerator. Makes 1 loaf (16 servings).

Per serving: 163 calories, 2 g protein, 23 g carbohydrate, 7 g total fat (1 g saturated), 13 mg cholesterol, 65 mg sodium, 51 mg potassium.

Apple-Peanut Loaf

2 cups all-purpose flour
½ cup packed brown sugar
½ cup granulated sugar
1 teaspoon baking soda
1 teaspoon ground
    cinnamon
½ teaspoon ground nutmeg
¼ teaspoon salt
1 cup finely shredded peeled
    apple
½ cup apple butter
2 beaten eggs
¼ cup cooking oil
2 tablespoons orange juice
1 cup coarsely chopped
    unsalted peanuts

In a mixing bowl stir together flour, brown sugar, granulated sugar, baking soda, cinnamon, nutmeg, and salt. In another mixing bowl combine shredded apple, apple butter, eggs, oil, and orange juice; add all at once to flour mixture. Stir just till moistened (batter should be lumpy). Fold peanuts into batter.

Pour batter into a greased 9x5x3-inch loaf pan. Bake in a 350° oven for 1 to 1¼ hours or till a toothpick inserted near the center comes out clean.

Cool in the pan for 10 minutes. Remove from pan; cool thoroughly on a wire rack. Wrap and store overnight before slicing. Makes 1 loaf (16 servings).

Per serving: 218 calories, 5 g protein, 32 g carbohydrate, 9 g total fat (1 g saturated), 27 mg cholesterol, 95 mg sodium, 145 mg potassium.

Orange-Poppy Seed Bread with Blueberries

1¾ **cups all-purpose flour**
½ **cup sugar**
1½ **teaspoons baking powder**
1 **tablespoon poppy seed**
¼ **teaspoon salt**
¾ **cup milk**
¼ **cup cooking oil**
1 **beaten egg**
1 **tablespoon finely shredded orange peel**
1 **tablespoon orange juice**
¾ **cup fresh *or* frozen blueberries**

In a mixing bowl combine flour, sugar, baking powder, poppy seed, and salt. In another mixing bowl combine milk, oil, egg, orange peel, and orange juice; add to flour mixture all at once. Stir just till moistened (batter should be lumpy). Fold in blueberries.

Pour batter into a greased 8x4x2-inch loaf pan. Bake in a 350° oven for 45 to 50 minutes or till a toothpick inserted near center comes out clean. Cool in the pan for 10 minutes. Remove from pan; cool thoroughly on a wire rack. Wrap and store overnight before slicing. Makes 1 loaf (16 servings).

Per serving: 118 calories, 2 g protein, 18 g carbohydrate, 4 g total fat (1 g saturated), 14 mg cholesterol, 45 mg sodium, 48 mg potassium.

Cocoa Muffins

1⅔ cups all-purpose flour
⅔ cup sugar
¼ cup unsweetened cocoa
   powder
1½ teaspoons baking powder
½ teaspoon baking soda
½ teaspoon ground
   cinnamon
⅛ teaspoon salt
1 beaten egg
1 slightly beaten egg white
1 8-ounce carton low-fat
   vanilla yogurt
⅓ cup cooking oil
⅓ cup chopped pecans
   Sugar

In a mixing bowl combine flour, the ⅔ cup sugar, cocoa powder, baking powder, baking soda, cinnamon, and salt. Make a well in the center. Combine egg, egg white, yogurt, and oil; stir till smooth. Add all at once to flour mixture. Stir just till moistened (batter should be lumpy). Fold in nuts.

Line muffin cups with paper baking cups; fill ⅔ full. Sprinkle tops lightly with the 2 tablespoons sugar. Bake in a 400° oven about 20 minutes or till a toothpick inserted in center comes out clean. Remove from pans; serve warm. Makes 12.

Per serving: 208 calories, 4 g protein, 28 g carbohydrate, 9 g total fat (1 g saturated), 19 mg cholesterol, 80 mg sodium, 66 mg potassium.

Cheddar-Blueberry Corn Muffins

1 cup all-purpose flour
¾ cup cornmeal
½ cup shredded cheddar
   cheese (2 ounces)
¼ cup sugar
2 teaspoons baking powder
¼ teaspoon salt
1 beaten egg
¾ cup milk
¼ cup cooking oil
¾ cup fresh *or* frozen
   blueberries

In a mixing bowl combine flour, cornmeal, shredded cheese, sugar, baking powder, and salt. Make a well in the center. Combine egg, milk, and oil; add all at once to flour mixture. Stir just till moistened (batter should be lumpy). Fold in blueberries.

Lightly grease muffin cups; fill ⅔ full. Bake in a 400° oven about 15 minutes or till golden. Makes 10 to 12.

Per serving: 193 calories, 5 g protein, 24 g carbohydrate, 9 g total fat (2 g saturated), 29 mg cholesterol, 107 mg sodium, 79 mg potassium.

Basic Muffins

1¾ cups all-purpose flour
⅓ cup sugar
2 teaspoons baking powder
¼ teaspoon salt
1 beaten egg
¾ cup milk
¼ cup cooking oil

In a mixing bowl combine flour, sugar, baking powder, and salt. **1** Make a well in the center. **2** Combine egg, milk, and oil; add all at once to flour mixture. **3** Stir just till moistened (batter should be lumpy). **4** Lightly grease muffin cups or line with paper baking cups; fill ⅔ full. Bake in a 400° oven about 20 minutes or till golden. Remove from pans; serve warm. Makes 10 to 12.

Per serving: 165 calories, 3 g protein, 23 g carbohydrate, 6 g total fat (1 g saturated), 23 mg cholesterol, 72 mg sodium, 57 mg potassium.

Blueberry Muffins: Prepare as above, *except* fold ¾ cup fresh or frozen *blueberries* and, if desired, 1 teaspoon finely shredded *lemon peel* into muffin batter.

Per serving: 171 calories, 3 g protein, 25 g carbohydrate, 7 g total fat (1 g saturated), 23 mg cholesterol, 73 mg sodium, 67 mg potassium.

Pumpkin Muffins: Prepare as above, *except* add 1 teaspoon ground *cinnamon*, ½ teaspoon ground *nutmeg*, and ⅛ teaspoon ground *cloves* to flour mixture. Add ½ cup canned *pumpkin* to egg mixture. Stir ¼ cup chopped *nuts* into batter. Do not use paper baking cups.

Per serving: 189 calories, 4 g protein, 25 g carbohydrate, 8 g total fat (1 g saturated), 23 mg cholesterol, 74 mg sodium, 99 mg potassium.

1 Gently push flour mixture against sides of bowl to make a well.

2 Add egg mixture to flour mixture all at once, pouring into well.

3 Stir mixture just till dry ingredients are moistened. Batter will be lumpy.

4 Fill greased muffin cups only ⅔ full to allow space for rising.

Raspberry-Bran Muffins

3 **cups bran flakes cereal**
1½ **cups all-purpose flour**
½ **cup packed brown sugar**
2 **teaspoons baking powder**
¼ **teaspoon salt**
1 **beaten egg**
1½ **cups milk**
¼ **cup cooking oil**
1 **cup fresh raspberries** *or*
   blueberries

In a mixing bowl combine cereal, flour, brown sugar, baking powder, and salt. Make a well in the center. Combine egg, milk, and oil; add all at once to flour mixture. Stir just till moistened (batter should be lumpy). Gently fold in raspberries or blueberries.

Lightly grease muffin cups; fill ¾ full. Bake in a 400° oven about 20 minutes or till golden. Remove from pans; serve warm. Makes 18.

Per serving: 135 calories, 3 g protein, 22 g carbohydrate, 4 g total fat (1 g saturated), 13 mg cholesterol, 120 mg sodium, 122 mg potassium.

Hearty Breakfast Muffins

1½ **cups all-purpose flour**
¾ **cup chopped pitted dates**
¼ **cup sugar**
2 **tablespoons wheat germ**
1½ **teaspoons baking powder**
¼ **teaspoon baking soda**
¼ **teaspoon salt**
¾ **cup orange juice**
¼ **cup cooking oil**
1 **beaten egg**

In a mixing bowl combine flour, dates, sugar, wheat germ, baking powder, baking soda, and salt. Make a well in the center. Combine orange juice, oil, and egg; add all at once to flour mixture. Stir just till moistened (batter should be lumpy).

Lightly grease muffin cups or line with paper baking cups; fill ⅔ full. Bake in a 400° oven about 15 minutes or till golden. Remove from pans; serve warm. Makes 12.

Per serving: 157 calories, 3 g protein, 26 g carbohydrate, 5 g total fat (1 g saturated), 18 mg cholesterol, 70 mg sodium, 136 mg potassium.

Almond Popovers

1 **tablespoon shortening** *or*
   nonstick spray coating
2 **beaten eggs**
1 **cup milk**
1 **tablespoon cooking oil**
½ **teaspoon almond extract**
1 **cup all-purpose flour**
¼ **teaspoon salt**
¼ **cup sliced almonds**

Using ½ *teaspoon* shortening for each cup, grease the bottom and sides of six 6-ounce custard cups or the cups of a popover pan. *Or,* spray cups with nonstick coating. Place the custard cups on a 15x10x1-inch baking pan; set aside.

In a medium mixing bowl combine beaten eggs, milk, cooking oil, and almond extract. Add flour and salt. Beat with a rotary beater or wire whisk till mixture is smooth. Fill the greased cups *half* full. Sprinkle with sliced almonds. Bake in a 400° oven about 40 minutes or till very firm.

Immediately after removal from the oven, prick each popover with a fork to let steam escape. Then, if crisper popovers are desired, return the popovers to the oven for 5 to 10 minutes more or till desired crispness (be sure the oven is turned off). Serve hot. Makes 6 popovers.

Per serving: 180 calories, 7 g protein, 18 g carbohydrate, 9 g total fat (2 g saturated), 74 mg cholesterol, 131 mg sodium, 135 mg potassium.

Raisin-Nut Coffee Cake

¼ **cup light raisins, coarsely chopped**
¼ **cup finely chopped walnuts**
2 **tablespoons brown sugar**
1 **tablespoon honey**
2 **teaspoons unsweetened cocoa powder**
1 **3-ounce package cream cheese**
¼ **cup margarine *or* butter**
2 **cups packaged biscuit mix**
¼ **cup milk**
4 **teaspoons margarine *or* butter, melted**
2 **tablespoons granulated sugar**
1 **teaspoon ground cinnamon**

For filling, in a mixing bowl combine raisins, walnuts, brown sugar, honey, and cocoa powder. Set filling aside.

Cut cream cheese and the ¼ cup margarine or butter into biscuit mix till crumbly. Add milk; stir till combined. On a floured surface, knead dough 10 to 12 strokes. **1** On waxed paper, roll or pat dough into a 12x8-inch rectangle. **2** Invert dough onto a greased baking sheet; remove paper. **3** Spread filling down center of dough.

4 Make 2½-inch cuts from long sides toward the center at 1-inch intervals. **5** Fold strips alternately over filling. Brush with melted margarine or butter. Combine granulated sugar and cinnamon; sprinkle on dough.

Bake in a 375° oven for 20 to 25 minutes or till golden brown. Serve warm. Makes 12 servings.

Per serving: 201 calories, 3 g protein, 22 g carbohydrate, 12 g total fat (3 g saturated), 8 mg cholesterol, 318 mg sodium, 61 mg potassium.

1 Roll or pat dough into a 12 x 8-inch rectangle on a sheet of waxed paper.

2 Invert dough onto a greased baking sheet; remove waxed paper.

3 Spread filling mixture in a 3-inch strip down center of dough.

4 Make 2½-inch cuts from the side edges to the center, keeping the cuts 1 inch apart.

5 Starting at one end, alternately fold opposite strips of dough at an angle across filling.

Glazed Raisin-Sour Cream Coffee Cake

1¼ **cups all-purpose flour**
¾ **cup sugar**
¼ **teaspoon salt**
⅓ **cup margarine *or* butter**
1 **teaspoon baking powder**
½ **teaspoon ground cinnamon**
¼ **teaspoon baking soda**
¼ **teaspoon ground nutmeg**
¼ **teaspoon ground allspice**
1 **beaten egg**
½ **cup dairy sour cream**
½ **cup raisins**
¼ **cup chopped nuts**
½ **cup sifted powdered sugar**
1 **tablespoon milk**
1 **teaspoon lemon juice**

In a mixing bowl combine flour, sugar, and salt; cut in margarine or butter till crumbly. Set aside ¼ *cup* of the flour mixture. To the remaining flour mixture add baking powder, cinnamon, baking soda, nutmeg, and allspice. Mix well. Stir in egg, sour cream, and raisins; mix well.

Spread batter into a greased 8x8x2-inch baking pan. Stir together reserved flour mixture and chopped nuts; sprinkle atop batter. Bake in a 350° oven for 30 to 35 minutes or till a toothpick inserted near the center comes out clean.

For glaze, combine powdered sugar, milk, and lemon juice. Drizzle over warm coffee cake. Makes 9 servings.

Per serving: 286 calories, 4 g protein, 42 g carbohydrate, 12 g total fat (3 g saturated), 29 mg cholesterol, 180 mg sodium, 120 mg potassium.

Chocolate-Pecan Sticky Rolls

⅓ **cup packed brown sugar**
2 **tablespoons margarine *or* butter**
1 **tablespoon light corn syrup**
⅓ **cup chopped pecans**
2 **cups all-purpose flour**
2 **teaspoons baking powder**
¼ **teaspoon salt**
⅓ **cup shortening**
¾ **cup milk**
1 **tablespoon melted margarine *or* butter**
¼ **cup granulated sugar**
½ **teaspoon ground cinnamon**
¼ **cup miniature semisweet chocolate pieces**
¼ **cup chopped raisins**

In a small saucepan combine brown sugar, the 2 tablespoons margarine or butter, and corn syrup. Cook and stir till combined. Spread mixture into an 8x8x2-inch baking pan. Sprinkle with chopped pecans. Set pan aside.

In a mixing bowl stir together flour, baking powder, and salt. Cut in shortening till mixture resembles coarse crumbs. Make a well in the center; add milk all at once, stirring just till dough clings together.

On a lightly floured surface, knead dough gently for 15 to 20 strokes. Roll dough into a 12x10-inch rectangle. Brush dough with the 1 tablespoon melted margarine or butter. Combine granulated sugar and cinnamon; sprinkle over dough. Top with chocolate pieces and raisins. Roll up from one of the long sides. Seal seams. Slice dough into 1-inch pieces. Place rolls, cut side down, in baking pan.

Bake in a 425° oven about 25 minutes or till golden. Immediately loosen sides and invert onto a serving plate. Serve warm. Makes 12.

Per serving: 242 calories, 3 g protein, 32 g carbohydrate, 12 g total fat (2 g saturated), 1 mg cholesterol, 115 mg sodium, 113 mg potassium.

Fruit 'n' Nut-Filled Sour Cream Coffee Cake

½ **cup chopped pecans**
½ **cup mixed dried fruit bits**
¼ **cup packed brown sugar**
1 **teaspoon ground cinnamon**
3 **cups all-purpose flour**
1 **tablespoon baking powder**
1 **teaspoon baking soda**
¼ **teaspoon salt**
1 **cup margarine *or* butter, softened**
1⅓ **cups granulated sugar**
1½ **cups dairy sour cream**
3 **eggs**
Sifted powdered sugar

For filling, in a mixing bowl combine pecans, fruit bits, brown sugar, and cinnamon; mix well. Set filling aside.

In a bowl combine flour, baking powder, baking soda, and salt. In a large bowl beat margarine or butter and granulated sugar with an electric mixer on medium to high speed till light and fluffy. Add sour cream; beat well. Add eggs, one at a time, beating well after each addition. Add dry ingredients; beat just till smooth.

Spoon *half* of the batter evenly into a greased and floured 10-inch fluted tube pan. Make a groove in the batter with the back of a spoon; sprinkle filling into groove. Carefully spoon remaining batter over filling, spreading evenly.

Bake in a 350° oven for 50 to 55 minutes or till a toothpick inserted near center comes out clean. Cool in pan for 10 minutes. Remove from pan and sprinkle with powdered sugar. Makes 16 servings.

Per serving: 353 calories, 5 g protein, 41 g carbohydrate, 20 g total fat (6 g saturated), 50 mg cholesterol, 249 mg sodium, 130 mg potassium.

BREADS

Puffed Oven Pancake

2 tablespoons margarine *or* butter
3 eggs
½ cup all-purpose flour
½ cup milk
1 teaspoon finely shredded orange peel
¼ teaspoon salt
¼ teaspoon vanilla
3 tablespoons chopped pecans *or* sliced almonds
Peach Butter
½ cup fresh red raspberries

Place margarine or butter in a 10-inch oven-proof skillet. Place in a 450° oven for 3 to 5 minutes or till margarine or butter melts.

In a bowl beat eggs with a rotary beater till combined. Add flour, milk, orange peel, salt, and vanilla. Beat till smooth. Immediately pour batter into the hot skillet. Sprinkle with nuts. Bake for 15 to 20 minutes or till puffed and well browned. Cut pancake into wedges. Serve with Peach Butter. Sprinkle each serving with raspberries. Makes 6 servings.

Peach Butter: In a medium bowl beat ⅓ cup softened *margarine or butter* with an electric mixer on medium speed till fluffy. Gradually beat in ¼ cup *peach preserves*. Chill till serving time. Makes about ½ cup.

Per serving with Peach Butter: 271 calories, 5 g protein, 20 g carbohydrate, 19 g total fat (4 g saturated), 108 mg cholesterol, 322 mg sodium, 120 mg potassium.

Apple-Cheddar Scones

1¾ cups all-purpose flour
1 tablespoon sugar
½ teaspoon baking powder
½ teaspoon baking soda
½ teaspoon ground cinnamon
¼ teaspoon salt
¼ cup margarine *or* butter
1 cup shredded sharp cheddar cheese
⅓ cup dried currants
1 beaten egg
½ cup applesauce
Milk

In a bowl combine flour, sugar, baking powder, baking soda, cinnamon, and salt. Cut in margarine or butter till mixture resembles coarse crumbs. Stir in cheese and currants.

Combine egg and applesauce; add to flour mixture. Stir just till moistened (dough will be sticky). On a lightly floured surface, knead dough gently 5 or 6 times. Pat dough into an 8-inch circle on an ungreased baking sheet. Cut into 12 wedges; separate wedges about 1 inch apart. Brush with milk. Bake in a 400° oven for 12 to 14 minutes or till lightly browned. Makes 12.

Per scones: 166 calories, 5 g protein, 20 g carbohydrate, 8 g total fat (3 g saturated), 28 mg cholesterol, 189 mg sodium, 79 mg potassium.

Basic Biscuits

2 **cups all-purpose flour**
1 **tablespoon baking powder**
2 **teaspoons sugar**
½ **teaspoon cream of tartar**
¼ **teaspoon salt**
½ **cup shortening, margarine,**
   or **butter**
⅔ **cup milk**

In a bowl stir together flour, baking powder, sugar, cream of tartar, and salt. **1 2** Cut in shortening, margarine, or butter till mixture resembles coarse crumbs. Make a well in the center; add milk all at once. **3** Stir just till dough clings together.

On a lightly floured surface, knead dough gently for 10 to 12 strokes. **4** Roll or pat dough to ½-inch thickness. **5** Cut with a 2½-inch biscuit cutter, dipping cutter into flour between cuts.

6 Transfer biscuits to a baking sheet. Bake in a 450° oven for 10 to 12 minutes or till golden. Serve warm. Makes 10.

Per biscuit: 188 calories, 3 g protein, 20 g carbohydrate, 11 g total fat (3 g saturated), 1 mg cholesterol, 67 mg sodium, 58 mg potassium.

1 Cut shortening into flour mixture with a pastry blender or two forks.

2 After cutting in shortening, the mixture should resemble coarse crumbs.

3 Stir liquid into dry ingredients with a fork till dough just holds together.

4 On a lightly floured surface, pat dough to ½ inch thickness.

5 Cut dough with a 2½-inch biscuit cutter. Dip cutter in flour between cuts to prevent sticking.

6 Using a metal spatula, carefully transfer cut biscuits to an ungreased baking sheet.

BREADS

Special Sweet Potato Biscuits

2 cups all-purpose flour
¼ cup sugar
1 tablespoon baking powder
¼ teaspoon salt
¼ teaspoon ground cinnamon
¼ cup margarine *or* butter
1 cup drained and mashed
   cooked sweet potato
⅓ cup half-and-half *or* light
   cream
   Sugar (optional)

In a mixing bowl combine flour, sugar, baking powder, salt, and cinnamon. Cut in margarine or butter till pieces resemble coarse crumbs. Add sweet potato and half-and-half or light cream all at once. Stir just till dough clings together.

On a lightly floured surface, knead dough gently for 10 to 12 strokes. Roll dough to ½-inch thickness. Cut with a 2½-inch biscuit cutter, dipping cutter into flour between cuts.

Transfer biscuits to a lightly greased baking sheet. Sprinkle tops with sugar, if desired. Bake in a 450° oven for 10 to 12 minutes or till golden brown. Makes 10 to 12.

Per biscuit: 190 calories, 3 g protein, 31 g carbohydrate, 6 g total fat (1 g saturated), 3 mg cholesterol, 120 mg sodium, 100 mg potassium.

Bacon-Herb Biscuits

2 cups all-purpose flour
1 tablespoon baking powder
1 teaspoon dried parsley
   flakes
½ teaspoon dry mustard
½ teaspoon dried basil or
   sage, crushed
⅛ teaspoon salt
⅓ cup shortening
¾ cup milk
6 slices bacon, crisp-cooked,
   drained, and crumbled

In a medium mixing bowl stir together flour, baking powder, parsley flakes, mustard, sage, and salt. Cut in shortening till mixture resembles coarse crumbs. Make a well in center; add milk and crumbled bacon all at once. Stir just till dough clings together.

On a lightly floured surface, knead dough gently for 10 to 12 strokes. Roll or pat dough to ½ inch thickness. Cut with a 2½-inch biscuit cutter, dipping cutter into flour between cuts.

Transfer biscuits to a baking sheet. Bake in a 450° oven for 10 to 13 minutes or till golden. Serve warm. Makes 8 to 10.

Per biscuit: 224 calories, 5 g protein, 24 g carbohydrate, 12 g total fat (3 g saturated), 6 mg cholesterol, 127 mg sodium, 95 mg potassium.

Cherry Scones

2½ cups all-purpose flour
¼ cup sugar
2 teaspoons baking powder
½ teaspoon baking soda
¼ teaspoon salt
⅓ cup margarine *or* butter
¾ cup dried cherries
2 teaspoons finely shredded
   orange peel
2 beaten eggs
½ cup vanilla yogurt

In a bowl combine flour, sugar, baking powder, baking soda, and salt. Cut in margarine or butter till mixture resembles coarse crumbs. Stir in dried cherries and orange peel.

Combine eggs and yogurt; add to flour mixture. Stir just till moistened (dough will be sticky). On a lightly floured surface, pat dough into a 12-inch circle. Cut into 16 wedges; place on a baking sheet. Brush lightly with *milk*. Bake in a 400° oven for 12 to 15 minutes or till lightly browned. Serve warm. Makes 16.

Per scone: 153 calories, 3 g protein, 23 g carbohydrate, 5 g total fat (1 g saturated), 27 mg cholesterol, 137 mg sodium, 49 mg potassium.

Cornmeal Pancakes

½ **cup all-purpose flour**
½ **cup cornmeal**
2 **teaspoons baking powder**
2 **teaspoons sugar**
¼ **teaspoon salt**
1 **beaten egg**
¾ **cup milk**
1 **tablespoon cooking oil**
½ **cup frozen whole kernel corn, thawed**
 Honey-Maple syrup

In a mixing bowl stir together flour, cornmeal, baking powder, sugar, and salt. In another mixing bowl combine egg, milk, and oil. Add to flour mixture all at once. **1** Stir mixture just till combined but still slightly lumpy. Fold in corn.

2 Pour about ¼ *cup* batter for *each* pancake onto a hot, lightly greased griddle or heavy skillet. **3** Cook till pancakes are golden brown, turning to cook second sides when pancakes have bubbly surfaces and slightly dry edges. Serve with Honey-Maple Syrup. Makes 8 to 10.

Honey-Maple Syrup: In a small saucepan combine ½ cup *maple syrup or maple-flavored syrup*, ¼ cup *honey*, 2 tablespoons *orange juice*, 1 tablespoon *margarine or butter*, and ¼ teaspoon ground *cinnamon*. Cook and stir over low heat till warm and margarine or butter melts. Store any remaining syrup in the refrigerator. Makes about 1 cup.

Per pancake with syrup: 209 calories, 3 g protein, 39 g carbohydrate, 5 g total fat (1 g saturated), 28 mg cholesterol, 110 mg sodium, 137 mg potassium.

1 Stir batter just till blended. Batter will be slightly lumpy.

2 Pour about ¼ cup batter for each pancake onto hot griddle. Leave enough space between pancakes to allow for expansion of batter during cooking.

3 Pancakes are ready to turn when tops are bubbly all over with a few broken bubbles. Edges will be slightly dry.

Aloha Waffles

1¾ cups all-purpose flour
½ cup toasted chopped
    macadamia nuts *or*
    toasted chopped almonds
1 tablespoon baking powder
¼ teaspoon salt
2 egg yolks
1½ cups milk
½ cup cooking oil
¼ cup unsweetened
    pineapple juice
2 egg whites
½ cup flaked coconut
    Cinnamon-Pineapple Sauce

In a mixing bowl combine flour, nuts, baking powder, and salt. In another bowl beat egg yolks slightly. Beat in milk, oil, and pineapple juice. Add egg yolk mixture to flour mixture all at once. Stir just till combined but still lumpy.

In a small bowl beat egg whites till stiff peaks form (tips stand straight). Gently fold beaten egg whites into flour and egg yolk mixture, leaving a few fluffs of egg white. *Do not overmix.*

Pour *1 to 1¼ cups* of the batter onto grids of a preheated, lightly greased waffle baker. Sprinkle about *1½ tablespoons* of coconut over batter. Close lid quickly; do not open during baking. Bake according to manufacturer's directions. When done, use a fork to lift waffle off grid. Repeat with remaining batter. Serve with Cinnamon-Pineapple Sauce. Makes 5 or 6 waffles.

Cinnamon-Pineapple Sauce: In a small saucepan combine 2 tablespoons *sugar*, 2 teaspoons *cornstarch*, and ¼ teaspoon ground *cinnamon*. Add one 15¼-ounce can *pineapple tidbits*. Cook and stir over medium heat till thickened and bubbly; cook and stir 2 minutes more. Add 1 tablespoon *margarine or butter*, stirring till melted. Serve warm. Makes about 1¾ cups.

Per serving with sauce: 635 calories, 11 g protein, 60 g carbohydrate, 41 g total fat (9 g saturated), 91 mg cholesterol, 243 mg sodium, 364 mg potassium.

Sausage and Cherry Crepes

1 pound bulk pork sausage
1½ cups milk
1 cup all-purpose flour
2 eggs
1 tablespoon cooking oil
¼ teaspoon salt
1 8-ounce carton dairy sour
    cream
1 20-ounce can cherry pie
    filling
1 teaspoon finely shredded
    orange peel
¼ cup orange juice

In a large skillet cook sausage till browned. Drain fat; keep warm.

For crepes, in a bowl combine milk, flour, eggs, oil, and salt. Beat with a rotary beater till well mixed. Heat a lightly greased 6-inch skillet. Remove from heat. Spoon in *2 tablespoons* batter; lift and tilt skillet to spread batter. Return to heat; brown on one side only. Invert pan over paper towels; remove crepe. Repeat with remaining batter, greasing skillet occasionally.

To assemble, spoon about *2 tablespoons* cooked sausage and *1 scant tablespoon* sour cream onto center of *each* of the 18 crepes. Fold bottom edge of crepe over filling, then fold in sides of crepe. Place crepes, seam side down, in a lightly greased 3-quart rectangular baking dish. Cover and bake in a 400° oven for 15 to 20 minutes or till heated through.

Meanwhile, for sauce, in a medium saucepan combine cherry pie filling, orange peel, and orange juice. Cook and stir till heated through. Serve sauce with crepes. Makes 9 servings.

Per serving: 322 calories, 10 g protein, 32 g carbohydrate, 17 g total fat (7 g saturated), 81 mg cholesterol, 415 mg sodium, 291 mg potassium.

CAKES

Lemon-Kissed White Chocolate Cake

Lemon-Kissed White Chocolate Cake

4 ounces white baking bar, coarsely chopped
½ cup boiling water
½ cup margarine *or* butter, softened
1¾ cups sugar
4 egg yolks
1 teaspoon vanilla
1 teaspoon finely shredded lemon peel
2 cups all-purpose flour
1½ teaspoons baking powder
½ teaspoon baking soda
1 cup buttermilk
4 egg whites
   Lemon Butter Cream Frosting

Grease and lightly flour three 9x1½-inch round baking pans; set aside.

Combine white baking bar and water in a small saucepan. Heat and stir constantly over low heat till baking bar melts; set aside to cool.

In a large mixing bowl beat margarine or butter with an electric mixer on medium-high speed for 30 seconds. Gradually add sugar, beating till well combined. Add egg yolks, one at a time, beating well after each addition. Stir in melted baking bar mixture, vanilla, and lemon peel.

Combine flour, baking powder, and baking soda. Add dry ingredients and buttermilk alternately to beaten mixture, mixing well after each addition.

Wash beaters. In another mixing bowl beat egg whites till stiff peaks form. Gently fold beaten egg whites into flour mixture. Pour batter into prepared pans.

Bake in a 350° oven about 25 minutes or till a wooden toothpick inserted in center comes out clean. Cool in pans on wire racks for 10 minutes. Loosen edges of cake from pans. Remove from pans. Cool thoroughly on racks.

Place one cake layer on a serving plate. Spread *½ cup* Lemon Butter Cream Frosting over top of cake layer. Repeat with second cake layer and another *½ cup* frosting. Top with third cake layer. Frost top and sides with remaining frosting. Makes 16 servings.

Lemon Butter Cream Frosting: In a mixing bowl beat ½ cup softened *margarine* or *butter* till fluffy. Gradually add 3 cups sifted *powdered sugar*, beating well. Slowly beat in ⅓ cup *lemon juice* (2 medium lemons) and 2 teaspoons *vanilla*. Slowly beat in another 3¾ cups sifted *powdered sugar*. Beat in additional sifted *powdered sugar* or *lemon juice*, if necessary, to make of spreading consistency.

Note: The third cake layer may be refrigerated while the first two bake: then bake as directed.

Per serving: 468 calories, 4 g protein, 81 g carbohydrate, 15 g total fat (4 g saturated), 54 mg cholesterol, 212 mg sodium, 91 mg potassium.

Yellow Cake

2¾ cups all-purpose flour
2½ teaspoons baking powder
½ teaspoon salt
½ cup margarine *or* butter
1¾ cups sugar
1½ teaspoons vanilla
2 eggs
1¼ cups milk

1 Grease and lightly flour two 8x1½-inch round cake pans; set aside. Combine flour, baking powder, and salt; set aside. In a large mixing bowl beat margarine or butter with an electric mixer on medium speed about 30 seconds. **2** Add sugar and vanilla; beat till well combined. Add eggs, one at a time, beating 1 minute after each addition. **3 4** Add dry ingredients and milk alternately to beaten mixture, beating after each addition. Pour batter into prepared pans.

5 Bake in a 375° oven for 30 to 35 minutes or till a toothpick inserted near center comes out clean. Cool in pans on wire racks for 10 minutes. **6** Loosen edges of cake from pans. Remove from pans. Cool thoroughly on racks. Frost as desired. Makes 12 servings.

Per serving (without frosting): 297 calories, 5 g protein, 50 g carbohydrate, 9 g total fat (2 g saturated), 37 mg cholesterol, 117 mg sodium, 83 mg potassium.

1 Grease and lightly flour cake pans, tilting and tapping the pan to distribute the flour evenly. Discard excess flour.

2 In a large bowl beat margarine or butter, sugar, and vanilla with an electric mixer on medium speed till well combined.

3 Add *one-third* of dry ingredients to sugar-egg mixture. Beat till thoroughly combined.

4 Add half of milk; beat till well combined. Add another *one-third* of dry ingredients, remaining milk and, finally, remaining dry ingredients.

5 To test for doneness, insert a toothpick near the center of the cake layer. When done, toothpick will come out clean.

6 Use a knife or spatula to loosen edges of cake from pans, then place a cooling rack atop cake. Invert and remove pan. Cool completely.

CAKES

Chocolate Raisin Cake

½ **cup chopped raisins**
¼ **cup orange juice**
2 **cups all-purpose flour**
½ **cup unsweetened cocoa**
    powder
2 **teaspoons baking powder**
½ **teaspoon baking soda**
¼ **teaspoon salt**
½ **cup shortening**
1¾ **cups sugar**
1 **teaspoon vanilla**
2 **eggs**
1¼ **cups milk**
    Chocolate-Orange Frosting

In a small bowl combine raisins and orange juice; let stand 15 minutes. Grease and lightly flour two 9x1½-inch round baking pans; set aside.

Stir together flour, cocoa powder, baking powder, baking soda, and salt; set aside. In a large mixing bowl beat shortening with an electric mixer on medium speed for 30 seconds. Add sugar and vanilla; beat till well combined. Add eggs, one at a time, beating well after each addition. Add dry ingredients and milk alternately to beaten mixture, beating on low speed after each addition just till combined. Add raisin mixture; beat on low speed just till combined.

Pour batter into prepared pans. Bake in a 350° oven for 30 to 35 minutes or till a toothpick inserted near center comes out clean. Cool in pans on wire racks for 10 minutes. Loosen edges of cake from pans. Remove from pans. Cool thoroughly on racks. Frost with Chocolate-Orange Frosting. Makes 12 servings.

Chocolate-Orange Frosting: In a medium mixing bowl beat ⅓ cup *margarine or butter* with an electric mixer on medium speed till fluffy. Gradually beat in 2 cups sifted *powdered sugar* and ½ cup *unsweetened cocoa powder*. Slowly beat in ¼ cup *orange juice* and 1 teaspoon *vanilla*. Gradually beat in an additional 2 cups *sifted powdered sugar*. Beat in additional *orange juice*, if necessary, to make of spreading consistency.

Per serving: 514 calories, 6 g protein, 87 g carbohydrate, 17 g total fat (4 g saturated), 37 mg cholesterol, 166 mg sodium, 141 mg potassium.

Buttermilk White Cake

2½ **cups all-purpose flour**
1 **teaspoon baking powder**
½ **teaspoon baking soda**
⅛ **teaspoon salt**
½ **cup shortening, margarine,**
    or **butter**
2 **cups sugar**
1 **teaspoon vanilla**
1½ **cups buttermilk** *or*
    sour milk
4 **egg whites**

Grease and lightly flour two 9x1½-inch round baking pans; set aside.

Combine flour, baking powder, baking soda, and salt. In a mixer bowl beat shortening, margarine, or butter with an electric mixer on medium speed about 30 seconds. Add sugar and vanilla and beat till fluffy. Add dry ingredients and buttermilk or sour milk alternately to beaten mixture, beating on low speed after each addition.

Wash beaters. In another mixing bowl beat egg whites till stiff peaks form. Gently fold beaten egg whites into flour mixture. Pour batter into prepared pans.

Bake in a 350° oven for 30 to 35 minutes or till a toothpick inserted near the center comes out clean. Cool in pans on wire racks for 10 minutes. Loosen edges of cake from pans. Remove from pans. Cool thoroughly on wire racks. Frost as desired. Makes 12 servings.

Per serving (without frosting): 310 calories, 5 g protein, 53 g carbohydrate, 9 g total fat (2 g saturated), 1 mg cholesterol, 124 mg sodium, 89 mg potassium.

Choco-Peanut Cupcakes

- **2 3-ounce packages cream cheese, softened**
- **3 tablespoons sugar**
- **1 egg yolk**
- **½ cup peanut butter-flavored pieces**
- **1½ cups all-purpose flour**
- **1 cup sugar**
- **¼ cup unsweetened cocoa powder**
- **1 teaspoon baking soda**
- **¼ teaspoon salt**
- **1 cup water**
- **⅓ cup shortening**
- **1 teaspoon vanilla**
- **¼ cup sugar**
- **⅓ cup chopped unsalted peanuts**

In a medium mixing bowl beat cream cheese, the 3 tablespoons sugar, and the egg yolk with an electric mixer on medium speed till smooth. Stir in peanut butter-flavored pieces. Set cream cheese mixture aside.

Combine flour, the 1 cup sugar, cocoa powder, baking soda, and salt. Add water, shortening, and vanilla. Beat with an electric mixer on low speed till combined. Beat on high speed for 2 minutes.

Line muffin pan with paper bake cups. **1** Fill paper bake cups about ½ full with batter. **2** Top each with about *1 tablespoon* of the cream cheese mixture. **3** Sprinkle with the ¼ cup sugar and the chopped peanuts.

Bake in a 350° oven for 25 to 30 minutes or till a toothpick inserted in chocolate portion comes out clean. Cool thorougly on wire racks. Makes 18 cupcakes.

Per cupcakes: 209 calories, 3 g protein, 27 g carbohydrate, 10 g total fat (5 g saturated), 23 mg cholesterol, 125 mg sodium, 40 mg potassium.

1 Spoon batter into paper-lined muffin cups, filling ½ full.

2 Usse a spoon to place about 1 tablespoon of the cream cheese filling atop batter.

3 Sprinkle sugar-peanut mixture evenly over each cupcake.

CAKES

Feathery Fudge Cake

3 ounces unsweetened
    chocolate, cut up
2 cups all-purpose flour
1¼ teaspoons baking soda
¼ teaspoon salt
⅔ cup margarine *or* butter
1¾ cups sugar
1 teaspoon vanilla
2 eggs
1¼ cups cold water
4¾ cups sifted powered sugar
½ cup unsweetened cocoa
    powder
½ cup margarine *or* butter,
    softened
⅓ cup boiling water
1 teaspoon vanilla

Grease and lightly flour two 9x1½-inch round baking pans; set aside.

In a small saucepan melt chocolate over low heat, stirring frequently. Remove from heat and let cool. Combine flour, baking soda, and salt; set aside.

In a large mixing bowl beat margarine or butter with an electric mixer on medium speed for 30 seconds. Add sugar and vanilla; beat till well combined. Add eggs, one at a time, beating 1 minute after each addition. Blend in cooled chocolate. Add dry ingredients and cold water alternately to beaten mixture, beating after each addition just till combined. Pour batter into prepared pans. Bake in a 350° oven for 30 to 35 minutes or till a toothpick inserted near the center comes out clean. Cool in pans on wire racks for 10 minutes. Loosen edges of cake from pans. Remove from pans. Cool thoroughly on racks.

For frosting, mix powdered sugar and cocoa. Add margarine, boiling water, and vanilla. Beat with an electric mixer on low speed till combined. Beat 1 minute on medium speed. Cool 20 to 30 minutes or till of spreading consistency. Frost tops and sides of cake. Serves 12.

Per serving: 558 calories, 5 g protein, 87 g carbohydrate, 23 g total fat (5 g saturated), 35 mg cholesterol, 390 mg sodium, 103 mg potassium.

Peanut Butter and Jelly Cake

2 cups all-purpose flour
1 tablespoon baking powder
¼ teaspoon salt
¾ cup margarine *or* butter,
    softened
1⅓ cups sugar
1 teaspoon vanilla
2 eggs
1 cup milk
1 cup peanut butter-flavored
    pieces
    Peanut Butter Frosting
⅓ cup currant jelly *or*
    strawberry jelly, melted
    and cooled slightly
¼ cup chopped unsalted
    peanuts

Grease and lightly flour two 9x1½-inch round baking pans; set aside.

Combine flour, baking powder, and salt; set aside. In a mixing bowl beat margarine or butter with an electric mixer on medium speed for 30 seconds. Add sugar and vanilla; beat till light and fluffy. Add eggs, one at a time, beating well after each addition.

Add dry ingredients and milk alternately to beaten mixture, beating on low speed till just combined. Stir in peanut butter-flavored pieces.

Pour batter into prepared pans. Bake in a 350° oven for 30 to 35 minutes or till a toothpick inserted near the center comes out clean. Cool in pans on wire racks for 10 minutes. Loosen edges of cake from pans. Remove from pans. Cool thoroughly on racks.

Frost with Peanut Butter Frosting. Drizzle melted jelly over the top of the frosted cake. Garnish with chopped peanuts. Makes 16 servings.

Peanut Butter Frosting: In a bowl beat ⅓ cup *creamy peanut butter* till fluffy. Gradually add 2 cups sifted *powdered sugar*, beating well. Slowly beat in ¼ cup *milk* and 2 teaspoons *vanilla*. Slowly beat in an additional 2½ cups sifted *powdered sugar*. Beat in additional *milk*, if necessary, to make of spreading consistency.

Per serving: 440 calories, 7 g protein, 68 g carbohydrate, 17 g total fat (4 g saturated), 28 mg cholesterol, 208 mg sodium, 171 mg potassium.

Banana-Pecan Cake with Browned Butter Frosting and Orange-Spice Pound Cake

Orange-Spice Pound Cake

1 cup butter
6 eggs
1 8-ounce carton low-fat vanilla yogurt
3 cups all-purpose flour
½ teaspoon salt
½ teaspoon ground cinnamon
¼ teaspoon baking soda
¼ teaspoon ground nutmeg
¼ teaspoon ground allspice
2 cups sugar
1 tablespoon finely shredded orange peel

Allow butter, eggs, and yogurt to stand at room temperature for 30 minutes. In a mixing bowl combine flour, salt, cinnamon, baking soda, nutmeg, and allspice; set aside.

In a large mixing bowl beat butter with an electric mixer on medium to high speed for 30 seconds. Gradually add sugar, beating about 10 minutes or till very light and fluffy. Add eggs, one at a time, beating 1 minute after each addition, scraping bowl often. Gradually add dry ingredients and yogurt alternately to butter mixture, beating on low speed just till combined. Stir in orange peel.

Pour batter into a greased and floured 10-inch tube pan. Bake in a 325° oven for 80 to 90 minutes or till a toothpick inserted near center comes out clean. Cool in pan on wire rack for 15 minutes. Loosen edges of cake from pan. Remove from pan. Cool thoroughly on wire rack. Makes 18 servings.

Per serving: 279 calories, 5 g protein, 38 g carbohydrate, 12 g total fat (7 g saturated), 99 mg cholesterol, 210 mg sodium, 74 mg potassium.

CAKES

Apple Cake

3 cups all-purpose flour
1 teaspoon baking powder
1 teaspoon baking soda
1 teaspoon ground cinnamon
¼ teaspoon ground allspice
¼ teaspoon salt
1 cup granulated sugar
1 cup packed brown sugar
1 cup cooking oil
2 beaten eggs
1 tablespoon vanilla
3 cups peeled, chopped apples
1 cup toasted chopped pecans
2 teaspoons finely shredded lemon peel
Sifted powdered sugar

In a bowl combine flour, baking powder, baking soda, cinnamon, allspice, and salt; set aside. In a mixing bowl combine granulated sugar, brown sugar, oil, eggs, and vanilla. Beat with an electric mixer on medium speed for 2 minutes. Add flour mixture and beat on low speed just till combined. Fold in apples, pecans, and lemon peel.

Pour batter into a greased and floured 10-inch tube pan. Bake in a 350° oven about 1 hour or till a toothpick inserted near the center comes out clean. Cool in pan on a wire rack for 10 minutes. Remove from pan. Cool thoroughly on rack. Sprinkle with powdered sugar. Store in refrigerator. Makes 12 servings.

Per serving: 495 calories, 5 g protein, 64 g carbohydrate, 25 g total fat (3 g saturated), 36 mg cholesterol, 65 mg sodium, 167 mg potassium.

Banana-Pecan Cake with Browned Butter Frosting

2 cups all-purpose flour
1 teaspoon baking powder
1 teaspoon baking soda
¼ teaspoon salt
½ cup margarine or butter, softened
1½ cups granulated sugar
1 teaspoon vanilla
2 eggs
1 8-ounce carton dairy sour cream
1 cup mashed ripe banana
¾ cup chopped pecans
⅓ cup margarine or butter
4 to 4½ cups sifted powdered sugar
¼ cup milk
1½ teaspoons vanilla

Combine flour, baking powder, baking soda, and salt. Set aside.

In a large mixing bowl beat the ½ cup margarine or butter with an electric mixer on medium-high speed for 30 seconds. Add granulated sugar and the 1 teaspoon vanilla, beating till combined. Add eggs, one at a time, beating well after each addition. Add dry ingredients and sour cream alternately to beaten mixture, beating on medium-low speed after each addition just till combined. Stir in mashed banana and pecans.

Pour batter into a greased 13x9x2-inch baking pan. Bake in a 350° oven for 30 to 35 minutes or till a toothpick inserted near the center comes out clean. Cool thoroughly on a wire rack.

Meanwhile, for frosting, in a small saucepan cook the ⅓ cup margarine or butter over medium heat for 5 to 8 minutes or till lightly browned. In a mixing bowl combine browned margarine or butter and *2 cups* of the powdered sugar; beat well. Slowly beat in milk and the 1½ teaspoons vanilla. Slowly beat in enough of the remaining powdered sugar to make frosting of spreading consistency. Frost top of cooled cake. Makes 12 servings.

Per serving: 551 calories, 5 g protein, 85 g carbohydrate, 23 g total fat (6 g saturated), 44 mg cholesterol, 287 mg sodium, 271 mg potassium.

Pumpkin Cake with Lemon Drizzle

1½ **cups all-purpose flour**
1 **teaspoon ground
    cinnamon**
¾ **teaspoon baking powder**
½ **teaspoon baking soda**
½ **teaspoon ground allspice**
¼ **teaspoon ground nutmeg**
¼ **teaspoon salt**
½ **cup margarine *or* butter**
1 **cup packed brown sugar**
1 **teaspoon vanilla**
2 **eggs**
1 **cup canned pumpkin**
½ **cup very finely chopped
    walnuts**
  Lemon Drizzle

Combine flour, cinnamon, baking powder, baking soda, allspice, nutmeg, and salt; set aside. In a large mixing bowl beat margarine or butter with an electric mixer on medium speed for 30 seconds. Add brown sugar and vanilla and continue beating 2 minutes or till light and fluffy. Add eggs, one at a time, beating well after each addition. With the electric mixer on low speed beat in about *half* of the dry ingredients. Beat in pumpkin till combined. Beat in remaining dry ingredients just till combined. Stir in walnuts.

Spread batter into a greased and floured 8x8x2-inch baking pan. Bake in a 350° oven for 30 to 35 minutes or till a toothpick inserted near the center comes out clean. Cool in pan on a wire rack. Serve warm with Lemon Drizzle. Makes 9 servings.

Lemon Drizzle: Stir together 1 cup sifted *powdered sugar* and enough *lemon juice* (1 to 2 tablespoons) to make of drizzling consistency.

Per serving: 368 calories, 5 g protein, 54 g carbohydrate, 16 g total fat (3 g saturated), 47 mg cholesterol, 262 mg sodium, 219 mg potassium.

Black Russian Cake

⅔ **cup margarine *or* butter**
1¾ **cups granulated sugar**
1 **teaspoon vanilla**
2 **eggs**
3 **ounces unsweetened
    chocolate, melted and
    cooled**
⅓ **cup coffee liqueur**
2 **cups all-purpose flour**
1 **teaspoon baking powder**
¾ **teaspoon baking soda**
¼ **teaspoon salt**
1 **cup milk**
1 **cup sifted powdered sugar**
2 **tablespoons unsweetened
    cocoa powder**
1 **tablespoon coffee liqueur**
½ **teaspoon vanilla**
  Milk

In a large mixing bowl beat margarine or butter with an electric mixer on medium speed for 30 seconds. Gradually add granulated sugar and the 1 teaspoon vanilla, beating till light and fluffy. Add eggs, one at a time, beating well after each addition. Beat in the melted and cooled chocolate and ⅓ cup coffee liqueur.

Combine flour, baking powder, baking soda, and salt. Add dry ingredients and milk alternately to beaten mixture, beating after each addition.

Pour batter into a greased and floured 10-inch fluted tube pan. Bake in a 350° oven for 45 to 50 minutes or till a toothpick inserted near the center comes out clean. Cool in pan on a wire rack for 10 minutes. Loosen edges of cake from pan. Remove from pan. Cool thoroughly on wire rack.

Meanwhile, for glaze, combine powdered sugar, cocoa powder, the 1 tablespoon coffee liqueur, and the ½ teaspoon vanilla. Stir in enough milk to make of drizzling consistency. Spoon glaze over cake. Makes 18 servings.

Per serving: 259 calories, 3 g protein, 39 g carbohydrate, 10 g total fat (3 g saturated), 25 mg cholesterol, 175 mg sodium, 89 mg potassium.

Apricot Upside-Down Cake

¼ cup margarine *or* butter,
    melted
½ cup packed brown sugar
1 tablespoon water
1 16-ounce can apricot
    halves, drained
¼ cup sliced almonds
1½ cups all-purpose flour
1½ teaspoons baking powder
½ teaspoon ground
    cinnamon
¼ teaspoon ground nutmeg
¼ teaspoon salt
⅓ cup margarine *or* butter,
    softened
⅔ cup granulated sugar
1 teaspoon vanilla
2 eggs
¾ cup milk

In a small bowl combine the ¼ cup melted margarine or butter, brown sugar, and water; spread mixture evenly in a 9x1½-inch round baking pan. Arrange apricots and almonds evenly over sugar mixture.

Stir together flour, baking powder, cinnamon, nutmeg, and salt. In a mixing bowl beat the ⅓ cup softened margarine or butter with an electric mixer on medium speed for 30 seconds. Add granulated sugar and vanilla; beat till fluffy. Add eggs, one at a time, beating well after each addition. Add dry ingredients and milk alternately to beaten mixture, beating on low speed after each addition till just combined. Spoon batter carefully over apricots in the prepared pan.

Bake in a 350° oven about 40 minutes or till a toothpick inserted near the center comes out clean. Cool in pan on a wire rack for 5 minutes. Loosen edges of cake from pan; invert onto a serving plate. Serve warm. Makes 8 servings.

Per serving: 433 calories, 7 g protein, 63 g carbohydrate, 19 g total fat (3 g saturated), 55 mg cholesterol, 260 mg sodium, 267 mg potassium.

Golden Fruitcake

1½ cups all-purpose flour
1 teaspoon ground
    cinnamon
½ teaspoon ground allspice
½ teaspoon baking powder
¼ teaspoon baking soda
¼ teaspoon ground nutmeg
1 cup snipped dried peaches
1 cup chopped pecans
½ cup light raisins
2 eggs
½ cup packed brown sugar
½ cup peach nectar
⅓ cup margarine *or* butter,
    melted
2 tablespoons honey
    Peach brandy *or* peach
    nectar

In a bowl combine flour, cinnamon, allspice, baking powder, baking soda, and nutmeg. Add dried peaches, pecans, and raisins; mix well. In another mixing bowl beat eggs; stir in brown sugar, peach nectar, margarine or butter, and honey till combined. Stir fruit mixture into egg mixture. Pour batter into a greased and floured 8x4x2-inch loaf pan.

Bake in a 300° oven for 1¼ to 1½ hours or till a toothpick inserted near the center comes out clean. Cool thoroughly in pan on a wire rack. Loosen edges of cake from pan. Remove from pan.

Wrap cake in peach brandy- or peach nectar-soaked 100% cotton cheesecloth. Overwrap with foil. Store in the refrigerator for 2 to 8 weeks to mellow flavors. Remoisten cheesecloth about once a week, or as needed. Makes 16 servings.

Per serving: 219 calories, 3 g protein, 31 g carbohydrate, 9 g total fat (1 g saturated), 27 mg cholesterol, 70 mg sodium, 213 mg potassium.

Angel Cake

1½ **cups egg whites (10 to 12 large)**
1½ **cups sifted powdered sugar**
 1 **cup sifted cake flour** *or* **sifted all-purpose flour**
1½ **teaspoons cream of tartar**
 1 **teaspoon vanilla**
 1 **cup sugar**

Bring egg whites to room temperature. Sift powdered sugar and flour together 3 times; set aside. **1** In a large bowl beat egg whites, cream of tartar, and vanilla with an electric mixer on medium speed till soft peaks form (tips curl). **2** Gradually add sugar, about 2 tablespoons at a time, beating till stiff peaks form (tips stand straight).

3 4 Sift about *one-fourth* of the flour mixture over beaten egg whites; fold in gently. (If bowl is too full, transfer to a larger bowl.) Repeat, folding in remaining flour mixture by fourths.

Pour into an ungreased 10-inch tube pan. **5** Gently cut through batter with a knife or narrow metal spatula. Bake on the lowest rack in a 350° oven for 40 to 45 minutes or till top springs back when lightly touched. **6** Immediately invert cake (leave in pan); cool thoroughly. Loosen sides of cake from pan; remove cake. Makes 12 servings.

Per serving: 160 calories, 4 g protein, 37 g carbohydrate, 0 g total fat (0 g saturated), 0 mg cholesterol, 46 mg sodium, 65 mg potassium.

1 Beat egg whites, cream of tartar, vanilla, and salt with an electric mixer till soft peaks form. The peak will curl when beaters are lifted from the egg white mixture.

2 Gradually add sugar, 2 tablespoons at a time, and continue beating till stiff peaks form. The peak will stand straight up when beaters are lifted from the mixture.

3 Sift *one-fourth* of the flour mixture over beaten egg whites.

4 Gently fold in flour mixture with a rubber spatula. Cut down through the mixture, scrape across bottom of bowl, and bring spatula up and over mixture close to the surface.

5 Gently cut through the cake batter with a knife or narrow metal spatula to remove air bubbles.

6 Turn cake upside down after removing it from the oven. Let it cool completely in that position to prevent the cake from losing volume.

Toasted Pecan Sponge Cake

6 **egg yolks**
½ **cup water**
1 **teaspoon vanilla**
½ **cup granulated sugar**
½ **cup packed brown sugar**
1¼ **cups all-purpose flour**
¼ **cup toasted very finely
     chopped pecans**
6 **egg whites**
½ **teaspoon cream of tartar**
½ **cup granulated sugar**
  Browned Butter Icing
  Pecan halves (optional)

In a medium mixing bowl beat egg yolks with an electric mixer on high speed about 5 minutes or till thick and lemon colored. Add water and vanilla. Beat on low speed till combined. Gradually beat in ½ cup granulated sugar and brown sugar on low speed. Increase to medium speed; beat till mixture thickens slightly and doubles in volume (about 5 minutes total).

Sprinkle ¼ *cup* of the flour and the chopped pecans over yolk mixture; fold in till combined. Repeat with remaining flour, ¼ cup at a time. Set yolk mixture aside.

Thoroughly wash beaters. In a large mixing bowl beat egg whites and cream of tartar on medium speed till soft peaks form. Gradually add ½ cup granulated sugar, beating on high speed till stiff peaks form.

Fold about *1 cup* of the beaten egg white mixture into the yolk mixture; fold yolk mixture into remaining egg white mixture. Pour into an ungreased 10-inch tube pan.

Bake in a 325° oven for 55 to 60 minutes or till cake springs back when lightly touched near center. Immediately invert cake (leave in pan); cool thoroughly. Loosen sides of cake from pan; remove cake from pan. Drizzle with Browned Butter Icing. Garnish with pecan halves, if desired. Makes 12 servings.

Browned Butter Icing: In a small saucepan heat ¼ cup *butter* (not margarine) over medium-low heat for 10 to 12 minutes or till lightly browned. Remove from heat. Stir in 2 cups sifted *powdered sugar* and enough *boiling water* (1 to 2 tablespoons) to make icing of drizzling consistency. Drizzle over cooled cake immediately. If icing becomes grainy, soften with a few drops of hot water.

Per serving: 294 calories, 5 g protein, 52 g carbohydrate, 8 g total fat (3 g saturated), 117 mg cholesterol, 74 mg sodium, 93 mg potassium.

Tropical Cream Cake Roll

½ **cup all-purpose flour**
½ **cup finely chopped**
    macadamia nuts *or*
    toasted almonds
4 **egg yolks**
½ **teaspoon vanilla**
⅔ **cup sugar**
4 **egg whites**
    Sifted powdered sugar
    Tropical Cream Filling
½ **cup whipping cream,**
    whipped
2 **tablespoons chopped**
    macadamia nuts *or*
    toasted coconut

Combine flour and ½ cup macadamia nuts or almonds; set aside. In a medium mixing bowl beat egg yolks and vanilla with an electric mixer on high speed for 5 minutes or till thick and lemon colored. Gradually add *half* of the sugar, beating on high speed till sugar is nearly dissolved.

Thoroughly wash beaters. In a large mixing bowl beat egg whites on medium speed till soft peaks form. Gradually add remaining sugar, beating till stiff peaks form. Fold yolk mixture into beaten egg whites. Sprinkle flour mixture over the egg mixture; fold in gently just till combined.

Spread batter evenly into a greased and floured 15x10x1-inch jelly-roll pan. Bake in a 375° oven for 12 to 15 minutes or till cake springs back when lightly touched near center.

1 **2** Immediately loosen edges of cake from pan and turn cake out onto a towel sprinkled with powdered sugar. **3** Roll up towel and cake, jellyroll style, starting from one of the short sides. Cool on a rack. **4** Unroll cake. Spread cake with Tropical Cream Filling to within 1 inch of edges. **5** Roll up cake. Spoon or pipe whipped cream lengthwise down center of cake. Sprinkle with 2 tablespoons chopped macadamia nuts or toasted coconut. Store in refrigerator. Makes 10 servings.

Tropical Cream Filling: In a small chilled mixing bowl beat 1 cup *whipping cream* and 3 tablespoons *powdered sugar* till stiff peaks form. Fold in one 8-ounce can well-drained *crushed pineapple* and ½ cup toasted *coconut*.

Per serving: 328 calories, 5 g protein, 28 g carbohydrate, 23 g total fat (10 g saturated), 134 mg cholesterol, 47 mg sodium, 133 mg potassium.

1 Using a narrow spatula, loosen edges of the warm cake from pan.

2 Invert pan over a towel sprinkled with powdered sugar and shake gently to remove cake.

3 Starting at the narrow end, roll the cake and towel together.

Tropical Cream Cake Roll (continued)

4 Carefully unroll cooled cake and towel. Spread cream filling over cake, leaving a 1-inch border around edges.

5 Again starting at short side, roll up cake and filling.

Chocolate Angel Cake with Coffee Liqueur Glaze

1½ **cups egg whites**
 (10 to 12 large)
1½ **cups sifted powdered sugar**
 1 **cup sifted cake flour or**
 sifted all-purpose flour
 ¼ **cup unsweetened cocoa**
 powder
1½ **teaspoons cream of tartar**
 1 **teaspoon vanilla**
 1 **cup granulated sugar**
 1 **cup sifted powdered sugar**
 ¼ **teaspoon vanilla**
 2 **tablespoon Coffee liqueur**

In a very large mixing bowl bring egg whites to room temperature. Meanwhile, sift the 1½ cups powdered sugar, flour, and cocoa powder together 3 times; set aside.

Add cream of tartar and the 1 teaspoon vanilla to egg whites; beat with an electric mixer on medium to high speed till soft peaks form (tips curl). Gradually add granulated sugar, about 2 tablespoons at a time, beating on medium to high speed till stiff peaks form (tips stand straight).

Sift about *one-fourth* of the flour mixture over the beaten egg whites; fold in gently. Repeat sifting and folding in of the remaining flour mixture, using one-fourth of the flour mixture each time.

Gently pour the batter evenly into an ungreased 10-inch tube pan. Gently cut through the cake batter with a knife or narrow metal spatula. Bake on the lowest rack in a 350° oven for 40 to 45 minutes or till the top springs back when lightly touched.

Immediately invert the cake (leave in the pan) and cool thoroughly. Using a narrow metal spatula, loosen the sides of the cake from the pan. Remove the cake from the pan.

For glaze, stir together the 1 cup powdered sugar, the ¼ teaspoon vanilla, and enough of the coffee liqueur (about 2 tablespoons), 1 teaspoon at a time, to make of drizzling consistency. Drizzle over top of cake. Makes 12 servings.

Per serving: 206 calories, 4 g protein, 47 g carbohydrate, 0 g total fat (0 g saturated), 0 mg cholesterol, 47 mg sodium, 66 mg potassium.

COOKIES

Double Nut Bars, Party Sandwich Cookies, Chocolate-Cherry Pinwheels, Marmalade Thumbprints

COOKIES

Marmalade Thumbprints

⅔ **cup margarine *or* butter**
½ **cup sugar**
2 **teaspoons finely shredded orange peel**
2 **egg yolks**
1 **teaspoon vanilla**
1½ **cups all-purpose flour**
2 **slightly beaten egg whites**
1 **cup finely chopped toasted almonds**
⅓ **to ½ cup orange marmalade**

In a large mixing bowl beat margarine or butter with an electric mixer on medium to high speed for 30 seconds. Add the sugar and orange peel and beat till thoroughly combined. Beat in egg yolks and vanilla till combined. Beat in as much of the flour as you can with the mixer. Stir in any remaining flour with a wooden spoon.

Shape dough into 1-inch balls. Roll balls in egg whites; then in almonds. Place 1 inch apart on a greased cookie sheet. Press the center with your thumb to form an indentation. Bake in a 375° oven for 10 to 12 minutes or till edges are lightly browned. Remove cookies from cookie sheet; cool on wire racks. Just before serving fill centers with orange marmalade. Makes about 42.

Note: Strawberry jam, raspberry jam, and currant jelly make equally delicious fillings for these rich cookies.

Per cookie: 78 calories, 1 g protein, 8 g carbohydrate, 5 g total fat (1 g saturated), 10 mg cholesterol, 38 mg sodium, 33 mg potassium.

Old-Fashioned Sugar Cookies

1 **cup margarine *or* butter, softened**
1½ **cups sugar**
2 **eggs**
2 **teaspoons cream of tartar**
1 **teaspoon baking soda**
¼ **teaspoon salt**
1 **teaspoon vanilla**
2¾ **cups all-purpose flour**
¼ **to ⅓ cup sugar**

In a large mixing bowl beat the margarine or butter with an electric mixer on medium to high speed for 30 seconds. Add the 1½ cups sugar; beat till combined. Beat in eggs, cream of tartar, baking soda, salt, and vanilla till combined. Beat in as much of the flour as you can with the mixer. Stir in any remaining flour with a wooden spoon. Cover and chill for 2 to 3 hours.

Shape dough into 1-inch balls. Roll balls in the ¼ to ⅓ cup sugar. Place 2 inches apart on an ungreased cookie sheet. Bake in a 375° oven for 7 to 8 minutes or till lightly browned. Cool. Makes about 60.

Per cookie: 70 calories, 1 g protein, 10 g carbohydrate, 3 g total fat (1 g saturated), 7 mg cholesterol, 61 mg sodium, 13 mg potassium.

Rolled Sugar Cookies

⅓ **cup margarine *or* butter**
⅓ **cup shortening**
¾ **cup sugar**
1 **teaspoon baking powder**
  Dash salt
1 **egg**
1 **tablespoon milk**
1 **teaspoon vanilla**
2 **cups all-purpose flour**

In a mixing bowl beat the margarine or butter and shortening with an electric mixer on medium to high speed for 30 seconds. Add sugar, baking powder, and salt and beat till combined. Beat in egg, milk, and vanilla. Beat in as much of the flour as you can with the mixer. Stir in any remaining flour with a wooden spoon. Divide dough in half. Cover and chill for 3 hours.

1 On a lightly floured surface, roll *half* of the dough at a time to ⅛-inch thickness. **2** Cut into desired shapes with a 2½-inch cookie cutter. **3** Place on an ungreased cookie sheet.

Bake in a 375° oven for 7 to 8 minutes or till edges are firm and bottoms are very lightly browned. Cool cookies on wire racks. Makes 36 to 40.

Per cookie: 73 calories, 1 g protein, 9 g carbohydrate, 4 g total fat (1 g saturated), 6 mg cholesterol, 26 mg sodium, 10 mg potassium.

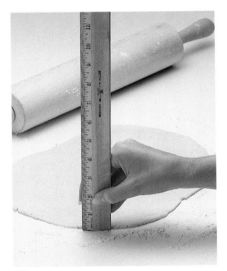

1 On a floured surface, roll out chilled dough from center to edges. Use a ruler to measure thickness of dough.

2 Cut dough into desired shapes using floured cookie cutters. Place cutouts as close together as possible to minimize rerolling dough.

3 Remove cut cookies from floured surface with a pancake turner or wide metal spatula. Place on an ungreased cookie sheet.

Triple Chocolate Cookies

½ **cup margarine *or* butter**
½ **cup granulated sugar**
½ **cup packed brown sugar**
½ **teaspoon baking soda**
1 **egg**
¼ **cup buttermilk**
1 **teaspoon vanilla**
½ **cup unsweetened cocoa**
    powder
2 **cups all-purpose flour**
1 **6-ounce package (1 cup)**
    semisweet chocolate
    pieces
½ **cup chopped nuts**
4 **ounces white baking bar**
4 **teaspoons shortening**

In a large mixing bowl beat margarine or butter with an electric mixer on medium to high speed for 30 seconds. Add granulated sugar, brown sugar, and baking soda; beat till combined. Beat in egg, buttermilk, and vanilla. Beat in cocoa powder and as much of the flour as you can with the mixer. Stir in any remaining flour with a wooden spoon. Stir in chocolate pieces and nuts.

Drop by rounded teaspoons 2 inches apart onto a lightly greased cookie sheet. Bake in a 375° oven about 10 minutes or till cookies look set. Remove cookies from cookie sheet. Cool cookies on a wire rack.

In a small heavy saucepan combine white baking bar and shortening. Cook over low heat till smooth, stirring constantly. Drizzle over cooled cookies. Makes about 50.

Per cookie: 93 calories, 1 g protein, 12 g carbohydrate, 5 g total fat (1 g saturated), 4 mg cholesterol, 39 mg sodium, 40 mg potassium.

Milk Chocolate-Coconut Chippers

½ **cup margarine *or* butter**
½ **cup shortening**
¾ **cup granulated sugar**
¾ **cup packed brown sugar**
½ **teaspoon baking soda**
2 **eggs**
1 **teaspoon vanilla**
2½ **cups all-purpose flour**
1 **6-ounce package (1 cup)**
    milk chocolate pieces
1 **cup flaked coconut**
1 **cup chopped pecans**

In a large mixing bowl beat margarine or butter and shortening with an electric mixer on medium to high speed for 30 seconds. Add granulated sugar, brown sugar, and baking soda; beat till combined. Beat in eggs and vanilla. Beat in as much of the flour as you can with the mixer. Stir in any remaining flour with a wooden spoon. Stir in milk chocolate pieces, coconut, and pecans.

Drop dough by rounded teaspoons 2 inches apart onto an ungreased cookie sheet. Bake in a 375° oven for 8 to 10 minutes or till edges are light brown. Remove cookies from cookie sheet; cool on a wire rack. Makes about 60.

Per cookie: 100 calories, 1 g protein, 11 g carbohydrate, 6 g total fat (1 g saturated), 8 mg cholesterol, 34 mg sodium, 38 mg potassium.

Chewy Orange Drops

- **1 cup snipped orange slice-shaped jelly candies**
- **½ cup coconut**
- **½ cup margarine *or* butter**
- **½ cup sugar**
- **⅛ teaspoon baking soda**
- **1 egg**
- **1 teaspoon vanilla**
- **1¼ cups all-purpose flour**
- **2 teaspoons finely shredded orange peel**

1 Use kitchen shears to snip the jelly candies into tiny pieces; set aside. **2 3** Toast coconut; set aside. **4** In a large mixing bowl beat margarine or butter with an electric mixer on medium to high speed for 30 seconds. Add sugar and baking soda; beat till combined. Beat in egg and vanilla. Beat in as much of the flour as you can with the mixer. Stir in any remaining flour with a wooden spoon. **5** Stir in jelly candies, coconut, and orange peel.

6 Drop by rounded teaspoons 2 inches apart onto an ungreased cookie sheet. Bake in a 375° oven for 8 to 10 minutes or till edges are golden. Remove from cookie sheet; cool on a wire rack. Makes 24.

Per cookie: 103 calories, 1 g protein, 15 g carbohydrate, 5 g total fat (1 g saturated), 9 mg cholesterol, 56 mg sodium, 17 mg potassium.

1 Snip jellied orange slices with kitchen shears. Spray blades lightly with vegetable cooking spray to keep candy from sticking.

2 To toast coconut, spread in a thin layer in a shallow baking pan. Bake in a 350° oven for 5 to 10 minutes.

3 Stir coconut once or twice during baking to prevent overbrowning.

4 Combine dry ingredients, margarine, sugar, baking soda, egg, and vanilla thoroughly. Beat in as much flour as you can with the mixer.

5 Use a wooden spoon to stir in any remaining flour and the snipped orange slices, coconut, and orange peel.

6 Drop dough by rounded teaspoons onto an ungreased cookie sheet.

Fruitcake Cookies

¼ **cup margarine *or* butter**
½ **cup packed brown sugar**
2 **eggs**
1 **tablespoon orange juice**
1 **cup all-purpose flour**
½ **teaspoon ground**
    cinnamon
¼ **teaspoon baking powder**
1 **cup diced mixed candied**
    fruits and peels
½ **cup light raisins**
½ **cup chopped pecans**
1 **cup sifted powdered sugar**
2 **to 3 teaspoons milk**

In a large bowl beat margarine or butter with an electric mixer on medium to high speed for 30 seconds. Add brown sugar; beat till well combined. Add eggs and orange juice, beating well. Add flour, cinnamon, and baking powder; mix well. Stir in candied fruits and peels, raisins, and pecans.

Drop by rounded teaspoons onto a lightly greased cookie sheet. Bake in a 375° oven for 10 to 12 minutes. Cool on wire racks.

Meanwhile, for glaze, in a small bowl stir together powdered sugar and enough milk to make drizzling consistency. Drizzle over cookies. Makes about 30.

Per cookie: 84 calories, 1 g protein, 13 g carbohydrate, 3 g total fat (0 g saturated), 14 mg cholesterol, 24 mg sodium, 48 mg potassium.

Almond Biscotti Bites

⅓ **cup margarine *or* butter**
⅔ **cup sugar**
2 **eggs**
2 **teaspoons baking powder**
2 **teaspoons finely shredded**
    orange peel *or* lemon
    peel
1 **teaspoon vanilla**
2 **cups all-purpose flour**
1½ **cups slivered almonds *or***
    hazelnuts (filberts), very
    finely chopped
1 **beaten egg yolk (optional)**
1 **tablespoon milk (optional)**
½ **cup semisweet chocolate**
    pieces (optional)
1 **tablespoon shortening**
    (optional)
    Ground almonds

In a medium mixing bowl beat margarine or butter with an electric mixer on medium to high speed about 30 seconds or till softened. Add sugar and beat till combined. Add eggs, baking powder, orange or lemon peel, and vanilla; beat well. Beat in as much of the flour as you can with the mixer. Stir in any remaining flour with a wooden spoon. Stir in the chopped nuts.

Shape dough into three 14-inch rolls. Place rolls about 3 inches apart on a lightly greased cookie sheet. Slightly flatten to ¾-inch thickness. Brush with mixture of egg yolk and milk, if desired. Bake in a 375° oven for 15 to 20 minutes or till lightly browned. Cool on cookie sheet about 1 hour.

Cut each cookie roll into ¼ inch-thick slices. Lay slices, cut sides down, on an ungreased cookie sheet. Bake in a 325° oven for 5 minutes. Turn slices over; bake for 5 to 10 minutes more or till dry and crisp. Remove cookies; cool on a wire rack.

If desired, melt chocolate and shortening over low heat. Dip *half* of each cookie in the melted chocolate mixture. Allow excess chocolate to drip off; roll in the ground nuts. Place cookies on waxed paper and let stand till dry. Makes about 168.

Per cookie: 27 calories, 1 g protein, 3 g carbohydrate, 1 g total fat (0 g saturated), 4 g cholesterol, 7 mg sodium, 15 mg potassium.

Merry Christmas Bars

1 **cup all-purpose flour**
½ **cup packed brown sugar**
⅓ **cup margarine *or* butter,
   softened**
½ **cup chopped pecans**
1 **8-ounce package cream
   cheese, softened**
1 **egg**
¼ **cup granulated sugar**
2 **tablespoons milk**
2 **tablespoons lemon juice**
½ **teaspoon vanilla**
¼ **teaspoon almond extract**
¼ **cup each red and green
   maraschino cherries,
   finely chopped and well
   drained**

In a large mixing bowl combine flour, brown sugar, and margarine or butter; beat with an electric mixer on low speed until mixture resembles fine crumbs. Stir in nuts. Reserve *1 cup* of the nut mixture for topping. Press remaining nut mixture into an ungreased 8x8x2-inch baking pan. Bake in a 350° oven for 8 to 10 minutes or till light brown.

For filling, combine cream cheese, egg, granulated sugar, milk, lemon juice, vanilla, and almond extract; beat until smooth. Stir in red and green cherries. Spread filling over partially baked crust. Sprinkle with reserved nut mixture. Bake in the 350° oven for 25 to 30 minutes or till light brown and set. Cool in pan on a wire rack. Cut into bars. Store in refrigerator. Makes 24.

Per bar: 121 calories, 2 g protein, 12 g carbohydrate, 8 g total fat (3 g saturated), 19 g cholesterol, 63 mg sodium, 52 mg potassium.

Citrus Hazelnut Bars

⅓ **cup margarine *or* butter, softened**
¼ **cup sugar**
1 **cup all-purpose flour**
⅓ **cup finely chopped toasted hazelnuts**
2 **eggs**
¾ **cup sugar**
2 **tablespoons all-purpose flour**
1 **teaspoon finely shredded orange peel**
1 **teaspoon finely shredded lemon peel**
2 **tablespoons orange juice**
1 **tablespoon lemon juice**
½ **teaspoon baking powder**
  Powdered sugar (optional)

In a medium mixing bowl beat the margarine or butter with an electric mixer on medium to high speed for 30 seconds. Add ¼ cup granulated sugar. Beat till thoroughly combined. Beat 1 cup flour and about *half* of the nuts till crumbly. Press mixture into the bottom of an ungreased 8x8x2-inch baking pan. Bake in a 350° oven for 10 minutes till lightly browned.

Meanwhile, combine eggs, the ¾ cup granulated sugar, 2 tablespoons flour, peels, orange juice, lemon juice, and baking powder. Beat for 2 minutes at medium speed or till thoroughly combined. Pour over hot baked layer. Sprinkle with remaining nuts.

Bake in a 350° oven about 20 minutes more or till light brown around edges and center is set. Cool on a wire rack. Sift powdered sugar over top; if desired. Cut into bars. Store in refrigerator. Makes 20 bars.

Note: Chopped almonds may be substituted for the chopped toasted hazelnuts. Do not toast almonds.

Per bar: 108 calories, 2 g protein, 15 g carbohydrate, 5 g total fat (1 g saturated), 21 mg cholesterol, 43 mg sodium, 28 mg potassium.

Cashew-Topped Toffee Bars

½ **cup margarine *or* butter**
½ **cup sugar**
1 **cup all-purpose flour**
1 **14-ounce can (1¼ cups) sweetened condensed milk**
2 **tablespoons margarine *or* butter**
2 **teaspoons vanilla**
1 **6-ounce package (1 cup) semisweet chocolate pieces**
⅔ **cup coarsely chopped cashews *or* peanuts**

In a mixing bowl beat ½ cup margarine or butter and the sugar with an electric mixer on medium to high speed till thoroughly combined. Stir in flour. Press into the bottom of an ungreased 13x9x2-inch baking pan. Bake in a 350° oven about 15 minutes or till edges are lightly browned.

In a heavy medium saucepan heat sweetened condensed milk and 2 tablespoons margarine or butter over medium heat till bubbly, stirring constantly. Cook and stir for 5 minutes more. (Mixture will thicken and become smooth.) Stir in the 2 teaspoons vanilla. Spread over baked layer. Bake for 12 to 15 minutes or till golden.

Sprinkle with chocolate pieces *immediately* after removing from the oven. Let stand for 2 to 3 minutes or till softened. Spread chocolate evenly over top. Sprinkle with cashews or peanuts. Cool; chill for 5 to 10 minutes or till chocolate layer is set before cutting. Cut into bars. Makes 36 bars.

Per bar: 123 calories, 2 g protein, 15 g carbohydrate, 7 g total fat (1 g saturated), 4 mg cholesterol, 68 mg sodium, 75 mg potassium.

Chocolate-Cherry Pinwheels

½ **cup shortening**
½ **cup margarine *or* butter**
1 **cup sugar**
½ **teaspoon baking powder**
¼ **teaspoon salt**
1 **egg**
2 **tablespoons milk**
½ **teaspoon almond extract**
½ **teaspoon vanilla**
3 **cups all-purpose flour**
½ **cup maraschino cherries, patted dry and finely chopped**
¼ **cup unsweetened cocoa powder**
½ **cup finely chopped toasted almonds**

In a large mixing bowl beat shortening and margarine or butter with an electric mixer on medium to high speed for 30 seconds. Add the sugar, baking powder, and salt; beat till combined. Beat in egg, milk, almond extract, and vanilla. Beat till thoroughly combined. Stir in the flour. Divide the mixture in half. Stir the cherries and cocoa powder into one portion. Chill dough till easy to handle.

Place each half between 2 sheets of waxed paper. **1** Using a rolling pin, roll each half into a 12x11-inch rectangle. Remove top sheets of waxed paper. **2** Carefully invert chocolate-cherry dough atop vanilla dough. Pat the 2 layers together. Remove waxed paper from top. **3** Trim dough around edges. **4** Beginning at long side, roll up dough jelly-roll style; remove bottom sheet of waxed paper as you roll. **5** Cut roll in half. Roll each half evenly in chopped almonds. Wrap in waxed paper; chill for 4 to 48 hours. **6** Cut into ¼ inch-thick thick slices. Place 2 inches apart on an ungreased cookie sheet. Bake in a 375° oven for 10 to 12 minutes or till done. Cool on a wire rack. Makes about 4 dozen.

Per cookie: 90 calories, 1 g protein, 11 g carbohydrate, 5 g total fat (1 g saturated), 4 mg cholesterol, 35 mg sodium, 22 mg potassium.

1 Roll each half of dough between 2 sheets of waxed paper into a 12 x 11 inch rectangle.

2 Remove top sheets of waxed paper; invert chocolate-cherry dough atop vanilla dough; pat.

3 Remove waxed paper from top layer. Trim dough around edges.

4 From long side, roll dough tightly, removing waxed paper.

5 Cut roll in half. Roll each half in chopped almonds to coat evenly.

6 Using a sharp knife, cut chilled dough with a gentle sawing motion.

COOKIES

Lemon-Poppy Seed Slices

¾ **cup margarine *or* butter**
1 **cup sugar**
1 **egg**
1 **tablespoon milk**
2 **teaspoons finely shredded lemon peel**
½ **teaspoon vanilla**
½ **teaspoon lemon extract (optional)**
2¼ **cups all-purpose flour**
2 **tablespoons poppy seeds**

In a large mixing bowl beat margarine or butter with an electric mixer on medium to high speed for 30 seconds. Add the sugar; beat till combined. Beat in egg, milk, lemon peel, vanilla, and, if desired, lemon extract. Beat in as much of the flour as you can with the mixer. Stir in any remaining flour with a wooden spoon. Stir in poppy seeds.

Shape the dough into two 8-inch rolls. Wrap in waxed paper or plastic wrap. Chill for 3 to 24 hours.

Cut the dough into ¼-inch slices. Place on an ungreased cookie sheet. Bake in a 375° oven for 11 to 12 minutes or till edges are golden. Remove cookies from cookie sheet; cool on a wire rack. Makes about 60.

Per cookie: 51 calories, 1 g protein, 7 g carbohydrate, 3 g total fat (0 g saturated), 4 mg cholesterol, 28 mg sodium, 9 mg potassium.

Party Sandwich Cookies

1½ **cups all-purpose flour**
1 **cup ground pecans**
½ **cup sugar**
⅔ **cup margarine *or* butter**
3 **tablespoons cold water**
½ **teaspoon vanilla**
¼ **cup raspberry *or* strawberry jam**
½ **cup semisweet chocolate pieces**
1 **tablespoon shortening**

In a large mixing bowl combine flour, nuts, and sugar. Cut in margarine or butter till pieces are the size of coarse crumbs. Combine water and vanilla. Sprinkle over flour mixture a little at a time and mix with a fork till dough forms a ball. Wrap in clear plastic wrap and chill for 1 to 2 hours or till dough is easy to handle.

On a lightly floured surface, roll dough to ⅛ inch thickness. Cut into desired shape with a 2-inch cookie cutter (if using a non-symmetrical cutter, invert half of cookies onto baking sheet in order to be able to sandwich them together). Place on an ungreased cookie sheet. Bake in a 375° oven for 7 to 10 minutes or till light golden brown. Remove cookies from cookie sheet; cool on a wire rack.

Up to 1 hour before serving, spread *half* of the cookies with raspberry or strawberry jam, using about *1 teaspoon* for each cookie. Top with remaining cookies.

In a heavy small saucepan combine semisweet chocolate pieces and shortening. Heat over low heat, stirring constantly, till melted. Drizzle over tops of cookies. Makes about 24.

Note: Use your microwave oven to melt the chocolate and shortening mixture. Combine the semisweet chocolate pieces and the shortening in a microwave-safe bowl. Micro-cook on 100% power (high) for 1 to 2 minutes or till melted, stirring every 30 seconds.

Per sandwich: 157 calories, 1 g protein, 17 g carbohydrate, 10 g total fat (1 g saturated), 0 mg cholesterol, 61 mg sodium, 45 mg potassium.

Peanut Butter Spritz Fingers

1 cup margarine *or* butter
½ cup creamy peanut butter
½ cup granulated sugar
½ cup packed brown sugar
1 teaspoon baking powder
1 egg
1 teaspoon vanilla
3 cups all-purpose flour
½ cup semisweet chocolate
    pieces
1 teaspoon shortening
¼ cup finely chopped
    unsalted peanuts

In a mixing bowl beat the margarine or butter and peanut butter with an electric mixer on medium to high speed for 30 seconds. Add the granulated sugar, brown sugar, and baking powder; beat till combined. Beat in egg and vanilla till combined. Beat in as much of the flour as you can with the mixer. Stir in any remaining flour with a wooden spoon.

1 2 Force *unchilled* dough through a cookie press fitted with star plate or ½-inch tip into 2-inch-long fingers onto an ungreased cookie sheet. Bake in a 375° oven for 8 to 10 minutes or till edges are firm but not brown. Cool cookies on a wire rack.

In a small saucepan heat chocolate pieces and shortening over low heat, stirring till smooth. (To melt chocolate in the microwave, see Note on page 191.) **3** Dip ends of cooled cookies, on a diagonal, halfway into melted chocolate. **4** Sprinkle nuts over chocolate. Let stand on waxed paper till set. Store cookies in an airtight container. Makes about 80.

Per cookie: 64 calories, 1 g protein, 7 g carbohydrate, 4 g total fat (1 g saturated), 3 mg cholesterol, 36 mg sodium, 28 mg potassium.

1 Pack dough into a cookie press fitted with a star plate or ½ inch tip.

2 Holding cookie press at an angle, force dough through the cookie press onto an ungreased cookie sheet.

3 Dip ends of cooled baked cookies diagonally into melted chocolate.

4 Sprinkle finely chopped peanuts over chocolate coated ends.

Peach Rugelach

2 cups all-purpose flour
1 cup margarine *or* butter
¾ cup dairy sour cream
¾ cup peach preserves
1 teaspoon finely shredded
    lemon peel
¼ teaspoon ground ginger
¼ teaspoon almond extract
2 tablespoons margarine *or*
    butter, melted
2 tablespoons sugar
⅛ teaspoon ground
    cinnamon

In a large mixing bowl place flour. Cut in the 1 cup margarine or butter till pieces are the size of small peas. Add sour cream; mix with a fork till dough is just moist enough to hold together. Divide dough into thirds. Form each third into a ball. Wrap in plastic wrap and chill about 1 hour or till firm enough to handle.

On a lightly floured surface, flatten one ball of dough with hands. Roll dough from center to edge, forming a circle about 11 inches in diameter. (Keep remaining dough in the refrigerator till ready to use.)

For filling, stir together peach preserves, lemon peel, ginger, and almond extract. Spread *¼ cup* of the filling evenly over dough. Cut the circle into 12 wedges. Starting at the wide edge, roll up each wedge, jelly-roll style. Place, point side up, about 1½ inches apart on an ungreased cookie sheet. Repeat with remaining dough and filling.

Brush melted margarine or butter over cookies. In a small bowl combine sugar and cinnamon. Sprinkle over cookies. Bake in a 375° oven for 20 to 25 minutes or till golden brown. Remove from cookie sheet; cool on a wire rack. Makes 36.

Per cookie: 105 calories, 1 g protein, 11 g carbohydrate, 7 g total fat (2 g saturated), 2 mg cholesterol, 70 mg sodium, 23 mg potassium.

Chocolate Raisin-Oatmeal Cookies

¾ cup margarine *or* butter
1 cup packed brown sugar
½ cup granulated sugar
1 teaspoon baking powder
¼ teaspoon baking soda
1 egg
1 teaspoon vanilla
1¾ cups all-purpose flour
2 cups rolled oats
1 cup chocolate-covered
    raisins
½ cup chopped pecans

In a large mixing bowl beat margarine or butter with an electric mixer on medium to high speed for 30 seconds. Add the brown sugar, granulated sugar, baking powder, and baking soda; beat till combined. Beat in egg and vanilla. Beat in as much of the flour as you can with the mixer. Stir in any remaining flour with a wooden spoon. Stir in oats; mix well. Stir in chocolate-covered raisins and nuts.

Drop dough by rounded teaspoons 2 inches apart onto an ungreased cookie sheet. Bake in a 375° oven for 10 to 12 minutes or till edges are golden. Remove cookies from cookie sheet; cool on a wire rack. Makes about 54.

Per cookie: 85 calories, 1 g protein, 12 g carbohydrate, 4 g total fat (1 g saturated), 4 mg cholesterol, 39 mg sodium, 46 mg potassium.

Frosted Fig Bars

1 cup all-purpose flour
1 cup rolled oats
⅔ cup packed brown sugar
¼ teaspoon baking soda
½ cup margarine *or* butter
Fig Filling
½ cup sifted powdered sugar
¼ teaspoon vanilla
1 to 2 teaspoons orange juice

In a mixing bowl combine flour, oats, brown sugar, and baking soda. Cut in margarine or butter till mixture resembles coarse crumbs. Reserve *½ cup* of the flour mixture. Press remaining flour mixture in bottom of an ungreased 9x9x2-inch baking pan. Spread with Fig Filling. Sprinkle with reserved flour mixture.

Bake in a 350° oven about 30 minutes or till golden. Cool in the pan on a wire rack.

For glaze, mix powdered sugar, vanilla, and enough orange juice to make of drizzling consistency. Drizzle over top. Cut into bars. Makes 20 to 24 bars.

Fig Filling: In a medium saucepan combine 1½ cups finely chopped *dried figs*, ⅓ cup *water*, ¼ cup *orange juice*, 3 tablespoons *sugar,* and 1 teaspoon finely shredded *orange peel*. Bring to boiling. Reduce heat and simmer, uncovered, 5 to 10 minutes or till thick.

Per bar: 161 calories, 2 g protein, 29 g carbohydrate, 5 g total fat (1 g saturated), 0 mg cholesterol, 68 mg sodium, 161 mg potassium.

Double Nut Bars

½ **cup margarine *or* butter, melted**
¼ **cup granulated sugar**
2 **cups chocolate wafer crumbs (about 38 cookies)**
1 **8-ounce package cream cheese, softened**
¼ **cup margarine *or* butter**
⅓ **cup sifted powdered sugar**
½ **cup finely chopped pecans**
1 **teaspoon vanilla**
2 **tablespoons creamy peanut butter**
1 **cup sifted powdered sugar**
1 **to 2 tablespoons milk**
½ **teaspoon vanilla**

For first layer, combine ½ cup melted margarine or butter and granulated sugar. Add chocolate wafer crumbs; mix well. Press mixture into the bottom of an ungreased 8x8x2-inch baking pan; chill about 20 minutes or till firm. Cool.

For second layer, in a large mixing bowl beat cream cheese and ¼ cup margarine or butter with an electric mixer on medium speed till fluffy. Add ⅓ cup powdered sugar; beat till combined. Stir in pecans and 1 teaspoon vanilla. Spread over crumb layer. Chill about 30 minutes or till set.

For third layer, beat peanut butter and *half* of the 1 cup powdered sugar till combined. Add *1 tablespoon* of the milk and ½ teaspoon vanilla. Beat till smooth. Gradually add remaining powdered sugar, beating till smooth. Add additional milk, if necessary, to make a spreading consistency. Spread over cream cheese layer. Cover and chill at least 2 hours before serving. Store in the refrigerator. Makes 24 bars.

Per bar: 201 calories, 2 g protein, 18 g carbohydrate, 14 g total fat (4 g saturated), 16 mg cholesterol, 172 mg sodium, 43 mg potassium.

Black Walnut Balls

1 **cup margarine *or* butter**
¼ **cup granulated sugar**
1 **teaspoon vanilla**
2 **cups all-purpose flour**
1½ **cups finely chopped black walnuts**
   Powdered sugar

In a large mixing bowl beat margarine or butter with an electric mixer on medium to high speed for 30 seconds. Add granulated sugar and vanilla; beat till combined. Beat in as much of the flour as you can with the mixer. Stir in any remaining flour with a wooden spoon. Stir in walnuts.

Shape dough into 1-inch balls; place on an ungreased cookie sheet. Bake in a 325° oven about 20 minutes or till bottoms are light brown. Remove cookies from baking sheet; cool slightly on a wire rack. While still warm, roll cookies in powdered sugar. If desired, let cookies cool completely and roll cookies again in additional powdered sugar. Makes about 60.

Per cookie: 65 calories, 1 g protein, 5 g carbohydrate, 5 g total fat (1 g saturated), 0 mg cholesterol, 36 mg sodium, 22 mg potassium.

PIES AND PASTRIES

Easy Cherry Turnovers and Chocolate-Peanut Butter Pie

Chocolate-Peanut Butter Pie

1½ cups finely crushed vanilla wafers (36 to 40 wafers)
¼ cup sugar
⅓ cup margarine *or* butter, melted
1 8-ounce package cream cheese, softened
1 cup sugar
1 cup creamy peanut butter
2 tablespoons milk
1 8-ounce carton frozen whipped dessert topping, thawed
½ cup fudge ice cream topping
¾ cup chopped unsalted peanuts
  Chopped peanuts (optional)
  Fudge ice cream topping (optional)

For crust, combine the crushed wafers, the ¼ cup sugar, and the melted margarine or butter; toss to mix well. Spread mixture evenly into a 9-inch pie plate. Press onto bottom and sides to form a firm, even crust. Bake in a 375° oven for 7 to 10 minutes or till edges are golden. Cool thoroughly on a wire rack.

Meanwhile, in a medium mixing bowl beat cream cheese and the 1 cup sugar with an electric mixer on medium to high speed till smooth. Add peanut butter and milk; beat till combined. Stir in 1 cup of the whipped dessert topping to soften; fold in remaining whipped dessert topping.

Spread the ½ cup fudge ice cream topping over the bottom of the cooled pie crust. Sprinkle with the ¾ cup peanuts, pressing gently into topping. Spoon cream cheese mixture over ice cream topping. Cover and chill about 4 hours or till firm. Garnish with additional chopped peanuts and drizzle with additional fudge ice cream topping, if desired. Makes 8 servings.

Per serving: 773 calories, 15 g protein, 71 g carbohydrate, 53 g total fat (14 g saturated), 43 mg cholesterol, 395 mg sodium, 431 mg potassium.

Easy Cherry Turnovers

1¼ cups cherry pie filling
⅓ cup chopped almonds
½ teaspoon almond extract
  Pastry for Double-Crust Pie (see recipe, page 199)
2 to 3 teaspoons honey

For filling, in a medium bowl combine cherry pie filling, almonds, and almond extract. Set filling aside.

Prepare pastry for double-crust pie as directed. Divide dough in half; roll each half to a ¹⁄₁₆-inch thickness. Cut six 5-inch circles from each dough half, rerolling as necessary.

Place about *1 tablespoon* of the filling on each pastry circle. Moisten edges with water. Fold dough in half over filling. Press edges with a fork to seal. Place turnovers on an ungreased baking sheet. Prick tops with a fork.

Bake in a 425° oven for 15 to 20 minutes or till golden. Transfer turnovers to a wire rack to cool. While still warm, brush with honey. Serve warm or cool. Makes 12 turnovers.

Per serving: 226 calories, 3 g protein, 24 g carbohydrate, 14 g total fat (3 g saturated), 0 mg cholesterol, 97 mg sodium, 68 mg potassium.

Pumpkin-Praline Pie

**Pastry for Single-Crust Pie
(see recipe, page 199)**
1 cup finely chopped pecans
½ cup packed brown sugar
**3 tablespoons margarine _or_
butter, softened**
**2 tablespoons all-purpose
flour**
1 16-ounce can pumpkin
⅔ cup packed brown sugar
**1½ teaspoons pumpkin pie
spice**
3 eggs
**1 5-ounce can (⅔ cup)
evaporated milk**
½ cup milk
Whipped cream (optional)

1 2 3 4 Prepare pastry for single crust pie as directed. For praline layer, combine pecans, the ½ cup brown sugar, margarine or butter, and flour. Toss with a fork till combined. Spoon _half_ of mixture evenly into a pastry-lined 9-inch pie plate. Press firmly onto bottom.

For filling, in a mixing bowl combine pumpkin, the ⅔ cup brown sugar, and pumpkin pie spice. Add eggs. Beat lightly with a fork. Gradually stir in evaporated milk and milk. Mix well.

5 Place pie plate on oven rack; pour filling over pecan mixture. Cover edge with foil. Bake in a 375° oven for 25 minutes. Remove foil. Sprinkle with remaining pecan mixture. **6** Bake for 25 minutes more or till done. Cool on a wire rack. Serve with whipped cream, if desired. Cover and chill to store. Makes 8 servings.

Per serving: 476 calories, 8 g protein, 56 g carbohydrate, 26 g total fat (5 g saturated), 86 mg cholesterol, 180 mg sodium, 407 mg potassium.

1 Using a pastry blender or two forks, cut in the shortening till pieces are the size of small peas.

2 On a lightly floured surface, flatten the ball of dough. Smooth the edges, keeping pastry in a circle.

3 Wrap rolled pastry around rolling pin. Loosely unroll pastry from rolling pin and ease into pie plate.

4 Trim pastry to ½ inch beyond edge of pie plate. Fold under extra pastry even with rim of pie plate.

5 Place pie plate on oven rack. Pour filling into pastry-lined pie plate.

6 To test for doneness, insert a knife near center of filling. When done, knife will come out clean.

PIES AND PASTRIES

Pastry for Single-Crust Pie

1¼ **cups all-purpose flour**
¼ **teaspoon salt**
⅓ **cup shortening *or* lard**
3 **to 4 tablespoons cold**
   water

In a mixing bowl stir together flour and salt. Cut in shortening or lard with a pastry blender till pieces are the size of small peas. Sprinkle *1 tablespoon* of the water over part of the mixture; gently toss with a fork. Push to side of bowl. Repeat till all is moistened. Form dough into a ball.

On a lightly floured surface, flatten dough with hands. Roll dough from center to edges, forming a circle about 12 inches in diameter. Wrap pastry around rolling pin. Unroll onto a 9-inch pie plate. Ease pastry into pie plate; do not stretch pastry.

Trim to ½ inch beyond edge of pie plate; fold under extra pastry. Make a fluted, rope-shape, or scalloped edge. *Do not prick pastry*. Bake as directed in individual recipes.

Baked Pastry Shell: Prepare as above, *except* prick bottom and sides of pastry generously with the tines of a fork. Prick where bottom and sides meet all around pie shell. Line pastry shell with a double thickness of foil. Bake in a 450° oven for 8 minutes. Remove foil and bake for 5 to 6 minutes more or till golden. Cool on a wire rack.

Per serving: 141 calories, 2 g protein, 14 g carbohydrate, 9 g total fat (2 g saturated), 0 mg cholesterol, 67 mg sodium, 19 mg potassium.

Pastry for Double-Crust Pie

2 **cups all-purpose flour**
½ **teaspoon salt**
⅔ **cup shortening *or* lard**
6 **to 7 tablespoons cold**
   water

In a mixing bowl stir together flour and salt. Cut in shortening or lard with a pastry blender till pieces are the size of small peas. Sprinkle *1 tablespoon* of the water over part of the mixture; gently toss with a fork. Push to side of bowl. Repeat till all is moistened. Divide dough in half. Form each half into a ball.

On a lightly floured surface, flatten one ball of dough. Roll dough from center to edges, forming a circle 12 inches in diameter. Wrap pastry around rolling pin. Unroll onto a 9-inch pie plate. Ease pastry into pie plate; do not stretch pastry. Trim even with rim of pie plate.

For top crust, roll remaining dough. Fill pastry in pie plate with desired filling. Place top crust on filling and cut slits to allow steam to escape. Trim top crust ½ inch beyond edge of plate. Fold top crust under bottom crust; flute edge. Bake as directed in individual recipes.

Pastry for Lattice-Top Pie: Prepare as directed above, *except* trim bottom pastry to ½ inch beyond edge of pie plate. Cut top pastry into ½-inch-wide strips. Fill pastry in pie plate with desired filling. Weave strips atop filling to make a lattice. Press ends of strips into rim of crust. Fold bottom pastry over strips; seal and flute edge. Bake as directed in individual recipes.

Per serving: 256 calories, 3 g protein, 22 g carbohydrate, 17 g total fat (4 g saturated), 0 mg cholesterol, 134 mg sodium, 31 mg potassium.

Apple-Raisin Pie

**Pastry for Double-Crust Pie
(see recipe, page 199)**
⅓ **cup finely chopped pecans**
½ **cup raisins**
2 **tablespoons brandy**
¾ **cup packed brown sugar**
2 **tablespoons all-purpose
flour**
¼ **teaspoon ground nutmeg**
⅛ **teaspoon salt**
6 **cups thinly sliced, peeled
cooking apples**
2 **tablespoons margarine *or*
butter**
Milk
Sugar

Prepare pastry as directed *except* stir in the pecans with the flour.
1 Roll out pastry and arrange in a 9-inch pie plate; set aside. In a small bowl stir together raisins and brandy. Soak for 10 minutes. Meanwhile, for filling, in a mixing bowl combine brown sugar, flour, nutmeg, and salt. Add apples; toss to coat. Drain raisins, discarding brandy. Toss raisins with apple mixture. Transfer filling to pie plate. Dot with margarine or butter. **2** Place top crust over filling; cut slits in top crust. **3** Trim, seal, and flute edges. Brush top crust with milk and sprinkle with sugar. **4 5** Cover edge of pie with foil.

Bake in a 375° oven for 25 minutes. Remove foil. Bake for 20 to 25 minutes more or till crust is golden and filling is bubbly. Makes 8 servings.

Per serving: 483 calories, 4 g protein, 64 g carbohydrate, 24 g total fat (5 g saturated), 0 mg cholesterol, 210 mg sodium, 269 mg potassium.

1 Using a floured rolling pin or one with a floured cover, roll from the center to the edge of the pastry with light, even strokes.

2 Place top crust over filling. Cut slits in the top crust to let steam escape during baking.

3 Trim top crust; fold extra pastry under bottom crust. To flute edge, press index finger flat against inside of pie shell. Press dough around finger, pinching to form a point.

4 To keep edge from overbrowning, make foil rim by folding a 12-inch square of foil into quarters. Cut out center portion, making a 7½-inch circle.

5 Unfold foil and loosely mold the foil rim over the edge of pie.

Ginger-Pear Pie with Cheddar Crust

6 **cups thinly sliced, peeled
     pears**
2 **teaspoons orange juice**
½ **cup sugar**
¼ **cup all-purpose flour**
1 **tablespoon finely chopped
     crystallized ginger**
2 **cups all-purpose flour**
½ **cup shredded sharp
     cheddar cheese**
½ **teaspoon salt**
⅔ **cup shortening**
6 **to 7 tablespoons cold
     water**

Place pears in a mixing bowl; sprinkle with orange juice. Combine sugar, the ¼ cup flour, and ginger; add to pears, tossing gently to coat. Set aside.

In a mixing bowl stir together the 2 cups flour, cheese, and salt. Cut in shortening with a pastry blender till pieces are the size of small peas. Sprinkle 1 tablespoon of the water over part of the mixture; gently toss with a fork. Push to side of bowl. Repeat till all is moistened. Divide dough in half. Form each half into a ball.

On a lightly floured surface, flatten one ball of dough with hands. Roll dough from center to edges, forming a circle about 12 inches in diameter. Wrap pastry around rolling pin. Unroll onto a 9-inch pie plate. Ease pastry into pie plate; do not stretch pastry. Trim pastry even with rim of pie plate.

For top crust, roll out remaining dough. Cut slits to allow steam to escape. Spoon pear mixture into pie plate. Place top crust on filling. Trim top crust ½ inch beyond edge of plate. Fold edge of top crust under bottom crust; flute edge. Cover edge with foil.

Bake in a 375° oven for 50 minutes. Remove foil; bake for 20 to 30 minutes more or till crust is golden and fruit is tender. Makes 8 servings.

Per serving: 432 calories, 6 g protein, 60 g carbohydrate, 20 g total fat (6 g saturated), 7 mg cholesterol, 178 mg sodium, 222 mg potassium.

Mixed Berry Pie

1 **cup sugar**
3 **tablespoons cornstarch**
1 **teaspoon finely shredded
     orange peel**
½ **teaspoon ground
     cinnamon**
¼ **teaspoon ground nutmeg**
⅛ **teaspoon ground ginger**
2 **cups sliced fresh
     strawberries**
2 **cups fresh blackberries *or*
     raspberries**
1 **cup fresh blueberries
     Pastry for Double-Crust Pie
     (see recipe, page 199)**
   Milk
   Sugar

In a large mixing bowl combine sugar, cornstarch, orange peel, cinnamon, nutmeg, and ginger. Add strawberries, blackberries or raspberries, and blueberries; toss gently to coat. Transfer to a pastry-lined 9-inch pie plate. Cut slits in top crust. Adjust top crust over filling. Seal and flute edge. Brush top crust with milk and sprinkle with sugar. Cover edge with foil.

Bake in a 375° oven for 25 minutes. Remove foil. Bake for 20 to 25 minutes more or till top is golden and filling is bubbly. Makes 8 servings.

Per serving: 405 calories, 4 g protein, 60 g carbohydrate, 18 g total fat (4 g saturated), 0 mg cholesterol, 137 mg sodium, 184 mg potassium.

Banana Split Tart

1¼ cups all-purpose flour
¼ cup sugar
½ cup margarine *or* butter
2 beaten egg yolks
1 tablespoon water
½ cup sugar
¼ cup all-purpose flour
2 cups milk
1 beaten egg
1 tablespoon margarine *or* butter
2 teaspoons vanilla
1 banana, peeled and sliced
½ of a 13½-ounce can pineapple tidbits, drained
7 *or* 8 strawberries
2 tablespoons fudge ice cream topping

Combine the 1¼ cups flour and the ¼ cup sugar. Cut in the ½ cup margarine or butter till pieces are the size of small peas. Combine egg yolks and water; add to flour mixture, mixing with a fork till moistened. Form dough into a ball. Wrap in plastic wrap and chill 30 minutes.

On a lightly floured surface, roll dough to ⅛-inch thickness. Ease into a 9-inch fluted tart pan with a removable bottom. Press dough into sides of tart pan; trim edges. Prick bottom and sides generously with a fork. Bake in a 450° oven for 10 minutes or till golden. Cool on a wire rack.

Meanwhile, for filling, combine the ½ cup sugar and the ¼ cup flour in a saucepan. Stir in milk all at once. Cook and stir over medium heat till thickened and bubbly. Stir a small amount of hot filling into the egg. Return all to saucepan. Cook and stir 1 minute more. Remove from heat. Stir in the 1 tablespoon margarine or butter and vanilla. Cool.

To assemble, spread banana slices evenly over bottom of tart shell. Add filling. Cover; chill 4 to 24 hours. To serve, thinly slice strawberries, cutting to but not through the stem end. Arrange pineapple and strawberries over filling; drizzle with ice cream topping. Serves 8.

Per serving: 370 calories, 6 g protein, 49 g carbohydrate, 17 g total fat (4 g saturated), 84 mg cholesterol, 195 mg sodium, 251 mg potassium.

Peach and Blueberry Tartlets

**Pastry for Double-Crust Pie
(see recipe, page 199)**
¼ **teaspoon ground
cinnamon**
⅛ **teaspoon ground nutmeg**
1 **8-ounce container soft-
style cream cheese**
¾ **cup fresh blueberries *or*
raspberries**
¾ **cup chopped, peeled
peaches**
1 **kiwi fruit, peeled,
quartered, and sliced**
⅔ **cup peach preserves**

Prepare Pastry for Double-Crust Pie as directed *except* stir cinnamon and nutmeg into the flour. Divide dough into 8 equal portions. Roll each portion out to ⅛-inch thickness; press into eight 3- to 4-inch fluted tartlet pans. Prick generously with a fork. Bake in a 450° oven for 12 to 15 minutes or till golden. Cool; carefully remove pastry shells from pans.

For filling, stir cream cheese till smooth; divide evenly among the pastry shells. Divide blueberries or raspberries, peaches, and kiwi fruit among the pastry shells. In a small saucepan, stir peach preserves over low heat till melted; strain and drizzle over fruit. Chill tartlets for 2 hours. Makes 8 servings.

Per serving: 450 calories, 5 g protein, 47 g carbohydrate, 28 g total fat (9 g saturated), 30 mg cholesterol, 240 mg sodium, 170 mg potassium.

Apricot-Mascarpone Mousse in Phyllo Cups

8 **18x12-inch sheets frozen
phyllo dough, thawed**
⅓ **cup margarine *or* butter,
melted**
¾ **cup sugar**
½ **cup margarine *or* butter**
⅓ **cup apricot nectar**
1 **tablespoon lemon juice**
4 **egg yolks**
½ **of an 8-ounce package
mascarpone cheese *or*
cream cheese, softened**
½ **cup whipping cream,
whipped**
**Fresh raspberries
(optional)**
Mint leaves (optional)

Grease six 6-ounce custard cups. Set cups aside. Unfold phyllo dough. Place *one* sheet of phyllo dough on a large cutting board; brush lightly with some of the melted margarine or butter. Top with a second sheet of phyllo; brush with more margarine or butter. Repeat layering with the remaining phyllo sheets and melted margarine or butter. Using a sharp knife, cut the stack *crosswise* into six 3-inch-wide strips. Then cut the stack *lengthwise* into thirds, forming eighteen 4x3-inch rectangles.

Press *three* rectangles into each custard cup, overlapping shorter edges in bottoms of cups. Place cups in a 15x10x1-inch baking pan. Bake in a 350° oven for 15 to 18 minutes or till golden. Cool on a wire rack.

Meanwhile, for filling, in a medium saucepan combine sugar, the ½ cup margarine or butter, apricot nectar, and lemon juice. Cook over medium heat till sugar dissolves and margarine or butter melts, stirring constantly.

In a mixing bowl beat egg yolks with an electric mixer on high speed for 2 minutes. With mixer on low speed, gradually add the apricot mixture till combined. Return mixture to saucepan. Cook and stir over medium-low heat for 5 to 7 minutes or till thickened and bubbly. Pour filling into a large bowl. Cover and chill for 2 hours.

Stir mascarpone or cream cheese into apricot mixture. Fold in whipped cream and chill till mixture mounds when dropped from a spoon. Divide filling evenly among phyllo cups. Garnish with fresh raspberries and mint leaves, if desired. Makes 6 servings.

Per serving: 567 calories, 8 g protein, 43 g carbohydrate, 43 g total fat (13 g saturated), 180 mg cholesterol, 439 mg sodium, 85 mg potassium.

Rhubarb-Raspberry Lattice Pie

1¼ **to 1½ cups sugar**
3 **tablespoons quick-cooking tapioca**
½ **teaspoon ground cinnamon**
3 **cups fresh *or* frozen unsweetened sliced rhubarb**
2 **cups fresh *or* frozen unsweetened raspberries**
1 **teaspoon lemon juice**
½ **teaspoon finely shredded orange peel**
  Pastry for Lattice-Top Pie (see recipe, page 199)

In a large mixing bowl stir together sugar, tapioca, and cinnamon. Add rhubarb, raspberries, lemon juice, and orange peel; toss gently to coat. Let fruit mixture stand for 15 to 30 minutes or till a syrup forms, stirring mixture occasionally. Prepare pastry for lattice-top pie as directed. Transfer fruit mixture to a pastry-lined 9-inch pie plate. 1 2 3 4 Top with lattice crust. 5 Trim pastry strips even with edge of bottom crust. Seal and flute edge. Cover edge of pie with foil.

Bake in a 375° oven for 25 minutes (50 minutes if using frozen fruit). Remove foil. Bake for 20 to 25 minutes more or till top is golden. Cool on a wire rack. Makes 8 servings.

Per serving: 413 calories, 4 g protein, 62 g carbohydrate, 18 g total fat (4 g saturated), 0 mg cholesterol, 136 mg sodium, 212 mg potassium.

1 Using a decorative pastry wheel or sharp knife, cut dough for lattice top into strips ½ to ¾ inch wide.

2 Lay half of the strips at 1-inch intervals atop the filling.

3 Fold back alternate strips halfway. Place another pastry strip in the center of pie at a right angle to the strips that are in place.

4 Unfold the folded strips and fold back remaining strips. Place another pastry strip parallel to the strip in the center. Repeat weaving process until lattice top is completed.

5 Trim the pastry strips even with the edge of the bottom crust. Fold bottom pastry over the ends of the lattice strips to build up edge.

Mango-Raspberry Swirl Ice Cream Pie

⅓ **cup margarine *or* butter**
3 **tablespoons brown sugar**
1¼ **cups finely crushed graham cracker crumbs**
1 **10-ounce package frozen raspberries in light syrup, thawed**
1 **tablespoon orange juice**
2 **teaspoons cornstarch**
½ **of a ripe mango, peeled and pitted**
1 **pint vanilla ice cream, softened**
Fresh raspberries (optional)
Fresh mint leaves (optional)

For crust, melt margarine or butter. Stir in brown sugar. Add crushed graham crackers; toss to mix well. Spread mixture evenly into a 9-inch pie plate. Press onto bottom and sides to form a firm, even crust. Chill about 1 hour or till firm.

For sauce, drain raspberries, reserving syrup. Press raspberries through a sieve; discard seeds. Combine reserved raspberry syrup and raspberry puree in a small saucepan. Combine orange juice and cornstarch; add to raspberry mixture. Cook and stir over medium heat till thickened and bubbly. Cook and stir 2 minutes more. Remove from heat; cool.

Place mango in a blender container or food processor bowl. Cover and blend or process till smooth (you should have about ¾ cup puree). Stir mango puree into ice cream; stir till combined. Spoon ice cream mixture into prepared crust. Drizzle ⅓ *cup* of the sauce over ice cream, reserving the remaining sauce. Carefully swirl raspberry sauce through ice cream.

Cover and freeze at least 6 hours or overnight. Let pie stand at room temperature for 15 minutes before serving. Garnish with fresh raspberries and mint leaves, if desired. Serve with the reserved raspberry sauce. Makes 8 servings.

Per serving: 271 calories, 3 g protein, 38 g carbohydrate, 12 g total fat (4 g saturated), 15 mg cholesterol, 193 mg sodium, 231 mg potassium.

Fruity Cream Pie

¾ **cup sugar**
¼ **cup cornstarch**
3 **cups milk**
4 **lightly beaten egg yolks**
1 **tablespoon margarine *or* butter**
1 **teaspoon vanilla**
Baked Pastry Shell (see recipe, page 199)
1 **cup sliced strawberries *or* sliced, peeled peaches *or* 1 cup red raspberries**
1 **cup whipping cream, whipped**

For filling, in a medium saucepan combine sugar and cornstarch. Gradually stir in milk. Cook and stir over medium heat till thickened and bubbly. Reduce heat; cook and stir for 2 minutes more. Remove saucepan from heat. Gradually stir about 1 cup of hot filling into egg yolks. Return all to saucepan. Bring to a gentle boil. Cook and stir 2 minutes more. Remove saucepan from heat; stir in margarine or butter and vanilla. Cool filling.

Arrange sliced strawberries, peaches, or raspberries over bottom of Baked Pastry Shell. Pour filling over fruit. Cover and refrigerate about 2 hours or till set. Just before serving, top with whipped cream. Makes 8 servings.

Per serving: 358 calories, 7 g protein, 25 g carbohydrate, 26 g total fat (11 g saturated), 154 mg cholesterol, 145 mg sodium, 223 mg potassium.

Pineapple Meringue Pie

**Baked Pastry Shell
(see recipe, page 199)**
1 **cup sugar**
⅓ **cup cornstarch**
1½ **cups unsweetened
pineapple juice**
½ **cup water**
3 **eggs**
3 **tablespoons margarine**
2 **teaspoons finely shredded
lemon peel**
1 **tablespoon lemon juice**
3 **egg whites**
½ **teaspoon vanilla**
¼ **teaspoon cream of tartar**
6 **tablespoons sugar**

1 Prepare baked pastry shell. For filling, in a medium saucepan combine sugar and cornstarch. Gradually stir in pineapple juice and water. Cook and stir over medium-high heat till thickened and bubbly. Reduce heat; cook and stir 2 minutes more. Remove from heat.

Separate egg yolks from whites; set whites aside. Beat yolks slightly. Gradually stir 1 cup hot filling into yolks; return to saucepan. Bring to a gentle boil. Cook and stir 2 minutes more. Remove from heat. Stir in margarine, lemon peel, and lemon juice. **2** Pour hot filling into baked pastry shell.

For meringue, allow egg whites to stand at room temperature for 30 minutes. In a mixing bowl combine egg whites, vanilla, and cream of tartar. **3** Beat with an electric mixer on medium speed for 1 minute or till soft peaks form. **4 5** Gradually add sugar, beating on high speed till mixture forms stiff, glossy peaks and sugar dissolves. **6** Immediately spread meringue over hot pie filling, sealing to edge of pastry to prevent shrinkage. Bake in a 350° oven for 15 minutes or till meringue is golden. Cool. Cover and chill to store. Makes 8 servings.

Per serving: 387 calories, 4 g protein, 60 g carbohydrate, 15 g total fat (4 g saturated), 80 mg cholesterol, 143 mg sodium, 116 mg potassium.

1 Prick the bottom and sides of pastry generously to prevent shrinkage during baking.

2 Pour hot filling into the baked pastry shell.

3 Beat egg white mixture with electric mixer on medium speed till soft peaks form.

4 Gradually add sugar, 1 tablespoon at a time, beating on high speed.

5 Beat egg white mixture till stiff glossy peaks form and sugar dissolves, about 4 minutes.

6 Using a spatula, spread the meringue over the hot filling, sealing it to the edge of pastry shell.

Coconut-Almond Tassies

½ **cup margarine _or_ butter, softened**
1 **3-ounce package cream cheese, softened**
1½ **cups all-purpose flour**
¼ **cup granulated sugar**
1 **cup packed brown sugar**
2 **tablespoons margarine _or_ butter, softened**
2 **eggs**
½ **cup milk chocolate pieces**
⅓ **cup coconut**
⅓ **cup finely chopped almonds**
1 **teaspoon vanilla**

For pastry, in a mixing bowl beat the ½ cup margarine _or_ butter and cream cheese till thoroughly combined. Stir in flour and granulated sugar.

Press a rounded _teaspoon_ of pastry evenly into the bottom and up the sides of _each_ of 36 ungreased 1¾-inch muffin cups. Set aside.

For filling, in a medium mixing bowl combine brown sugar and the 2 tablespoons margarine or butter; beat till smooth. Add eggs, mixing well. Stir in milk chocolate pieces, coconut, almonds, and vanilla. Spoon 1 _heaping teaspoon_ of the filling into _each_ pastry shell.

Bake in a 325° oven for 25 to 30 minutes or till lightly browned. Cool in pans 10 minutes. Remove from pans and cool on wire racks. Makes 36.

Per serving: 107 calories, 1 g protein, 13 g carbohydrate, 6 g total fat (1 g saturated), 15 mg cholesterol, 52 mg sodium, 51 mg potassium.

Cranberry-Walnut Pie

Pastry for Single-Crust Pie (see recipe, page 199)
3 **eggs**
1 **cup light corn syrup**
⅔ **cup packed brown sugar**
¼ **cup margarine _or_ butter, melted**
1 **teaspoon finely shredded orange peel**
½ **teaspoon ground cinnamon**
⅛ **teaspoon salt**
1 **cup chopped walnuts**
1 **cup cranberries**

Prepare pastry for single-crust pie as directed.

For filling, in a large mixing bowl beat eggs lightly with a fork till combined. Stir in corn syrup, brown sugar, melted margarine or butter, orange peel, cinnamon, and salt. Stir in walnuts.

Spread cranberries evenly in bottom of pastry-lined 9-inch pie plate. Pour filling over cranberries in pie plate. Cover edge of pie with foil. Bake in a 350° oven for 25 minutes. Remove foil; bake for 20 to 25 minutes more or till a knife inserted in the center comes out clean. Cool on a wire rack. Cover and chill to store. Makes 8 servings.

Per serving: 505 calories, 6 g protein, 67 g carbohydrate, 24 g total fat (5 g saturated), 80 mg cholesterol, 227 mg sodium, 158 mg potassium.

Pumpkin-Pecan Cheesecake

DESSERTS

Pumpkin-Pecan Cheesecake

1¾ cups finely crushed
    gingersnaps
⅓ cup margarine *or* butter,
    melted
4 8-ounce packages cream
    cheese, softened
1 cup packed brown sugar
1 16-ounce can pumpkin
3 tablespoons all-purpose
    flour
2 teaspoons pumpkin pie
    spice
1 teaspoon vanilla
½ teaspoon ground allspice
3 eggs
½ cup toasted chopped pecans
1½ teaspoons finely shredded
    orange peel (optional)
1 8-ounce carton dairy sour
    cream
1 tablespoon granulated
    sugar
    Pecan halves (optional)
    Orange slices (optional)

For crust, combine crushed gingersnaps and margarine or butter. Press mixture onto bottom and about 2 inches up sides of a 9-inch springform pan.

In a large mixing bowl beat cream cheese and brown sugar with an electric mixer on medium to high speed till well combined. Beat in pumpkin, flour, pumpkin pie spice, vanilla, and allspice. Add eggs all at once. Beat on low speed just till combined. Stir in chopped pecans and orange peel, if desired. Pour into crust-lined pan. Place in a shallow baking pan in oven.

Bake in a 375° oven for 45 to 50 minutes or till center appears nearly set when shaken. Cool on a wire rack for 10 minutes. Stir together sour cream and granulated sugar; spread over top of cheesecake. Loosen crust from sides of pan. Cool 30 minutes more; remove sides of pan. Cool completely. Chill at least 4 hours. Garnish with pecan halves and orange slices, if desired. Makes 12 to 16 servings.

Note: To make decorative cookie "fence" around cheesecake, cut gingersnaps in half and press cut edge gently into filling.

Per serving: 555 calories, 9 g protein, 38 g carbohydrate, 41 g total fat (22 g saturated), 145 mg cholesterol, 400 mg sodium, 300 mg potassium.

Chocolate-Almond Soufflé

2 tablespoons margarine *or*
    butter
3 tablespoons all-purpose
    flour
1 teaspoon instant coffee
    crystals
¼ teaspoon ground cinnamon
¾ cup milk
½ cup semisweet chocolate
    pieces
4 beaten egg yolks
¼ cup toasted chopped
    almonds
4 egg whites
½ teaspoon vanilla
¼ cup sugar
    Sifted powdered sugar

Grease the sides of a 2-quart soufflé dish. Sprinkle sides with a little sugar. Set dish aside.

In a small saucepan melt margarine or butter. Stir in flour, coffee crystals, and cinnamon. Add milk all at once. Cook and stir till thickened and bubbly. Add chocolate; stir till melted. Remove from heat. Gradually stir chocolate mixture into beaten egg yolks. Add almonds; set aside.

In a bowl beat egg whites and vanilla till soft peaks form. Gradually add sugar, beating till stiff peaks form. Fold about *1 cup* of the beaten egg whites into the chocolate mixture. Then fold chocolate mixture into remaining beaten whites. Transfer to prepared dish.

Bake in a 350° oven for 40 to 45 minutes or till a knife inserted near center comes out clean. Sift powdered sugar over top of hot soufflé. Serve immediately. Makes 6 servings.

Per serving: 254 calories, 7 g protein, 25 g carbohydrate, 14 g total fat (3 g saturated), 144 mg cholesterol, 164 mg sodium, 224 mg potassium.

Pear-Cranberry Crisp

5 cups sliced, peeled pears
1 cup coarsely chopped cranberries
¼ cup granulated sugar
¼ cup water
1 tablespoon lemon juice
½ cup all-purpose flour
¼ cup packed brown sugar
½ teaspoon ground cinnamon
¼ cup margarine *or* butter
Vanilla ice cream, *or* half-and-half *or* light cream (optional)

1 Combine pears, cranberries, and the granulated sugar. Transfer to an 8x1½-inch round baking dish. In a small mixing bowl combine water and lemon juice; pour over fruit in dish.

For topping, in a mixing bowl combine flour, brown sugar, and cinnamon. **2** Cut in margarine or butter till mixture resembles coarse crumbs. **3** Sprinkle topping over fruit.

Bake in a 375° oven for 30 to 35 minutes or till fruit is tender and topping is golden. Serve warm with ice cream, or half-and-half or light cream, if desired. Makes 6 servings.

Per serving: 235 calories, 1 g protein, 41 g carbohydrate, 8 g fat (2 g saturated), 0 mg cholesterol, 95 mg sodium, 166 mg potassium.

1 Place fruit mixture evenly in an 8x1½-inch round baking dish.

2 Cut margarine or butter into flour mixture till mixture resembles coarse crumbs.

3 Sprinkle crumb topping evenly over the fruit filling.

DESSERTS

Peach-Blackberry Crisp

3 cups sliced, peeled peaches
    ***or* frozen unsweetened**
    peach slices
2 cups fresh *or* frozen
    unsweetened
    blackberries
½ cup granulated sugar
3 tablespoons all-purpose
    flour
½ cup rolled oats
⅓ cup packed brown sugar
¼ cup all-purpose flour
¼ teaspoon ground
    cinnamon
¼ teaspoon ground nutmeg
¼ cup margarine *or* butter
½ cup chopped walnuts

For filling, thaw fruit, if frozen. *Do not drain.* In a large mixing bowl stir together granulated sugar and the 3 tablespoons flour. Add peaches and blackberries and their juices; toss gently till coated. Transfer fruit filling to an ungreased 2-quart square baking dish. Set aside.

For topping, in a mixing bowl combine rolled oats, brown sugar, the ¼ cup flour, cinnamon, and nutmeg. Cut in margarine or butter till mixture resembles coarse crumbs. Stir in nuts. Sprinkle topping over filling.

Bake in a 375° oven for 30 to 35 minutes or till peaches are tender and topping is golden. Serve warm. Makes 6 servings.

Per serving: 367 calories, 5 g protein, 59 g carbohydrate, 15 g total fat (2 g saturated), 0 mg cholesterol, 94 mg sodium, 439 mg potassium.

Steamed Cranberry Pudding

2 cups cranberries
2 tablespoons all-purpose
    flour
2 cups all-purpose flour
½ cup packed brown sugar
⅓ cup granulated sugar
1 teaspoon baking soda
1 teaspoon ground
    cinnamon
½ teaspoon ground nutmeg
¼ teaspoon ground allspice
1 cup milk
1 egg
2 tablespoons margarine *or*
    butter, melted
    Hard Sauce

In a small bowl toss together cranberries and the 2 tablespoons flour. Set aside.

In a large mixing bowl stir together the 2 cups flour, brown sugar, granulated sugar, baking soda, cinnamon, nutmeg, and allspice. Add milk, egg, and margarine or butter; stir till well combined. Stir in cranberry mixture.

Transfer cranberry mixture to a well-greased 6-cup metal mold. Cover mold tightly with foil. Place mold on a rack in a Dutch oven or roasting pan. Add *boiling water* to just below rack; cover.

Bring to a very gentle boil over medium heat. Steam for 1 to 1½ hours or till a toothpick inserted in center comes out clean, adding more *boiling water* to Dutch oven or roasting pan occasionally to maintain desired water level.

Remove pudding from Dutch oven or roasting pan and let stand 2 to 3 minutes. Remove foil and unmold onto a serving dish. Serve with Hard Sauce. Makes 12 servings.

Hard Sauce: In a small mixing bowl beat together 1 cup sifted *powdered sugar* and ¼ cup softened *margarine or butter* with an electric mixer on medium speed for 3 to 5 minutes or till mixture is well combined. Beat in ½ teaspoon *vanilla.* Spoon into a serving bowl. Chill to harden. Makes ⅔ cup.

Per serving: 240 calories, 3 g protein, 42 g carbohydrate, 7 g total fat (2 g saturated), 19 mg cholesterol, 192 mg sodium, 108 mg potassium.

Apple Dumplings

1¾ cups water
1¼ cups sugar
½ teaspoon ground cinnamon
½ teaspoon ground nutmeg
2 tablespoons margarine or butter
2¼ cups all-purpose flour
¼ teaspoon salt
⅔ cup shortening
6 to 8 tablespoons cold apple juice *or* apple cider
2 tablespoons finely chopped walnuts
6 small apples

For syrup, in a small saucepan combine water, *1 cup* of the sugar, *¼ teaspoon* of the cinnamon, and *¼ teaspoon* of the nutmeg. Bring to boiling. Reduce heat and simmer, uncovered, for 5 minutes. Remove from heat; stir in margarine or butter. Set aside.

For pastry, in mixing bowl stir together flour and salt. Cut in shortening till mixture resembles coarse crumbs. Sprinkle *1 tablespoon* apple juice or cider over part of mixture; gently toss with fork. Push to side of bowl. Repeat till all is moistened. Form into ball. On a lightly floured surface, roll dough into a 19x13-inch rectangle. Trim to an 18x12-inch rectangle. Cut into six 6-inch squares. Save extra dough to make leaf cutouts, if desired. **1** Peel and core apples. Combine remaining sugar, cinnamon, nutmeg, and the walnuts. **2** Place *one* apple on each pastry square. Sprinkle spice mixture over fruit. **3 4** Moisten edges of pastry; fold corners to center atop fruit. Pinch to seal. Decorate with leaf cutouts, if desired. Place in a 2-quart rectangular baking dish. Pour syrup over dumplings. Bake in a 375° oven about 45 minutes or till fruit is tender and pastry is brown. Makes 6 servings.

Per serving: 629 calories, 5 g protein, 91 g carbohydrate, 29 g total fat (7 g saturated), 0 mg cholesterol, 139 mg sodium, 181 mg potassium.

1 Using an apple corer, remove the core from the center of the apple.

2 Place an apple in the center of a pastry square. Sprinkle spices in and over the apple.

3 With a pastry brush, moisten the edges of the pastry.

4 Bring each corner of the pastry square up to the top of the apple and pinch to seal.

Southern Blackberry Cobbler

- 1½ cups all-purpose flour
- ¼ cup granulated sugar
- 2 teaspoons baking powder
- ¼ teaspoon salt
- ¼ teaspoon ground cinnamon
- ⅛ teaspoon ground nutmeg
- ⅓ cup shortening
- ¾ cup packed brown sugar *or* granulated sugar
- 4 teaspoons cornstarch
- 5 cups fresh *or* frozen blackberries
- ¾ cup water
- 2 teaspoons finely shredded orange peel
- ½ teaspoon vanilla
- 1 egg
- ½ cup milk
- Whipped cream *or* vanilla ice cream (optional)

For topping, in a large mixing bowl stir together flour, the granulated sugar, baking powder, salt, cinnamon, and nutmeg. Cut in shortening till the mixture resembles coarse crumbs. Make a well in the center. Set the dry ingredients aside.

For filling, in a medium saucepan stir together the brown sugar and cornstarch. Stir in fresh or frozen blackberries, water, and orange peel. Cook and stir till thickened and bubbly. Stir in the vanilla. Keep filling hot.

In a small bowl, use a fork to beat together egg and milk. Add egg mixture all at once to the dry ingredients; stir just till moistened. Transfer hot filling to an ungreased 2-quart rectangular baking dish. Immediately drop topping into 8 mounds atop the hot filling.

Bake in a 400° oven for 20 to 25 minutes or till a toothpick inserted into topping comes out clean. Serve warm with whipped cream or ice cream, if desired. Makes 8 servings.

Per serving: 325 calories, 4 g protein, 57 g carbohydrate, 10 g total fat (3 g saturated), 28 mg cholesterol, 94 mg sodium, 305 mg potassium.

Apricot Bread Pudding

- 4 eggs
- 2¼ cups milk
- ⅓ cup sugar
- ¼ cup Amaretto *or* milk
- ½ teaspoon ground cinnamon
- ½ teaspoon vanilla
- ¼ teaspoon ground nutmeg
- 3 cups French bread cubes, dried
- 1 cup snipped dried apricots
- ⅓ cup whipping cream
- 2 tablespoons sugar

In a large mixing bowl beat together eggs, milk, the ⅓ cup sugar, Amaretto or milk, cinnamon, vanilla, and nutmeg.

In an ungreased 2-quart square baking dish toss together dry bread cubes and apricots. Pour the egg mixture evenly over the bread mixture.

Bake in a 350° oven for 40 to 45 minutes or till a knife inserted near the center comes out clean. Meanwhile, beat whipping cream and the 2 tablespoons sugar till soft peaks form. Serve pudding warm with whipped cream. Makes 9 servings.

Note: To dry bread cubes, bake them in a 300° oven about 15 minutes.

Per serving: 207 calories, 6 g protein, 28 g carbohydrate, 7 g total fat (4 g saturated), 111 mg cholesterol, 115 mg sodium, 340 mg potassium.

Apricot Bavarian Creme with Raspberry Sauce and Peach-Strawberry Shortcake

Peach-Strawberry Shortcake

**2 cups fresh strawberries,
   sliced**
⅓ cup sugar
2 cups all-purpose flour
⅓ cup sugar
2 teaspoons baking powder
¼ teaspoon salt
½ cup margarine *or* butter
1 beaten egg
⅔ cup milk
½ teaspoon vanilla
**¼ teaspoon almond extract
   (optional)**
3 cups sliced, peeled peaches
**1 cup whipping cream,
   whipped**

Stir together strawberries and ⅓ cup sugar; set aside. Combine flour, ⅓ cup sugar, baking powder, and salt. Cut in margarine or butter till mixture resembles coarse crumbs. Combine egg, milk, vanilla, and almond extract, if desired; add all at once to dry ingredients. Stir just to moisten. Spread into a greased 8x1½-inch round baking pan.

Bake in a 450° oven for 20 to 25 minutes or till a toothpick inserted near center comes out clean. Cool in pan 10 minutes. Remove from pan; split into 2 layers. Add peaches to berry mixture; stir gently. Spoon fruit and whipped cream between layers and over top. Garnish with sliced almonds, if desired. Serve immediately. Makes 8 servings.

Per serving: 433 calories, 6 g protein, 51 g carbohydrate, 24 g total fat (9 g saturated), 63 g cholesterol, 235 mg sodium, 288 mg potassium.

Apricot Bavarian Creme with Raspberry Sauce

½ cup sugar
1 envelope unflavored
  gelatin
1 6-ounce can (¾ cup) apricot
  nectar
1 cup whipping cream
1 teaspoon vanilla
1 8-ounce carton low-fat
  vanilla yogurt
  Raspberry Sauce

In a saucepan combine sugar and gelatin. Stir in apricot nectar. Cook and stir over medium heat till gelatin dissolves. Stir in whipping cream and vanilla. Gradually whisk yogurt into gelatin mixture till well combined. Pour mixture into a lightly oiled 3- or 4-cup mold. Cover and chill for 8 to 24 hours or till firm.

To serve, unmold onto a serving dish (see photos 2 and 3, page 118). Top with Raspberry Sauce. If desired, swirl additional vanilla yogurt into sauce. Makes 6 servings.

Raspberry Sauce: Thaw one 10-ounce package frozen *raspberries*. In a blender container or food processor bowl combine thawed raspberries, 2 tablespoons *powdered sugar*, and 1 tablespoon *orange juice*. Cover and blend or process till smooth. Press through a sieve to remove seeds; discard seeds.

Per serving: 315 calories, 4 g protein, 42 g carbohydrate, 16 g total fat (10 g saturated), 56 mg cholesterol, 39 mg sodium, 203 mg potassium.

Stirred Honey-Rice Pudding

3 cups milk
1 cup long grain rice
½ cup light raisins
⅓ cup honey
2 teaspoons finely shredded
  orange peel
1 teaspoon vanilla
  Ground cinnamon
  Whipping cream *or* half-
  and-half *or* light cream
  (optional)

In a heavy medium saucepan bring milk to boiling. Stir in *uncooked* rice and raisins. Cover and cook over low heat, stirring occasionally, for 30 to 40 minutes or till most of the milk is absorbed. (Mixture may appear curdled.)

Stir in honey, orange peel, and vanilla. Spoon into dessert dishes. Sprinkle lightly with cinnamon. Serve warm with whipping cream, half-and-half, or light cream, if desired. Makes 6 servings.

Per serving: 274 calories, 7 g protein, 57 g carbohydrate, 3 g total fat (2 g saturated), 9 mg cholesterol, 65 mg sodium, 340 mg potassium.

DESSERTS

Peaches and Cream in Spiced Cream Puffs

½ **cup margarine** *or* **butter**
1 **cup water**
¼ **teaspoon ground cinnamon**
⅛ **teaspoon ground nutmeg**
⅛ **teaspoon ground ginger**
⅛ **teaspoon salt**
1 **cup all-purpose flour**
4 **eggs**
½ **cup whipping cream**
¼ **cup sifted powdered sugar**
1 **8-ounce package cream cheese, softened**
2 **tablespoons peach preserves**
½ **teaspoon almond extract**
2 **medium peaches, peeled and coarsely chopped**

In a medium saucepan combine margarine or butter, water, cinnamon, nutmeg, ginger, and salt. Bring to boiling. Add flour all at once, stirring vigorously. **1** Cook and stir till mixture forms a ball that doesn't separate. Remove from heat. Cool 10 minutes. **2** Add eggs, one at a time, beating with a wooden spoon after each addition till smooth.

3 Drop batter by heaping tablespoons, 3 inches apart, onto a greased baking sheet. Bake in a 400° oven for 30 to 35 minutes or till golden. Cool on a wire rack.

Meanwhile, in a small bowl beat whipping cream with an electric mixer on high speed till soft peaks form. Gradually add the ¼ cup powdered sugar. Continue beating till stiff peaks form. Add cream cheese, peach preserves, and almond extract. Continue beating till smooth. Stir in chopped peaches.

4 To assemble, cut off top one-fourth of each puff. **5** Remove any soft dough from inside. **6** Fill each puff with peach mixture. Replace tops. Sprinkle with additional *powdered sugar*. If desired, filled puffs may be stored in refrigerator up to 1 hour before serving. Makes 12 servings.

Per serving: 258 calories, 5 g protein, 15 g carbohydrate, 20 g total fat (9 g saturated), 106 mg cholesterol, 194 mg sodium, 96 mg potassium.

1 After adding the flour to the boiling mixture, stir constantly until mixture forms a ball.

2 Add eggs, one at a time, beating mixture with a wooden spoon till smooth.

3 Using a tablespoon, drop batter onto a greased baking sheet.

4 After puffs have cooled, cut off the tops with a serrated knife.

5 Use a fork to remove the moist soft dough from the inside.

6 Fill each puff with cream mixture and replace the tops.

DESSERTS

Piña Colada Mousse

6 **ounces white baking bar, chopped**
1 **egg**
1 **egg yolk**
½ **cup pineapple juice**
2 **tablespoons light rum**
1 **teaspoon coconut extract or pineapple extract**
1 **teaspoon unflavored gelatin**
1 **cup whipping cream**
   Toasted coconut
   Maraschino cherries

In a heavy 1-quart saucepan, melt white baking bar over low heat, stirring constantly. In the top of a double boiler beat egg and egg yolk with an electric mixer on high speed about 4 minutes or till thick and lemon colored. Gradually add melted baking bar to egg mixture, beating on low speed. Place the top of the double boiler over, but not touching, hot water (*not boiling water*). Cook for 18 to 20 minutes, beating constantly. Pour egg mixture into a large bowl. Cover surface with plastic wrap and cool.

In a 1-cup glass measure combine pineapple juice, rum, and coconut or pineapple extract. Sprinkle gelatin over pineapple juice mixture. Let stand 5 minutes to soften. Place glass measure in a small saucepan with 1 inch of water. Heat and stir till gelatin dissolves. Gradually add gelatin mixture to egg mixture, beating till smooth.

Whip cream till soft peaks form. Gently fold into egg mixture. Chill for 15 to 20 minutes or till mixture mounds when spooned. Spoon mousse into individual dessert dishes. Cover and chill for 4 to 24 hours. Garnish with toasted coconut and maraschino cherries. Makes 6 servings.

Per serving: 376 calories, 5 g protein, 27 g carbohydrate, 27 g total fat (15 g saturated), 127 mg cholesterol, 64 mg sodium, 190 mg potassium.

Coffee Cream in Chocolate Cups

9 **foil bake cups**
1 **6-ounce package (1 cup) semisweet chocolate pieces**
1 **2-ounce square chocolate-flavored candy coating**
2 **cups tiny marshmallows**
⅓ **cup milk**
½ **cup whipping cream, whipped**
2 **tablespoons coffee liqueur**
   Fresh fruit such as raspberries, strawberries, or blueberries

For chocolate cups, place foil bake cups on a baking sheet. In a heavy medium saucepan combine chocolate pieces and candy coating; stir constantly over low heat till melted. Remove saucepan from heat; let stand 10 minutes.

Spoon *one rounded tablespoon* of the melted chocolate into each bake cup. With a small paint brush, brush melted chocolate onto bottom and up side of each bake cup till about ⅛ inch thick. (If chocolate becomes too firm to brush, reheat it.) Chill chocolate-coated bake cups for 10 minutes. Carefully peel foil away from chocolate cup. Keep chocolate cups refrigerated.

For filling, place marshmallows and milk in a 1½-quart saucepan. Cook and stir over medium heat for 3 to 4 minutes or till marshmallows are almost melted. Stir till smooth. Chill for 25 to 30 minutes or till mixture thickens, stirring occasionally. Fold in whipped cream and coffee liqueur. Chill mixture till it mounds, stirring occasionally.

Place chocolate cups on individual dessert plates. Spoon a scant ¼ *cup* filling into each chocolate cup. Garnish each serving with desired fresh fruit. Makes 9 servings.

Per serving: 224 calories, 2 g protein, 30 g carbohydrate, 11 g total fat (4 g saturated), 19 mg cholesterol, 33 mg sodium, 170 mg potassium.

Pecan Crunch Ice Cream

- ⅔ **cup chopped pecans**
- ¼ **cup sugar**
- 1 **tablespoon margarine** *or* **butter**
- 4 **cups half-and-half** *or* **light cream**
- 1½ **cups sugar**
- 1 **tablespoon vanilla**
- 2 **cups whipping cream**

In a skillet cook pecans, ¼ cup sugar, and margarine over medium heat till sugar begins to melt *(do not stir)*, shaking skillet occasionally. **1** Reduce heat to low. Cook and stir till sugar turns golden. Immediately spread on a baking sheet lined with greased foil. Cool; break into chunks. Set aside.

In a large mixing bowl combine half-and-half or light cream, 1½ cups sugar, and the vanilla. Stir till sugar dissolves. Stir in whipping cream. **2** Pour into a 4- or 5-quart ice cream freezer can. Stir in pecan chunks. Fit can into freezer. Adjust dasher; cover. **3** Pack crushed ice and rock salt around can. (Use 6 parts ice to 1 part salt.) Begin freezing ice cream. It is ready when the motor can no longer turn the dasher in the can or the hand crank turns hard. **4** Remove ice to below lid. Remove lid and dasher, scraping off ice cream. **5** To ripen ice cream, cover freezer can with several thicknesses of waxed paper or foil. Plug opening in lid; replace lid. Pack more ice and salt around can (Use 4 parts ice to 1 part salt.) Cover with several layers of towels or newspaper. Let ripen 4 hours. Remove ice mixture to below lid; remove lid. Makes 2 quarts (16 to 20 servings).

Per serving: 303 calories, 3 g protein, 26 g carbohydrate, 22 g total fat (11 g saturated), 63 mg cholesterol, 42 mg sodium, 123 mg potassium.

1 Cook pecan-sugar mixture till melted sugar turns golden, stirring frequently with a wooden spoon.

2 Pour mixture into the freezer can, filling the can no more than ⅔ full. Stir in pecan chunks.

3 After can has been placed in the freezer container, alternately pack layers of crushed ice and rock salt.

4 After ice cream has processed, remove ice to below level of can to prevent salt from seeping into can. Remove the dasher and replace lid.

5 To ripen, pack additional layers of ice and salt around can. Cover freezer with several layers of towels or newspaper. Let stand 4 hours.

No-Cook Vanilla Ice Cream

3 cups light cream
1½ cups sugar
1 tablespoon vanilla
3 cups whipping cream

In a large mixing bowl combine light cream, sugar, and vanilla. Stir till sugar dissolves. Stir in whipping cream. Freeze in a 4 or 5-quart ice cream freezer according to the manufacturer's directions. Makes 2 quarts (16 to 20 servings).

Per serving: 316 calories, 2 g protein, 22 g carbohydrate, 25 g total fat (16 g saturated), 91 g cholesterol, 35 mg sodium, 88 mg potassium.

No-Cook Chocolate-Almond Ice Cream: Prepare as above, *except* reduce sugar to *1 cup*. Stir one 16-ounce can (1½ cups) *chocolate-flavored syrup* and ½ cup chopped toasted *almonds* into ice cream mixture before freezing. Makes 2 quarts (16 to 20 servings).

Per serving: 394 calories, 4 g protein, 39 g carbohydrate, 27 g total fat (16 g saturated), 91 mg cholesterol, 55 mg sodium, 216 mg potassium.

Grape Sorbet

1½ cups water
1 6-ounce can frozen grape juice concentrate, thawed
1 tablespoon orange juice
1½ teaspoons lemon juice
Mint leaves (optional)
Lemon peel curls (optional)

Combine water, thawed juice concentrate, orange juice, and lemon juice; mix well. Pour into an 8x8x2-inch baking pan. Cover and freeze about 3 hours or till almost firm.

Break frozen mixture into large pieces and transfer, half at a time, to a food processor bowl. Cover and process till fluffy but not thawed. Return to pan. Cover and freeze till firm. (*Or,* after combining ingredients, freeze in a 1-quart ice cream freezer according to manufacturer's directions.)

To serve, scoop sorbet into serving dishes. Garnish with mint leaves and lemon peel curls, if desired. Makes about 3½ cups (7 servings).

Per serving: 45 calories, 0 g protein, 11 g carbohydrate, 0 g total fat (0 g saturated), 0 mg cholesterol, 3 mg sodium, 24 mg potassium.

Sweet Cherry Sorbet

1 cup orange juice
1 cup apple juice
2 tablespoons sugar
1 16-ounce package frozen pitted dark sweet cherries, thawed
¼ cup kirsch
1 teaspoon lemon juice

Combine orange juice, apple juice, and sugar, stirring till sugar dissolves; set aside. Place cherries in a blender container or food processor bowl. Cover and blend or process till smooth. Combine pureed cherries, kirsch, lemon juice, and juice mixture. Freeze in a 2-quart ice cream freezer according to manufacturer's directions. Makes 1 quart (8 servings).

Per serving: 104 calories, 1 g protein, 21 g carbohydrate, 1 g total fat (0 g saturated), 0 mg cholesterol, 2 mg sodium, 231 mg potassium.

Poached Pears in Rosy Fruit Sauce

4 ripe medium pears
2 cups cranberry-raspberry drink
1 tablespoon lemon juice
3 inches stick cinnamon
4 whole allspice
1 3x½-inch orange peel strip
2 tablespoons cold water
1 tablespoon cornstarch
Mint leaves (optional)

Peel pears, leaving stems on; remove core from bottom end. In a large saucepan combine cranberry-raspberry drink, lemon juice, cinnamon, allspice, and orange peel. Place pears in juice mixture, stem ends up.

Bring to boiling. Reduce heat and simmer, covered, for 10 to 15 minutes or till pears are tender. Carefully remove pears from pan with a slotted spoon. Refrigerate in a covered container until serving time. Remove and discard spices and orange peel. Measure *1 cup* of the poaching liquid; discard remaining liquid. Return the 1 cup poaching liquid to the saucepan.

For sauce, combine water and cornstarch, stirring till smooth. Stir cornstarch mixture into poaching liquid. Cook and stir over medium heat till thickened and bubbly. Cook and stir 2 minutes more. Cool to room temperature. Cover and chill completely.

To serve, place pears in individual dessert dishes. Pour sauce over pears. Garnish with mint leaves, if desired. Makes 4 servings.

Per serving: 142 calories, 1 g protein, 36 g carbohydrate, 1 g total fat (0 g saturated), 0 mg cholesterol, 2 mg sodium, 231 mg potassium.

Meringue Sundaes with Brandied Peach Sauce

3 egg whites
1 teaspoon vanilla
¼ teaspoon cream of tartar
¼ teaspoon ground
   cinnamon
   Dash salt
1 cup granulated sugar
¼ cup finely chopped
   walnuts
1 16-ounce can sliced
   peaches
2 tablespoons margarine *or*
   butter
⅓ cup packed brown sugar
2 tablespoons brandy
2 tablespoons light raisins
1 quart raspberry sherbet

Let egg whites stand at room temperature for 30 minutes. Meanwhile, cover a baking sheet with plain brown paper. Draw eight 3-inch circles on paper.

For meringue, combine egg whites, vanilla, cream of tartar, cinnamon, and salt in a large bowl. Beat with an electric mixer on medium speed till soft peaks form (tips curl). Add granulated sugar, a tablespoon at a time, beating on high speed till stiff peaks form (tips stand straight) and sugar is almost dissolved. Gently fold in walnuts.

Pipe or spoon meringue onto the circles on the brown paper, building the sides up to form shells. Bake in a 300° oven for 35 minutes. Turn off oven. Let shells dry in oven, with door closed, for at least 1 hour. Remove shells from paper. Store in an airtight container.

For sauce, drain peaches, reserving *2 tablespoons* syrup. Chop peaches; set aside. In a small saucepan melt margarine or butter. Stir in brown sugar, brandy, and the reserved peach syrup. Cook and stir over medium heat till bubbly and sugar is dissolved. Remove from heat. Stir in chopped peaches and raisins. Serve warm or at room temperature.

To serve, place a scoop of raspberry sherbet in the center of each meringue shell. Spoon peach sauce over sherbet. Makes 8 servings.

Per serving: 385 calories, 3 g protein, 79 g carbohydrate, 7 g total fat (2 g saturated), 5 mg cholesterol, 109 mg sodium, 216 mg potassium.

Summer Fruit with Custard Sauce

3 beaten eggs
2 cups milk *or* half-and-half
   or light cream
¼ cup sugar
1 tablespoon rum (optional)
1 teaspoon vanilla
4 cups mixed fresh fruit,
   such as sliced, peeled
   plums *or* peaches; sliced
   nectarines, strawberries,
   raspberries, *or*
   blueberries

In a heavy medium saucepan combine eggs; milk, half-and-half, or light cream; and sugar. Cook and stir over medium heat. Continue cooking egg mixture till it just coats a metal spoon. Remove from heat. Stir in rum, if desired, and vanilla.

Quickly cool the custard by placing the saucepan in a sink or bowl of ice water for 1 to 2 minutes, stirring constantly. Pour custard mixture into a bowl. Cover surface with clear plastic wrap. Chill till serving time. Spoon desired fruit into individual dessert dishes. Pour custard atop fruit. Makes 6 servings.

Per serving: 158 calories, 7 g protein, 24 g carbohydrate, 5 g total fat (2 g saturated), 113 mg cholesterol, 74 mg sodium, 324 mg potassium.

DESSERTS

Orange Cheesecake

1½ cups finely crushed
    chocolate wafers
    (about 25 cookies)
3 tablespoons sugar
1 tablespoon all-purpose
    flour
¼ cup margarine *or* butter,
    melted
3 8-ounce packages cream
    cheese, softened
¾ cup sugar
3 tablespoons all-purpose
    flour
1 tablespoon finely shredded
    orange peel
1 teaspoon vanilla
3 eggs
1 8-ounce carton dairy sour
    cream
¾ cup orange juice
    Whipped cream (optional)
    Orange slices (optional)
    Mint sprigs (optional)

For crust, combine crushed chocolate wafers, the 3 tablespoons sugar, and the 1 tablespoon flour. Stir in margarine or butter. **1** Press mixture onto bottom and about 2 inches up sides of a 9-inch springform pan.

In a large mixing bowl combine cream cheese, the ¾ cup sugar, the 3 tablespoons flour, orange peel, and vanilla. Beat with an electric mixer till fluffy. Add eggs and sour cream, beating on low speed just till combined. Stir in orange juice. **2** Pour into crust-lined pan. Place in a shallow baking pan in oven.

3 Bake in a 350° oven for 45 to 50 minutes or till center appears nearly set when shaken. Cool 15 minutes. Loosen crust from sides of pan. **4** Cool for 30 minutes more; remove sides of pan. Cool completely. Chill at least 4 hours. Garnish with whipped cream, orange slices, and mint, if desired. Makes 16 servings.

Per serving: 322 calories, 6 g protein, 23 g carbohydrate, 23 g total fat (12 g saturated), 94 mg cholesterol, 249 mg sodium, 111 mg potassium.

1 Press crumb mixture about 2 inches up the sides of the spring-form pan.

2 Pour filling mixture into crust-lined pan.

3 Test for doneness by gently shaking the pan. Filling should be firm in the center.

4 After cooling 45 minutes, remove sides of pan; cool completely. Chill at least 4 hours.

Chocolate-Cherry Ice Cream Torte

1   10¾-ounce frozen loaf
      pound cake
1   pint vanilla ice cream
½   cup maraschino cherries,
      well drained and
      chopped
1   ounce semisweet
      chocolate, grated
1   3-ounce package cream
      cheese, softened
2   tablespoons margarine *or*
      butter
2   teaspoons milk
¼   teaspoon vanilla
1⅓ cups sifted powdered
      sugar
2   tablespoons unsweetened
      cocoa powder
1   to 2 tablespoons chocolate-
      flavored syrup
      Maraschino cherries with
      stems

Using a serrated knife, cut pound cake horizontally into 3 layers. Place bottom cake layer on a baking sheet; set aside.

In a chilled mixing bowl stir ice cream just enough to soften. Fold in the ½ cup chopped maraschino cherries and grated chocolate. Spread *half* of the ice cream mixture over the bottom cake layer. Place second cake layer atop ice cream mixture. Spread remaining ice cream mixture over the second cake layer. Top with remaining cake layer. Place in freezer.

For frosting, in a small mixing bowl beat cream cheese, margarine or butter, milk, and vanilla with an electric mixer on medium speed for 30 seconds or till fluffy. Gradually add powdered sugar and cocoa powder, beating till smooth.

Remove cake from freezer. Spread frosting over top and sides of cake. Drizzle chocolate-flavored syrup around top edge of cake, allowing syrup to drip down sides. Cover and freeze till firm.

To serve, remove cake from freezer and let stand, covered, at room temperature for 10 minutes. Unwrap and place on a serving plate. Garnish with maraschino cherries. Makes 8 servings.

Per serving: 399 calories, 4 g protein, 54 g carbohydrate, 20 g total fat (7 g saturated), 27 mg cholesterol, 211 mg sodium, 169 mg potassium.

Chocolate Pudding and Oat-Crunch Parfaits

⅔   cup quick-cooking rolled
      oats
⅓   cup chopped pecans
2   tablespoons brown sugar
2   tablespoons margarine *or*
      butter, melted
½   cup granulated sugar
¼   cup unsweetened cocoa
      powder
2   tablespoons cornstarch
2   cups milk
3   beaten egg yolks
2   teaspoons margarine *or*
      butter

For oat crunch, in a mixing bowl combine rolled oats, pecans, brown sugar, and the 2 tablespoons melted margarine or butter. Spread oat mixture in a 9-inch pie plate. Bake in a 350° oven for 15 to 20 minutes or till toasted, stirring occasionally. Set oat mixture aside to cool.

For pudding, in a medium saucepan combine granulated sugar, cocoa powder, and cornstarch. Stir in milk all at once. Cook and stir over medium heat till thickened and bubbly. Reduce heat; cook and stir 2 minutes more. Remove saucepan from heat.

Gradually stir about *1 cup* of the hot mixture into beaten egg yolks. Return all of egg mixture to saucepan. Bring to a gentle boil. Reduce heat; cook and stir 2 minutes more. Remove saucepan from heat. Stir in the 2 teaspoons margarine or butter. Pour pudding into a bowl. Cover the surface with plastic wrap. Chill.

To serve, spoon *half* of the chocolate pudding into the bottom of 6 parfait glasses. Sprinkle with *half* of the oat mixture. Repeat layers. Makes 6 servings.

Per serving: 292 calories, 7 g protein, 36 g carbohydrate, 14 g total fat (3 g saturated), 113 mg cholesterol, 106 mg sodium, 207 mg potassium.

CANDY

Easy Chocolate Almond Truffles, Walnut Caramels, and Cashew Brittle

CANDY

Walnut Caramels

1 cup chopped walnuts
1 cup margarine *or* butter
1 16-ounce package (2¼ cups) packed brown sugar
2 cups half-and-half *or* light cream
1 cup light corn syrup
1 teaspoon vanilla

Line an 8x8x2-inch baking pan with foil, extending foil over edges of pan. Butter the foil. Sprinkle chopped walnuts on the bottom of the foil-lined pan; set pan aside.

In a heavy 3-quart saucepan melt the butter or margarine over low heat. Add the brown sugar, half-and-half or light cream, and corn syrup; mix well. Cook and stir over medium-high heat to boiling. Carefully clip candy thermometer to the side of the pan. Cook and stir over medium heat to 248°, firm-ball stage (45 to 60 minutes).

Remove saucepan from heat; remove candy thermometer from saucepan. Stir in vanilla. Immediately pour the caramel mixture over the nuts in the prepared pan. When caramel mixture is firm, use foil to lift it out of pan. Use a buttered knife to cut into 1-inch squares. Wrap each piece in clear plastic wrap. Makes about 64 caramels.

Note: Check the accuracy of your candy thermometer each time it is used. To do this, place the thermometer in a saucepan of boiling water for a few minutes and then read the temperature. If the thermometer registers above or below 212°, add or subtract the same number of degrees from the recipe temperature, and cook to that temperature.

Per caramel: 89 calories, 1 g protein, 11 g carbohydrate, 5 g total fat (1 g saturated), 2 mg cholesterol, 43 mg sodium, 45 mg potassium.

Peanutty Fudge Log

1⅓ cups sugar
⅔ cup evaporated milk
⅛ teaspoon salt
1½ cups tiny marshmallows
¾ cup semisweet chocolate pieces
¾ cup butterscotch-flavored pieces
½ cup chopped dry roasted peanuts
1 teaspoon vanilla
⅓ cup finely chopped dry roasted peanuts

In a heavy medium saucepan combine sugar, evaporated milk, and salt. Bring to boiling. Reduce heat to medium-low; cook and stir for 5 minutes.

Remove saucepan from heat. Add marshmallows, chocolate pieces, butterscotch pieces, the ½ cup chopped peanuts, and vanilla. Stir till marshmallows melt. Chill, if necessary, till thick enough to handle. Shape mixture into a 15x2-inch log. Roll log in the ⅓ cup chopped peanuts. Chill log; cut into ½-inch-thick slices. Store tightly covered in the refrigerator. Makes about 1½ pounds (30 slices).

Per slice: 115 calories, 2 g protein, 18 g carbohydrate, 5 g total fat (2 g saturated), 2 mg cholesterol, 56 mg sodium, 74 mg potassium.

Cardamom Fudge

2 **cups sugar**
¾ **cup milk**
2 **ounces unsweetened chocolate, cut up**
1 **tablespoon light corn syrup**
2 **tablespoons margarine *or* butter**
1 **teaspoon vanilla**
¾ **teaspoon ground cardamom**
½ **cup toasted chopped almonds**

Check the accuracy of your candy thermometer (see Note, page 225).

Line a 9x5x3-inch loaf pan with foil, extending foil over edges of pan. Butter the foil; set aside.

Butter the sides of a heavy 2-quart saucepan to prevent sugar buildup. In saucepan combine sugar, milk, chocolate, and corn syrup. Cook and stir over medium-high heat to boiling. **1**Carefully clip a candy thermometer to side of pan. Cook and stir over medium-low heat to 234°, soft-ball stage (20 to 25 minutes).

Remove saucepan from heat. Add margarine or butter, vanilla, and cardamom, but do not stir. Cool, without stirring, to 110° (about 55 minutes). Remove thermometer from saucepan. Beat mixture vigorously with a spoon till fudge just begins to thicken. Add almonds. **2**Continue beating till fudge becomes thick and starts to lose its gloss (about 10 minutes).

3*Immediately* spread fudge into prepared pan. Score into squares while warm. When firm, use foil to lift candy out of pan and cut into squares. Store tightly covered. Makes 1¼ pounds (24 pieces).

Per piece: 102 calories, 1 g protein, 18 g carbohydrate, 4 g total fat (1 g saturated), 1 mg cholesterol, 16 mg sodium, 44 mg potassium.

1When the chocolate mixture has come to a boil, clip a candy thermometer to the side of the pan, making sure the tip is submersed in the sugar mixture.

2When fudge is ready, it will become very thick and start to lose its glossy appearance.

3Spread into a buttered-foil-lined pan. The foil will make the removal from the pan much easier.

Toffee Butter Crunch

½ **cup toasted coarsely chopped almonds *or* pecans**
1 **cup butter**
1 **cup sugar**
3 **tablespoons water**
1 **tablespoon light corn syrup**
¾ **cup semisweet chocolate pieces**
½ **cup toasted finely chopped almonds *or* pecans**

Check the accuracy of your candy thermometer (see Note, page 225).

Line a 13x9x2-inch baking pan with foil, extending foil over edges. Sprinkle the ½ cup coarsely chopped nuts in pan. Butter the sides of a heavy 2-quart saucepan. In the saucepan melt the butter. Add the sugar, water, and corn syrup. Cook and stir over medium-high heat to boiling.

Clip a candy thermometer to side of saucepan. Cook and stir over medium heat to 290°, soft-crack stage (about 15 minutes). Watch carefully after 280° to prevent scorching. Remove saucepan from heat; remove thermometer from saucepan. Pour mixture into prepared pan. Let stand for 5 minutes or till firm. Sprinkle with chocolate pieces; let stand for 1 to 2 minutes. When softened, spread chocolate over mixture. Sprinkle with the ½ cup finely chopped nuts. Chill till firm. Use the foil to lift the candy out of the pan. Break into pieces. Store tightly covered. Makes about 1½ pounds (48 pieces).

Per piece: 76 calories, 1 g protein, 7 g carbohydrate, 6 g total fat (2 g saturated), 10 mg cholesterol, 40 mg sodium, 24 mg potassium.

Sweet and Salty Treats

8 **2-ounce squares vanilla-flavored candy coating**
1 **3-ounce can (2 cups) chow mein noodles**
2 **cups salted peanuts**

In a large heavy saucepan melt candy coating over low heat, stirring constantly. Cool slightly. Stir in chow mein noodles and peanuts. Drop mixture by spoonfuls onto a foil-lined baking sheet. If necessary, chill about 20 minutes or till firm. Makes about 36 pieces.

Note: Place candy coating in a large microwave-safe bowl. Micro-cook, uncovered, on 100% power (high) for 1 to 3 minutes or till candy coating melts, stirring occasionally. Cool slightly. Continue as directed.

Per piece: 130 calories, 3 g protein, 11 g carbohydrate, 9 g total fat (3 g saturated), 1 mg cholesterol, 70 mg sodium, 95 mg potassium.

Maple-Pecan Divinity

1½ **cups granulated sugar**
1 **cup packed brown sugar**
½ **cup light corn syrup**
½ **cup water**
2 **egg whites**
½ **teaspoon vanilla**
½ **teaspoon maple flavoring**
½ **cup chopped pecans**

Check the accuracy of your candy thermometer (see Note, page 225).

In a heavy 2-quart saucepan mix granulated sugar, brown sugar, corn syrup, and water. Cook and stir over medium-high heat to boiling. Clip candy thermometer to pan. Cook over medium heat without stirring to 260°, hard-ball stage (10 to 15 minutes). Remove from heat. Remove candy thermometer.

1 In a large mixer bowl, beat egg whites with a sturdy free-standing electric mixer on medium speed till stiff peaks form. **2** Gradually pour hot mixture in a thin stream over whites, beating on high speed about 3 minutes; scrape bowl. Add vanilla and maple flavoring. **3** Continue beating on high speed just till candy starts to lose its gloss. When beaters are lifted, mixture should fall in a ribbon that mounds on itself. This final beating should take 5 to 6 minutes. Drop a spoonful of candy onto waxed paper. If it stays mounded, the mixture has been beaten sufficiently.

Immediately stir in nuts. **4** Quickly drop remaining mixture from a teaspoon onto waxed paper. If mixture flattens out, beat ½ to 1 minute more; check again. If mixture is too stiff, beat in a few drops of hot water till candy is a softer consistency. Store tightly covered. Makes about 40 pieces.

Per piece: 70 calories, 0 g protein, 16 g carbohydrate, 1 g total fat (0 g saturated), 0 mg cholesterol, 8 mg sodium, 27 mg potassium.

1 Beat the egg whites till stiff peaks form.

2 While mixer is running, gradually pour hot mixture in a thin stream over egg whites.

3 When the candy just starts to lose its gloss, lift the beaters. The candy should fall in a ribbon, but mound on itself and not dissappear into the remaining mixture.

4 With a teaspoon, quickly drop mounds onto wax paper. Use a second spoon to push the candy off the first one.

CANDY

Chocolate-Covered Cherries

60 **maraschino cherries with stems (about three 10-ounce jars)**
3 **tablespoons margarine *or* butter, softened**
3 **tablespoons light corn syrup**
2 **cups sifted powdered sugar**
8 **2-ounce squares chocolate-flavored candy coating**

Drain cherries thoroughly on paper towels for several hours. Combine margarine or butter and corn syrup. Stir in powdered sugar; knead mixture till smooth (chill if too soft to handle).

Shape about *½ teaspoon* of the powdered sugar mixture around each cherry. Place coated cherries upright on a waxed paper-lined baking sheet; chill about 1 hour or till firm (do not chill too long or sugar mixture will begin to dissolve).

Cook and stir candy coating over low heat till melted. Holding cherries by stems, dip into melted coating. (Be sure to completely seal cherries in coating to prevent cherry juice from leaking.) Let excess coating drip off cherries. Place cherries, stem side up, on a waxed paper-lined baking sheet. Chill till coating is firm.

Store cherries in a tightly covered container in the refrigerator. Let cherries ripen in refrigerator for 1 to 2 weeks before serving. (Ripening allows powdered sugar mixture around cherries to soften and liquefy.) Makes 60.

Per cherry: 68 calories, 1 g protein, 11 g carbohydrate, 3 g total fat (1 g saturated), 0 mg cholesterol, 14 mg sodium, 36 mg potassium.

Butter-Mallow Crunch

2 **cups broken pretzels**
1 **cup tiny marshmallows**
½ **cup chopped salted cashews *or* peanuts**
¾ **cup sugar**
⅓ **cup half-and-half *or* light cream**
2 **tablespoons margarine *or* butter**
1 **cup butterscotch-flavored pieces**

In a large mixing bowl combine pretzels, marshmallows, and cashews or peanuts; set aside. In a heavy saucepan combine sugar, half-and-half or light cream, and margarine or butter. Bring to boiling over medium heat, stirring constantly. Remove saucepan from heat.

Stir in butterscotch pieces till smooth. Cool for 10 minutes. Pour butterscotch mixture over pretzel mixture; stir to coat. Drop by rounded teaspoons onto waxed paper-lined baking sheets. Chill till firm. Store in a tightly covered container in the refrigerator. Makes about 30.

Per piece: 81 calories, 1 g protein, 12 g carbohydrate, 4 g total fat (2 g saturated), 1 mg cholesterol, 75 mg sodium, 28 mg potassium.

White Fudge

2 cups sugar
½ cup milk
½ cup half-and-half *or* light
    cream
1 tablespoon light corn
    syrup
1 tablespoon margarine *or*
    butter
1 teaspoon vanilla
⅓ cup finely chopped dried
    apricots
⅓ cup toasted finely chopped
    pecans

Check the accuracy of your candy thermometer (see Note, page 225).
Line an 8x4x2-inch loaf pan with foil, extending the foil over the
edges of the pan. Butter foil; set aside.

Butter the sides of a heavy 2-quart saucepan. In the saucepan combine
sugar, milk, half-and-half or light cream, and corn syrup. Cook and stir
over medium-high heat to boiling. Carefully clip a candy thermometer
to side of pan. Cook and stir over medium-low heat to 238°, soft-ball
stage (25 to 35 minutes).

Remove from heat. Add margarine or butter and vanilla; do not stir.
Cool, without stirring, to 110° (about 55 minutes). Remove
thermometer. Stir in apricots and nuts. Beat mixture vigorously with a
wooden spoon till fudge is very thick and just starts to lose its gloss
(about 7 minutes).

Immediately spread fudge into prepared pan. Score into squares while
warm. When candy is firm, use the foil to lift it out of the pan. Cut
fudge into 1-inch squares. Makes about 1 pound (32 pieces).

Per piece: 74 calories, 0 g protein, 14 g carbohydrate, 2 g total fat (1 g saturated), 2 mg cholesterol, 11 mg sodium,
35 mg potassium.

CANDY

Rum-Raisin Clusters

1 6-ounce package (1 cup)
   semisweet chocolate
   pieces
¼ cup whipping cream
1 tablespoon rum
1½ cups raisins
½ cup chopped pecans
2 ounces white baking bar

In a small saucepan combine chocolate pieces and whipping cream. Cook and stir over low heat till chocolate melts and mixture is smooth. Stir in rum till smooth. Stir in raisins and chopped pecans.

Drop mixture into 1-inch paper candy cups. In another small saucepan melt white baking bar over low heat, stirring constantly; drizzle over raisin clusters. Chill till firm. Store in a tightly covered container in the refrigerator. Makes about 36 clusters.

Per cluster: 65 calories, 1 g protein, 9 g carbohydrate, 3 g total fat (1 g saturated), 2 mg cholesterol, 6 mg sodium, 82 mg potassium.

Chocolate Pralines

1½ cups granulated sugar
1½ cups packed brown sugar
1 cup half-and-half *or* light
   cream
3 tablespoons margarine *or*
   butter
2 ounces finely chopped
   unsweetened chocolate
2 cups pecan halves

Check the accuracy of your candy thermometer (see Note, page 225). Butter the sides of a heavy 2-quart saucepan. In the saucepan combine granulated sugar, brown sugar, and half-and-half or light cream. Cook and stir over medium-high heat to boiling. Clip candy thermometer to side of pan. Cook and stir over medium-low heat to 234°, soft-ball stage (16 to 18 minutes). Remove saucepan from heat.

Add margarine or butter and chopped chocolate to saucepan, but do not stir. Cool, without stirring, to 150° (about 30 minutes). Remove thermometer from saucepan. Stir in pecans. Beat mixture with a wooden spoon till candy just begins to thicken but is still glossy (about 3 minutes). Quickly drop candy by spoonfuls onto waxed paper. If candy becomes too stiff to drop, stir in a few drops of hot water. Store tightly covered. Makes about 36 pralines.

Per praline: 133 calories, 1 g protein, 19 g carbohydrate, 7 g total fat (1 g saturated), 3 mg cholesterol, 19 mg sodium, 78 mg potassium.

Easy Chocolate-Almond Truffles

1 11½-ounce package milk
    chocolate pieces
⅓ cup whipping cream
¼ teaspoon almond extract
⅓ cup toasted ground
    almonds
4 2-ounce squares vanilla-
    flavored candy coating
½ cup semisweet chocolate
    pieces, melted

In a heavy saucepan combine milk chocolate pieces and whipping cream. Cook over low heat for 4 to 5 minutes or till chocolate melts, stirring frequently. Remove saucepan from heat. Cool slightly. Stir in almond extract. Beat mixture with an electric mixer on low speed till smooth. Cover and refrigerate about 1 hour or till firm.

1 Shape chocolate mixture into ¾-inch balls; roll in ground almonds. Place on a waxed paper-lined baking sheet. Freeze for 30 minutes.

Meanwhile, in a heavy medium saucepan melt candy coating over low heat, stirring constantly. **2** Quickly dip truffles into melted candy coating, allowing excess coating to drip off.

3 Place truffles on waxed paper and let stand about 30 minutes or till coating is set. **4** Decoratively drizzle the melted semisweet chocolate over the tops of the truffles. Store in a tightly covered container in the refrigerator. Makes about 2½ dozen truffles.

Note: In a small microwave-safe bowl micro-cook vanilla-flavored candy coating on 100% power (high) for 2 to 3 minutes or till almost melted; stir till smooth.

Per truffles: 124 calories, 2 g protein, 14 g carbohydrate, 8 g total fat (2 g saturated), 6 mg cholesterol, 19 mg sodium, 83 mg potassium.

1 Roll balls in ground almonds to coat evenly.

2 Drop centers, one at a time, into melted candy coating; turn to coat. Lift center out; draw fork across rim of pan to remove excess coating.

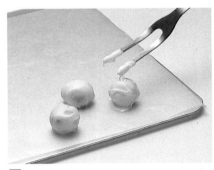

3 Invert onto a baking sheet lined with wax paper. Twist fork slightly as candy falls so you can swirl the top.

4 Using a small plastic bag with one corner snipped, carefully drizzle decoration on top of truffles.

Chocolate-Raspberry Truffles

⅔ **cup whipping cream**
3 **tablespoons unsalted butter**
1 **tablespoon granulated sugar**
6 **ounces semisweet chocolate, chopped**
2 **tablespoons raspberry liqueur**
¼ **cup unsweetened cocoa powder**
¼ **cup sifted powdered sugar**

Chek the accuracy of your candy thermometer (see Note, page 225). In a 1-quart saucepan combine the whipping cream, unsalted butter, and granulated sugar. Carefully clip candy thermometer to the side of the pan. Cook and stir till butter melts and mixture is very hot (180°). Remove saucepan from heat; remove candy thermometer from saucepan. Stir in the semisweet chocolate till melted and well combined. Stir in raspberry liqueur. Transfer mixture to a chilled bowl. Cover and chill about 1 hour or till mixture is completely cool, stirring often.

Drop mixture from a level tablespoon onto a waxed paper-lined baking sheet. Chill about 30 minutes or till firm. (If chocolate mixture is too soft to shape, quick-chill the mixture in the freezer for 5 to 10 minutes.) Working with a few at a time, shape drops into balls. Keep chilled. Roll the chilled chocolate balls in a mixture of cocoa powder and powdered sugar (or omit the powdered sugar and increase the cocoa powder to ½ cup). Store truffles in a tightly covered container in the refrigerator. Makes about 24 truffles.

Per truffle: 82 calories, 1 g protein, 7 g carbohydrate, 6 g total fat (4 g saturated), 13 mg cholesterol, 3 mg sodium, 34 mg potassium.

Date-Pecan Truffles

1 **cup chopped pitted dates**
2 **tablespoons orange juice**
¼ **cup whipping cream**
2 **tablespoons honey**
2 **tablespoons margarine** *or* **butter**
¼ **teaspoon ground cinnamon**
1 **6-ounce package (1 cup) semisweet chocolate pieces**
1 **cup finely chopped pecans**

In a mixing bowl combine chopped dates and orange juice; set aside. In a heavy medium saucepan combine whipping cream, honey, margarine or butter, and cinnamon. Bring just to boiling, stirring frequently. Remove saucepan from heat. Add chocolate pieces and stir till melted. Stir chocolate mixture into date mixture. Freeze mixture about 45 minutes or till firm enough to mound when dropped from a spoon, stirring after 20 minutes.

Drop by rounded teaspoons onto a foil-lined baking sheet. Freeze about 10 minutes or till almost firm. Shape drops into balls. Roll in chopped pecans. Chill till firm. Store in a tightly covered container in the refrigerator. Makes about 36.

Per serving: 71 calories, 1 g protein, 9 g carbohydrate, 4 g total fat (1 g saturated), 2 mg cholesterol, 12 mg sodium, 72 mg potassium.

Cashew Brittle

2 cups sugar
1 cup light corn syrup
1 cup butter
½ cup water
3 cups cashews, coarsely
  chopped
1½ teaspoons baking soda,
  sifted

Check the accuracy of your candy thermometer (see Note, page 225). Butter two large baking sheets; set baking sheets aside. Butter the sides of a heavy 3-quart saucepan. In the saucepan combine sugar, corn syrup, the 1 cup margarine or butter, and water. Cook and stir over medium-high heat to boiling. Carefully clip candy thermometer to side of pan.

1 Cook over medium heat, stirring occassionally to 275°, soft-crack stage (20 to 25 minutes). Stir in the chopped cashews. Continue cooking over medium heat, stirring frequently, to 295°, hard-crack stage (7 to 10 minutes).

Remove saucepan from heat; remove candy thermometer. **2** Quickly sprinkle sifted baking soda over mixture, stirring constantly. *Immediately* pour mixture onto prepared baking sheets. **3** With a greased spoon or spatula, carefully spread the candy into a thin sheet. Cool completely. Break candy into pieces. Store tightly covered. Makes about 2¼ pounds (72 servings).

Per serving: 181 calories, 2 g protein, 22 g carbohydrate, 11 g total fat (2 g saturated), 0 mg cholesterol, 189 mg sodium, 66 mg potassium.

1 Mixture should boil at a moderately steady rate over the entire surface.

2 Stir constantly as you sprinkle the baking soda over the candy mixture. The candy will foam as the baking soda reacts chemically. This makes the brittle porous.

3 Pour candy onto two large baking sheets. Using a greased spoon or spatula, carefully spread and pull the candy into a thin sheet.

Marbled Pecan Bark

4 2-ounce squares vanilla-
   flavored candy coating,
   coarsely chopped
1 12-ounce package (2 cups)
   semisweet chocolate
   pieces
1½ cups toasted chopped
   pecans

In a small heavy saucepan melt vanilla-flavored candy coating over low heat, stirring constantly; set aside. In another heavy saucepan melt chocolate pieces over low heat, stirring constantly; stir pecans into chocolate.

Spread pecan mixture thinly over a waxed paper-lined baking sheet. Drizzle melted candy coating over pecan mixture. Swirl candy coating through pecan mixture with the tip of a spoon or a thin metal spatula. Chill about 1 hour or till firm. Break into pieces. Store in an airtight container in the refrigerator. Makes about 1½ pounds.

Note: In a small microwave-safe bowl micro-cook vanilla-flavored candy coating on 100% power (high) for 2 to 3 minutes or till almost melted; stir till smooth. Set aside. In another microwave-safe bowl micro-cook semisweet chocolate pieces on 100% power (high) for 2 to 3 minutes or till almost melted; stir till smooth. Continue as directed.

Per serving: 171 calories, 2 g protein, 17 g carbohydrate, 11 g total fat (2 g saturated), 0 mg cholesterol, 18 mg sodium, 134 mg potassium.

Orange-Coconut Balls

1 12-ounce box vanilla
   wafers, crushed (3 cups)
1 3½-ounce can (1⅓ cups)
   flaked coconut
1 14-ounce can (1¼ cups)
   sweetened condensed
   milk
1 cup finely chopped pecans
1 cup light raisins
⅓ cup orange juice
2 tablespoons finely chopped
   crystallized ginger
1 cup flaked coconut

In a large mixing bowl combine crushed vanilla wafers, the 1⅓ cups flaked coconut, sweetened condensed milk, pecans, raisins, orange juice, and ginger. Chill for 1 hour.

Shape mixture into 1-inch balls. Roll in the 1 cup coconut. Store in a tightly covered container in the refrigerator. Makes about 6 dozen.

Per serving: 66 calories, 1 g protein, 9 g carbohydrate, 3 g total fat (1 g saturated), 5 mg cholesterol, 19 mg sodium, 59 mg potassium.

APPETIZERS AND BEVERAGES

Minted-Raspberry Iced Tea and Ham and Cheese Pinwheels

Ham and Cheese Pinwheels

1 **3-ounce package cream cheese, softened**
⅓ **cup diced fully cooked ham**
¼ **cup shredded Swiss *or* cheddar cheese (1 ounce)**
1 **tablespoon chopped onion *or* green onion**
2 **teaspoons snipped fresh parsley**
1 **teaspoon brown mustard *or* Dijon-style mustard**
1 **package (8) refrigerated crescent rolls**

For filling, in a mixing bowl combine cream cheese, ham, shredded cheese, onion, parsley, and mustard; mix well. Set filling aside.

Separate crescent rolls into 4 rectangles; press perforations to seal. Spread *one-fourth* of the filling over each crescent roll rectangle, leaving a ¼-inch margin on one short side and no margin on the other sides.

Starting at the short side with filling spread to the edge, roll up rectangles jelly roll style. Pinch seams to seal. Cut each roll into 8 slices. Place pinwheels, cut side down, on a greased baking sheet. Bake in a 375° oven for 10 to 12 minutes or till lightly browned. Makes 32.

Per serving: 40 calories, 1 g protein, 3 g carbohydrate, 3 g total fat (1 g saturated), 4 mg cholesterol, 88 mg sodium, 27 mg potassium.

Chicken Mousse

1 **envelope unflavored gelatin**
2 **tablespoons cold water**
½ **cup chicken broth**
1 **cup whipping cream**
1 **5-ounce can cooked chicken, drained and finely chopped**
¼ **cup mayonnaise *or* salad dressing**
3 **tablespoons chopped green onion**
1 **2-ounce jar sliced pimiento, drained and chopped**
1½ **teaspoons snipped fresh tarragon *or* ½ teaspoon dried tarragon, crushed**
¼ **teaspoon salt**
¼ **teaspoon white pepper**
Assorted crackers *or* sliced fresh vegetables

Soften gelatin in cold water; let stand 3 minutes. Bring chicken broth to boiling. Add to gelatin mixture, stirring till dissolved. Stir in whipping cream, chicken, mayonnaise, onion, pimiento, tarragon, salt, and pepper. Pour into a lightly greased 3-cup mold. Chill about 2 hours or till firm. Unmold onto a serving plate. Serve with assorted crackers or sliced fresh vegetables. Makes 3 cups (twenty-four 2-tablespoon servings).

Per 2 tablespoons: 63 calories, 2 g protein, 1 g carbohydrate, 6 g total fat (3 g saturated), 18 mg cholesterol, 86 mg sodium, 36 mg potassium.

Fruited Baked Brie

2 4-inch rounds Brie cheese (about 8 ounces each)
⅓ cup peach preserves
2 tablespoons chopped raisins
2 tablespoons toasted chopped pecans
¼ teaspoon ground ginger
Dash ground allspice
½ of a 17¼-ounce package (1 sheet) frozen puff pastry, thawed
Sliced fresh fruit *or* assorted crackers

1 Cut each round of Brie horizontally in half. Stir together peach preserves, raisins, pecans, ginger, and allspice. **2** Spread mixture over cut surface of bottom halves of Brie; replace top halves. Set aside.

Unfold puff pastry on a lightly floured surface. **3** Roll pastry into a 16x10-inch rectangle. Using a sharp knife, cut rectangle in half crosswise. **4** Place *one* Brie round in the center of each rectangle. Brush edges with water and bring up edges to completely cover top and sides of Brie, pressing to seal. **5** Trim off excess pastry and use it to make decorative cutouts for garnishing the top, if desired.

Place Brie rounds, smooth sides up, on an ungreased baking sheet. Cover and chill for 4 to 24 hours. Bake in a 400° oven for 15 to 18 minutes or till golden brown. Let stand 10 minutes before serving. Serve warm with fruit or crackers. Makes 16 servings.

Per serving: 189 calories, 7 g protein, 11 g carbohydrate, 13 g total fat (5 g saturated), 28 mg cholesterol, 236 mg sodium, 61 mg potassium.

1 With a sharp knife, cut Brie in half horizontally.

2 Spread peach preserve mixture evenly over bottom half of Brie. Replace top half.

3 On a lightly floured surface, roll pastry into a 16x10-inch rectangle. Cut pastry in half crosswise.

4 Place one round of Brie in the center of each pastry. Moisten edges of pastry with water and bring up edges to completely cover top and sides of Brie; press to seal.

5 Trim off excess pastry and use to make cutouts to garnish top, if desired.

Chinese Chicken Bites with Plum Sauce

3 tablespoons orange juice
1 tablespoon dry sherry
1 teaspoon soy sauce
12 ounces boneless, skinless chicken breast halves, cut into 1-inch pieces
½ cup cornflake crumbs
½ cup ground walnuts
⅛ teaspoon salt
⅛ teaspoon pepper
Plum Sauce

In a bowl stir together orange juice, sherry, and soy sauce; add chicken pieces, tossing to coat. In a plastic bag combine cornflake crumbs, ground walnuts, salt, and pepper. Add chicken pieces, a few at a time, closing bag and shaking to coat pieces well. Place chicken pieces in a single layer in a lightly greased 15x10x1-inch baking pan.

Bake in a 450° oven for 8 to 10 minutes or till no longer pink. Serve with Plum Sauce. Makes about 36.

Plum Sauce: In a small saucepan heat ½ cup *plum jam* over medium heat till melted. Stir in 1 tablespoon *orange juice*, 1½ teaspoons *prepared mustard*, 1 teaspoon finely shredded *orange peel*, ¼ teaspoon ground *ginger*, ⅛ teaspoon ground *cinnamon*, dash ground *cloves*, and dash *ground red pepper*. Bring to boiling. Cook for 1 minute, stirring constantly. Makes about ½ cup.

Per chicken bite with sauce: 16 calories, 2 g protein, 1 g carbohydrate, 0 g total fat (0 g saturated), 5 mg cholesterol, 29 mg sodium, 19 mg potassium.

Salmon Mousse

1 6½-ounce can boneless, skinless salmon
1 envelope unflavored gelatin
½ cup mayonnaise *or* salad dressing
2 tablespoons chili sauce
1 tablespoon lemon juice
2 hard-cooked eggs, finely chopped
¼ cup finely chopped celery
2 tablespoons chopped green onion
1 tablespoon snipped fresh chives
⅛ teaspoon pepper
½ cup whipping cream
Lettuce leaves
Assorted crackers

Drain salmon, reserving liquid. Add water to liquid to make *½ cup*. In a saucepan sprinkle gelatin over reserved liquid. Let stand 5 minutes. Heat and stir till gelatin dissolves. Remove saucepan from heat. Stir together mayonnaise or salad dressing, chili sauce, and lemon juice. Stir into gelatin. Chill till partially set (consistency of unbeaten egg whites). Fold in salmon, eggs, celery, green onion, chives, and pepper.

Beat whipping cream till soft peaks form; fold into gelatin mixture. Pour into a 3½- or 4-cup mold. Chill for 4 to 24 hours. Unmold onto a lettuce-lined serving platter. Serve with assorted crackers. Makes 24 servings.

Per serving: 70 calories, 2 g protein, 1 g carbohydrate, 7 g total fat (2 g saturated), 30 mg cholesterol, 85 mg sodium, 54 mg potassium.

Crab-Stuffed Miniature Popovers

2   6-ounce cans crabmeat,
    drained, flaked, and
    cartilage removed
⅓   cup mustard-mayonnaise
    sandwich and salad
    spread
¼   cup sliced green onion
¼   cup chopped red sweet
    pepper
1   teaspoon lemon juice
¼   teaspoon dried thyme,
    crushed
¼   teaspoon pepper
    Nonstick spray coating
2   eggs
1   cup milk
¾   cup all-purpose flour
¼   cup whole wheat flour
2   tablespoons grated
    Parmesan cheese
1   tablespoon cooking oil

For filling, in a medium bowl combine crabmeat, mustard-mayonnaise spread, green onion, sweet red pepper, lemon juice, thyme, and pepper; mix well. Cover and refrigerate.

Preheat oven to 450°. Spray 1¾-inch muffin cups with nonstick spray coating; set aside. In a blender container combine eggs, milk, all-purpose flour, whole wheat flour, Parmesan cheese, and oil. Cover and blend till smooth. **1** Fill prepared muffin cups *half* full of batter. Bake in a 450° oven for 10 minutes. Turn off oven; leave popovers in the oven for 5 minutes more. **2** Remove popovers from pan and cool on wire racks.

3 To serve, slice each popover in half, but not through to the other side. **4** Fill each popover with about *2 teaspoons* of the filling. Place filled popovers on a baking sheet. Bake in a 400° oven about 5 minutes or till heated through. Makes about 32.

Per popover: 44 calories, 3 g protein, 4 g carbohydrate, 2 g total fat (0 g saturated), 24 mg cholesterol, 85 mg sodium, 65 mg potassium.

1 Pour batter into muffin cups, filling half full.

2 Remove popovers from pan and cool on wire racks.

3 To fill, slice each popover in half crosswise, but not all the way through to the other side.

4 Fill each popover with about 2 teaspoons crabmeat mixture and place on baking sheet.

APPETIZERS AND BEVERAGES

Crab-Pine Nut Balls

1 7-ounce can crabmeat, drained, flaked, and cartilage removed
1 3-ounce package cream cheese with chives, softened
3 tablespoons fine dry bread crumbs
1 tablespoon soy sauce
¼ teaspoon white pepper
Several dashes bottled hot pepper sauce
½ cup toasted pine nuts, finely chopped

Stir together crabmeat, cream cheese, bread crumbs, soy sauce, white pepper, and pepper sauce in bowl till well combined. Form into 1-inch balls. Roll in nuts. Cover and chill for 1 to 24 hours. Makes 40 balls.

Per ball: 25 calories, 2 g protein, 1 g carbohydrate, 2 g total fat (1 g saturated), 7 mg cholesterol, 49 mg sodium, 35 mg potassium.

Crunchy Date Spread

½ of an 8-ounce package (4 ounces) cream cheese, softened
¼ cup creamy peanut butter
2 tablespoons milk
⅓ cup finely chopped pitted dates
¼ cup chopped unsalted peanuts
Apple slices *and/or* assorted crackers

In a small mixing bowl combine cream cheese, peanut butter, and milk; mix well. Stir in dates and peanuts. Cover and chill for 2 to 4 hours. Serve with apple slices and/or assorted crackers. Makes about 1 cup (sixteen 1-tablespoon servings).

Per tablespoon: 66 calories, 2 g protein, 4 g carbohydrate, 5 g total fat (2 g saturated), 8 mg cholesterol, 42 mg sodium, 72 mg potassium.

Texas Double Dip

1 cup chunky salsa
1 10-ounce can bean dip
1 6-ounce container frozen avocado dip, thawed
1 8-ounce carton dairy sour cream
2 tablespoons chopped ripe olives
Tortilla chips

Drain salsa, reserving juice; set salsa aside. In a small bowl stir enough juice (about 2 tablespoons) into bean dip to make dipping consistency.
Spread bean dip over half of a large plate to within 1 inch of edge. Spread avocado dip over other half of plate. Spread sour cream evenly over bean and avocado dips to within 1 inch of edge. Cover and chill till serving time.
To serve, top with drained salsa and olives. Serve with tortilla chips. Makes 8 servings.

Per serving: 276 calories, 6 g protein, 26 g carbohydrate, 17 g total fat (4 g saturated), 12 mg cholesterol, 744 mg sodium, 350 mg potassium.

Oriental Shrimp Dip

1 8-ounce carton dairy sour cream
1 4¼-ounce can shrimp, rinsed, drained, and chopped
½ cup finely chopped celery
½ cup finely chopped water chestnuts
¼ cup finely chopped green onion
¼ cup mayonnaise *or* salad dressing
2 teaspoons soy sauce
¼ teaspoon ground ginger
⅛ teaspoon garlic powder
Sugar snap peas
Celery sticks
Red sweet pepper pieces

In a mixing bowl combine sour cream, shrimp, celery, water chestnuts, green onion, mayonnaise or salad dressing, soy sauce, ginger, and garlic powder; mix well. Cover and chill for 2 to 8 hours. Serve with sugar snap peas, celery sticks, and red sweet pepper pieces. Makes about 2 cups (thirty-two 1-tablespoon servings).

Per tablespoon: 34 calories, 1 g protein, 1 g carbohydrate, 3 g total fat (1 g saturated), 11 mg cholesterol, 45 mg sodium, 33 mg potassium.

Apple-Nut Fruit Dip

1 **8-ounce package cream cheese**
½ **of a 6-ounce can frozen apple juice concentrate, thawed (⅓ cup)**
1 **tablespoon finely chopped toasted pecans**
4 **to 6 cups assorted fruit such as apple *or* pear wedges, pineapple spears, *and/or* strawberries**

In a small mixing bowl beat cream cheese and apple juice concentrate till smooth. Cover and chill, if desired. At serving time, sprinkle with pecans. Serve with fruit dippers. Makes 1⅓ cups dip (twenty-one 1-tablespoon servings).

Per tablespoon: 48 calories, 1 g protein, 2 g carbohydrate, 4 g total fat (2 g saturated), 12 mg cholesterol, 34 mg sodium, 37 mg potassium.

Honey-Mustard Pretzel Snacks

¼ **cup margarine *or* butter**
¼ **cup honey mustard**
1 **teaspoon Worcestershire sauce**
¼ **teaspoon garlic powder**
 Several dashes bottled hot pepper sauce
10 **cups small pretzels**

In a small saucepan melt margarine or butter. Remove saucepan from heat and stir in honey mustard, Worcestershire sauce, garlic powder, and hot pepper sauce.

Place pretzels in a foil-lined 15x10x1-inch baking pan. Pour mustard mixture over pretzels; toss gently to coat. Bake in a 300° oven for 25 minutes, stirring every 10 minutes. Spread on foil; cool. Store in an airtight container. Makes 10 cups (20 servings).

Per ½ cup serving: 112 calories, 2 g protein, 17 g carbohydrate, 3 g total fat (1 g saturated), 0 mg cholesterol, 483 mg sodium, 38 mg potassium.

Calypso Popcorn

2 **tablespoons margarine *or* butter**
¼ **teaspoon curry powder**
¼ **teaspoon ground ginger**
¼ **teaspoon ground cumin**
⅛ **teaspoon ground allspice**
⅛ **teaspoon ground red pepper**
4 **cups popped popcorn**
1 **cup dry roasted peanuts**
½ **cup mixed dried fruit bits**

In a small saucepan cook and stir margarine or butter, curry powder, ginger, cumin, allspice, and red pepper till margarine or butter melts. Cook and stir 1 minute more.

In a large mixing bowl combine popcorn, peanuts, and dried fruit bits. Drizzle margarine or butter mixture over popcorn mixture, tossing gently to coat evenly. Makes about 5 cups (10 servings).

Per ½ cup serving: 144 calories, 4 g protein, 12 g carbohydrate, 10 g total fat (1 g saturated), 0 mg cholesterol, 147 mg sodium, 180 mg potassium.

Sizzling Pecans and Raisins

3 tablespoons margarine *or* butter
1 tablespoon soy sauce
½ teaspoon five-spice powder
¼ teaspoon garlic salt
⅛ teaspoon ground red pepper
Dash bottled hot pepper sauce
2 cups pecan halves
1 cup raisins

1 In a small saucepan cook and stir margarine or butter, soy sauce, five-spice powder, garlic salt, ground red pepper, and hot pepper sauce till margarine or butter melts. **2** Spread pecan halves in a 9x9x2-inch baking pan; add margarine or butter mixture, stirring to coat.

3 Bake in a 350° oven for 12 to 15 minutes or till toasted, stirring occasionally. Remove from oven and stir in raisins. **4** Spread mixture on foil; cool. Store in an airtight container. Makes about 3 cups (13 servings).

Per ¼ cup serving: 169 calories, 2 g protein, 12 g carbohydrate, 14 g total fat (1 g saturated), 0 mg cholesterol, 151 mg sodium, 154 mg potassium.

1 In a small saucepan combine margarine or butter, soy sauce, and spices. Heat and stir over low heat till melted.

2 Pour margarine or butter mixture evenly over pecans; stir to thoroughly coat pecans with mixture.

3 Stir pecan mixture occasionally as it bakes.

4 Spread pecan-raisin mixture on aluminum foil to cool.

Pepperoni Biscuit Bites

2 cups packaged biscuit mix
1 3-ounce package
   pepperoni, finely
   chopped (¾ cup)
½ cup grated Romano cheese
3 tablespoons snipped fresh
   parsley
1 teaspoon dried Italian
   seasoning, crushed
¼ teaspoon garlic powder
⅔ cup milk

In a medium mixing bowl combine biscuit mix, chopped pepperoni, Romano cheese, parsley, Italian seasoning, and garlic powder. Add milk; stir till moistened.

Drop by rounded teaspoons onto a greased baking sheet. Bake in a 400° oven for 12 to 15 minutes or till golden brown. Makes about 36.

Per serving: 47 calories, 2 g protein, 5 g carbohydrate, 2 g total fat (1 g saturated), 4 mg cholesterol, 147 mg sodium, 19 mg potassium.

Chunky Guacamole

2 large ripe avocados,
   halved, seeded, peeled,
   and chopped
¼ cup sliced green onions
¼ cup chopped onion
1 teaspoon lemon juice
1 teaspoon salad oil
1 medium tomato, chopped
   Chopped tomato (optional)
   Tortilla chips

In medium mixing bowl combine avocados, onions, lemon juice, oil, dash *salt,* and dash *pepper.* Stir in chopped tomato. Transfer to serving bowl. Garnish with additional chopped tomato, if desired. Serve with tortilla chips. Makes 2 cups (thirty-two 1-tablespoon servings).

Note: To make ahead, increase lemon juice to 1 tablespoon; cover and chill till serving time.

Per tablespoon: 25 calories, 0 g protein, 0 g carbohydrates, 3 g total fat (0 g saturated), 0 mg cholesterol, 6 mg sodium, 114 mg potassium.

Marinated Mushrooms

1 pound small fresh
   mushrooms
½ cup sliced green onion
¼ cup salad oil
½ cup dry white wine
⅓ cup water
3 tablespoons lemon juice
1 clove garlic, minced
½ teaspoon dried rosemary,
   crushed
½ teaspoon ground coriander
½ teaspoon instant beef
   bouillon granules
¼ teaspoon salt

Wash mushrooms; trim stems to ¼ inch. Place in bowl with green onion. In a saucepan heat salad oil, wine, water, lemon juice, garlic, rosemary, coriander, bouillon granules, and salt till simmering. Pour over vegetables. Cover and chill at least 24 hours, stirring occasionally. Store in refrigerator up to 3 days. Makes 8 servings.

Per serving: 31 calories, 1 g protein, 3 g carbohydrates, 2 g total fat (0 g saturated), 0 mg cholesterol, 73 mg sodium, 223 mg potassium.

Plantation Punch with Pineapple Ice Ring

Water
Sliced fruit
2 **46-ounce cans unsweetened pineapple juice, chilled**
1 **6-ounce can frozen daiquiri mix concentrate**
1 **6-ounce can frozen orange juice concentrate**
1 **1-liter bottle lemon-lime carbonated beverage, chilled**
1 **cup rum**

1 For the ice ring, pour *½ inch* of water (about ¾ cup) into a 7-cup ring mold. Freeze till firm. **2** Arrange sliced fruit upside down on the ice. Carefully pour *¼ cup* water around the fruit. Freeze till firm. **3** Carefully pour in *4 cups* of the pineapple juice. Freeze about 8 hours or till firm. Turn mold upside down. Run warm water over mold to loosen ice ring. Unmold, wrap, and store ice ring in the freezer.

To serve, combine remaining pineapple juice, daiquiri mix concentrate, and orange juice concentrate in a large punch bowl. Stir in lemon-lime beverage, rum, and 4 cups *ice cold water*.

4 Unwrap ice ring; place fruit-side up in punch bowl. Makes about 32 (4-ounce) servings.

Per serving: 93 calories, 0 g protein, 19 g carbohydrate, 0 g total fat (0 g saturated), 0 mg cholesterol, 5 mg sodium, 148 mg potassium.

1 To make Pineapple Ice Ring, pour ½ inch of water into a 7-cup ring mold. Freeze till firm.

2 Arrange fruit upside down in a decorative pattern atop ice. Carefully pour ¼ cup water around fruit; freeze.

3 When fruit layer is firm, pour 4 cups pineapple juice over frozen layer. Freeze till firm.

4 At serving time, place ice ring fruit side up in punch mixture. Ice ring will float.

Minted-Raspberry Iced Tea

4 **cups water**
3 **tablespoons frozen**
   lemonade concentrate,
   thawed
⅓ **cup fresh *or* frozen**
   raspberries
¼ **to ½ cup fresh mint leaves**
3 **tablespoons sugar**
5 **raspberry-flavored tea bags**
   Ice cubes
   Fresh mint sprigs and
   raspberries (optional)

In a saucepan combine water and lemonade concentrate; bring to boiling. Place raspberries, mint leaves, sugar, and tea bags in a 2-quart heatproof container. Pour boiling water mixture over tea bag mixture. Steep for 5 minutes; remove and discard tea bags. Chill thoroughly.

To serve, strain mixture and discard mint leaves. Serve over ice. Garnish each serving with mint sprigs and fresh raspberries, if desired. Makes about 5 (6-ounce) servings.

Per serving: 48 calories, 0 g protein, 13 g carbohydrate, 0 g total fat (0 g saturated), 0 mg cholesterol, 6 mg sodium, 23 mg potassium.

Hot Spiced Cranberry-Apple Sipper

2½ **cups cranberry juice**
    cocktail
2 **cups apple cider**
½ **cup orange juice**
2 **tablespoons red cinnamon**
   candies
2 **tablespoons lemon juice**
3 **whole cloves**
1 **whole allspice**
   Lemon slices (optional)

In a saucepan combine cranberry juice cocktail, apple cider, orange juice, cinnamon candies, lemon juice, cloves, and allspice. Bring to boiling. Reduce heat and simmer, uncovered, about 10 minutes or till candies dissolve. Remove and discard whole cloves and allspice. Serve hot. Garnish each serving with a lemon slice, if desired. Makes 5 (8-ounce) servings.

Per serving: 104 calories, 0 g protein, 27 g carbohydrate, 0 g total fat (0 g saturated), 0 mg cholesterol, 7 mg sodium, 207 mg potassium.

Triple Strawberry Shake

1 **pint strawberry ice cream**
½ **cup milk**
½ **cup sliced fresh**
   strawberries
1 **tablespoon strawberry jam**
½ **teaspoon coconut**
   flavoring (optional)

Place ice cream, milk, strawberries, strawberry jam, and, if desired, coconut flavoring in a blender container. Cover and blend till smooth. Serve immediately. Makes 2 servings.

Per serving: 323 calories, 6 g protein, 49 g carbohydrate, 13 g total fat (8 g saturated), 43 mg cholesterol, 112 mg sodium, 413 mg potassium.

Mixed Fruit Cooler

1 cup sliced strawberries
1 cup sliced, peeled peaches
1 cup chopped, peeled
   mango
1 cup unsweetened
   pineapple juice
½ cup cream of coconut
2 tablespoons lemon juice
2 tablespoons lime juice
1 teaspoon rum flavoring
   (optional)
1½ to 2½ cups ice cubes

In a large bowl combine strawberries, peaches, mango, pineapple juice, cream of coconut, lemon juice, lime juice, and, if desired, rum flavoring. Add fruit mixture, half at a time, to blender container along with half of the ice cubes. Repeat with remaining fruit mixture and ice cubes. Cover and blend till frothy. Serve immediately. Makes about 5 (8-ounce) servings.

Per serving: 152 calories, 2 g protein, 20 g carbohydrate, 9 g total fat (7 g saturated), 0 mg cholesterol, 4 mg sodium, 319 mg potassium.

Papaya Smoothie

1 **ripe papaya, peeled,**
   seeded, and chopped
1 **cup milk**
¾ **cup orange juice**
4 **ice cubes**
1 **tablespoon honey**
2 **teaspoons lime juice**
¼ **teaspoon ground allspice**
⅛ **teaspoon ground**
   cinnamon
⅛ **teaspoon ground**
   cardamom

In a blender container combine papaya, milk, orange juice, ice cubes, honey, lime juice, allspice, cinnamon, and cardamom. Cover and blend till smooth. Makes 2 servings.

Per serving: 261 calories, 6 g protein, 54 g carbohydrate, 3 g total fat (1 g saturated), 9 mg cholesterol, 78 mg sodium, 805 mg potassium.

Dessert Coffee

⅔ **cup hot strong coffee**
2 **teaspoons rum**
1 **teaspoon dark brown**
   sugar
   Dash ground allspice
   Whipped cream (optional)
   Orange peel curl (optional)

Stir together hot coffee, rum, brown sugar, and allspice. Top with a dollop of whipped cream and an orange peel curl, if desired. Makes 1 (about 6-ounce) serving.

Per serving: 42 calories, 0 g protein, 5 g carbohydrate, 0 g total fat (0 g saturated), 0 mg cholesterol, 5 mg sodium, 103 mg potassium.

Cardamom-Ginger Cocoa

4 **cups milk**
¼ **cup sugar**
4 **teaspoons unsweetened**
   cocoa powder
¼ **teaspoon ground**
   cardamom
⅛ **teaspoon ground ginger**
⅓ **cup whipping cream,**
   whipped
   Grated semisweet
   chocolate

In a medium saucepan combine *1½ cups* of the milk, sugar, cocoa powder, cardamom, and ginger. Cook and stir over medium heat till mixture just comes to boiling. Stir in remaining milk; heat through. *Do not boil.* Serve hot in cups or mugs. Top each serving with a dollop of whipped cream. Sprinkle with grated chocolate. Makes about 5 (6-ounce) servings.

Per serving: 207 calories, 7 g protein, 22 g carbohydrate, 11 g total fat (7 g saturated), 36 mg cholesterol, 104 mg sodium, 327 mg potassium.

Jungle Trail Mix

Jungle Trail Mix

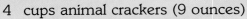

Ingredients:

4 cups animal crackers (9 ounces)

2 cups whole grain wheat and raisin squares

2 6-ounce packages mixed dried fruit bits

1 cup candy-coated milk chocolate pieces

Per ¼ cup: 88 calories, 1 g protein, 17 g carbohydrate, 2 g total fat (1 g saturated), 1 mg cholesterol, 50 mg sodium, 106 mg potassium.

1 In the **large bowl** combine all ingredients with **wooden spoon**; stir well.

2 Pour mixture into a **large storage container** with a loose fitting **cover**. Makes 9 cups (thirty-six ¼ cup servings).

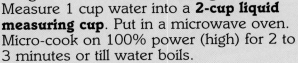

Cool Cupcakes

Ingredients:

Cooking oil

1 3-ounce package strawberry-flavored gelatin

1 cup water

1 cup cranberry-raspberry drink

¾ cup fresh sliced strawberries

1 medium banana, thinly sliced

Pressurized whipped dessert topping

Per serving: 120 calories, 2 g protein, 24 g carbohydrate, 3 g total fat (1 g saturated), 3 mg cholesterol, 44 mg sodium, 112 mg potassium.

1 Using a **paper towel**, lightly grease six **6-ounce custard cups** with cooking oil. Set aside until Step 4.

2 Put gelatin in a **medium mixing bowl**. Measure 1 cup water into a **2-cup liquid measuring cup**. Put in a microwave oven. Micro-cook on 100% power (high) for 2 to 3 minutes or till water boils.

3 Carefully remove measuring cup from microwave oven and pour water over gelatin in bowl. Stir till gelatin dissolves. Add cranberry-raspberry drink and stir.

4 Divide strawberries and banana slices evenly among the custard cups. Pour gelatin over fruit. Cover cups with plastic wrap and refrigerate. Chill 3 hours or till firm.

5 To unmold, dip each custard cup in bowl of warm water to loosen. Place **small plate** upside down on top of custard cup. Turn custard cup and plate together right side up. Lift off cup. Top with whipped topping. Makes 6 servings.

Orange-Almond Monkey Bread

1 Turn oven to 350°. To toast almonds, place in a **shallow baking pan** in oven for 5 to 10 minutes or till golden brown. Use **hot pads** to remove baking pan from oven. Raise oven temperature to 375°. Put a little bit of shortening on a piece of **paper towel**. Spread the shortening evenly over the inside of a **10-inch fluted tube pan**. Spoon orange marmalade evenly over bottom of greased pan. Sprinkle with toasted almonds. Set pan aside.

Ingredients:

- ¼ cup sliced almonds
- Shortening
- ½ cup orange marmalade
- ¼ cup margarine or butter
- 2 10-ounce packages refrigerated biscuits
- ⅓ cup light raisins
- ½ cup sugar
- ½ teaspoon ground cinnamon
- ¼ teaspoon ground nutmeg

Per serving: 261 calories, 3 g protein, 46 g carbohydrate, 9 g total fat (1 g saturated), 0 mg cholesterol, 418 mg sodium, 285 mg potassium.

2 Melt margarine or butter in the **small saucepan** with burner set on low heat, stirring constantly with a **wooden spoon**. Turn off the burner. Remove the pan from burner. Separate the biscuits. Use **kitchen shears** to cut each biscuit into quarters.

4 Place the sugar-cinnamon coated biscuit pieces on top of the raisins in pan. Put the pan in the oven. Bake about 25 minutes or till the biscuits are golden brown. Turn the oven off.

3 Place ⅓ of the biscuit pieces (26) in the greased pan. Sprinkle raisins evenly over biscuit layer. In a **small bowl** combine sugar, cinnamon, and nutmeg. Dip remaining biscuit pieces in the melted margarine or butter. Then roll in sugar-cinnamon mixture.

5 Use **hot pads** to remove the pan from the oven. Put pan on a **cooling rack**. Cool about 1 minute. Have an adult place a **plate** upside down on top of the pan. Carefully turn the pan and plate together right side up. Remove the pan. Cool about 10 minutes. Serve warm. Makes 10 servings.

Fruity Muffins

Ingredients:

1¾ cups all-purpose flour
⅓ cup sugar
2 teaspoons baking powder
½ teaspoon ground cinnamon
2 ripe medium bananas
½ cup strawberry low-fat yogurt
1 beaten egg
¼ cup cooking oil
¼ cup Grape Nuts cereal

Per serving: 165 calories, 3 g protein, 27 g carbohydrate, 5 g total fat
(1 g saturated), 18 mg cholesterol, 75 mg sodium, 126 mg potassium.

1 Turn oven to 400°. Line **muffin pan** with **paper bake cups**; set aside. In a **medium mixing bowl** combine flour, sugar, baking powder, cinnamon, and ¼ teaspoon salt.

2 Peel bananas and break into chunks; place in a **small bowl**. Mash banana with a **fork**. Measure the mashed banana; you should have ⅔ cup.

3 Add mashed banana, yogurt, egg, and oil to flour mixture. Stir just till flour mixture is moistened.

4 Fill muffin cups ⅔ full. Sprinkle evenly with cereal. Bake for 15 to 20 minutes or till golden. Use **hot pads** to remove muffin pan from oven. Turn oven off. Makes 12.

BBQ Chicken with Corn Muffins

Ingredients:

2 cups cubed cooked chicken
   (about 10 ounces)
1½ cups bottled barbecue sauce
1½ cups frozen mixed vegetables
¼ cup frozen chopped onion
1 11½-ounce package frozen corn
   muffins

Per serving: 361 calories, 18 g protein, 51 g carbohydrate, 8 g total fat
(2 g saturated), 66 mg cholesterol, 969 mg sodium, 234 mg potassium.

1 Turn oven to 350°. Put chicken, barbecue sauce, frozen vegetables, and onion in a **medium saucepan**. Turn the burner to medium. Cook the chicken mixture till hot, stirring occasionally with a **wooden spoon**.

2 While heating chicken mixture, remove corn muffins and baking tray from package. Put in oven. Bake for 16 to 20 minutes or till golden. Turn oven off. Use **hot pads** to remove tray from oven. Cool slightly.

3 Carefully remove hot muffins from paper bake cups. Cut muffins in half lengthwise and place on a serving plate.

4 Spoon chicken mixture over muffin halves. Makes 6 servings.

Popcorn-Nut Crunch

Ingredients:

1   12-ounce package chocolate-flavored candy coating

2   tablespoons peanut butter

6   cups popped popcorn

1   cup bite-size corn cereal squares

1   cup peanuts

1   cup dried banana chips or mixed dried fruit bits

½   cup raisins

Per ¼ cup serving: 85 calories, 2 g protein, 9 g carbohydrate, 5 g total fat (2 g saturated), 0 mg cholesterol, 32 mg sodium, 83 mg potassium.

1 In a **medium microwave-safe bowl** combine candy coating and peanut butter. Micro-cook on 100% power (high) for 1 to 2 minutes or till chocolate melts, stirring twice. Meanwhile, in a **large bowl** combine popcorn, cereal, peanuts, banana chips or dried fruit bits, and raisins.

2 Pour warm melted chocolate mixture over popcorn mixture, stirring gently to coat well.

3 Spread popcorn mixture onto a large piece of **foil**. Cool thoroughly. Break popcorn mixture apart and store in a **tightly covered container** for up to 5 days. Makes 11 cups.

Chocolate Chip-Oatmeal Cookies

Ingredients:

½ cup margarine or butter
1 egg
1 cup all-purpose flour
½ cup granulated sugar
½ cup packed brown sugar
1 teaspoon vanilla
½ teaspoon baking soda
1 cup quick-cooking rolled oats
1 6-ounce package (1 cup) semisweet chocolate pieces

Per cookie: 80 calories, 1 g protein, 11 g carbohydrate, 4 g total fat (0 g saturated), 5 mg cholesterol, 44 mg sodium, 36 mg potassium.

1 Remove the margarine or butter from the refrigerator at least 30 minutes before making the cookies.

2 Turn oven to 375°. Put margarine or butter in a **large bowl**. Position **electric mixer** over bowl. Turn mixer to medium speed. Beat 30 seconds. Turn off mixer.

3 Crack the egg into a **custard cup**. Add the egg, flour, granulated sugar, brown sugar, vanilla, and baking soda to the margarine. Beat on medium speed about 2 minutes or till well mixed. Stop occasionally to scrape sides of bowl with a **rubber scraper** as needed. Turn off mixer. Use a **wooden spoon** to stir in oats and chocolate pieces.

4 Scoop enough dough on a **small spoon** so the dough is slightly rounded. Use **another spoon** to push the dough from the spoon onto a **cookie sheet**. Repeat to fill cookie sheet. Leave about 2 inches between cookies.

5 Put the cookie sheet in the oven. Bake for 8 to 10 minutes or till brown. While the cookies bake, drop more cookie dough onto another cookie sheet.

6 Use **hot pads** to remove the cookie sheet from the oven and set on a **cooling rack**. Put the second cookie sheet into the oven. Use a **pancake turner** to lift the baked cookies onto a second cooling rack. When the first cookie sheet is cool, drop more dough onto it. Repeat with remaining dough. Turn the oven off. Makes about 40.

Rocky Road Fudge

Ingredients:

3⅔ cups sifted powdered sugar
½ cup unsweetened cocoa powder
½ cup margarine or butter
2 tablespoons milk
½ cup tiny marshmallows
¼ cup chopped nuts
1 tablespoon vanilla

Per serving: 75 calories, 0 g protein, 12 g carbohydrate, 3 g total fat (1 g saturated), 0 mg cholesterol, 31 mg sodium, 7 mg potassium.

 Line an **8x8x2-inch baking pan** with **foil**. Set pan aside until Step 5.

 In a **mixing bowl** combine powdered sugar and cocoa powder. Mix well with a **wooden spoon**. Set aside until Step 4.

In a **small saucepan** mix margarine or butter and milk. Put pan on burner. Turn to low. Heat and stir till margarine melts. Turn off burner; take pan off burner.

 Pour melted margarine or butter mixture over powdered sugar mixture. Stir with the wooden spoon till smooth. Add marshmallows, nuts, and vanilla; stir well.

 Pour into foil-lined pan. Spread evenly with a **rubber scraper**. Chill till firm. Cut into squares. Makes 36 pieces.

Peanutty S'Mores Bars

Ingredients:

18 graham cracker squares
    (2½-inch squares)
¼   cup marshmallow creme
¼   cup chopped peanuts
½   cup peanut butter-flavored pieces
½   cup milk chocolate pieces

Per serving: 161 calories, 3 g protein, 21 g carbohydrate, 8 g total fat
(4 g saturated), 0 mg cholesterol, 116 mg sodium, 91 mg potassium.

1 Place 9 of the graham cracker squares in the bottom of a **2-quart square baking dish** or place flat on a **microwave-safe plate**.

2 Using a **spoon,** scoop up about 1 teaspoon of the marshmallow creme. Use another spoon to push it onto a cracker in the dish. Repeat with remaining crackers.

3 Sprinkle chopped peanuts over marshmallow creme.

4 Sprinkle peanut butter-flavored pieces and chocolate pieces over the marshmallow-topped cracker squares.

5 Put the rest of the graham cracker squares on top of the chocolate pieces.

6 Put the baking dish or plate in a microwave oven. Micro-cook on 100% power (high) for 1 to 2 minutes or till the chocolate begins to melt.

7 Remove the baking dish or plate from the microwave oven with **hot pads**. Cool at least 5 minutes before serving. Makes 9.

Breakfast Pizzas

Ingredients:

½ cup soft-style cream cheese

4 6-inch whole wheat pita bread rounds

¼ cup chunky applesauce

4 brown-and-serve sausage links

1 cup shredded American or cheddar cheese (4 ounces)

Per serving: 329 calories, 13 g protein, 28 g carbohydrate, 20 g total fat (10 g saturated), 55 mg cholesterol, 751 mg sodium, 278 mg potassium.

1 Turn oven to 425°. Use a **table knife** to spread cream cheese over pita bread rounds. Place bread rounds on a **baking sheet**. Spoon applesauce over cream cheese.

2 Cut each sausage link into slices. Divide sausage slices evenly among the pita rounds.

3 Sprinkle each bread round with shredded cheese. Place baking sheet in oven. Bake for 8 to 10 minutes or till cheese is melted and bubbly. Turn oven off.

4 Use **hot pads** to take the baking sheet out of the oven. Use a **pancake turner** to remove pizzas from the baking sheet. Cool the pizzas slightly before serving. Makes 4 servings.

258

Easy Enchilada Casserole

Ingredients:

1 pound lean ground beef

½ cup frozen chopped onion

1 8-ounce can whole kernel corn, drained

1 8-ounce can tomato sauce

⅔ cup mild enchilada sauce or mild salsa

1 4-ounce can diced green chili peppers, drained

½ teaspoon chili powder

¼ teaspoon salt

10 6-inch corn tortillas

1 cup shredded cheddar cheese (4 ounces)

Per serving: 376 calories, 24 g protein, 31 g carbohydrate, 18 g total fat (8 g saturated), 67 mg cholesterol, 832 mg sodium, 492 mg potassium.

 1 Turn the oven to 350°. Place ground beef in a **large skillet**. Use a **wooden spoon** to break the meat into small chunks. Add the onion. Put the skillet on the burner. Turn burner to medium-high. Cook, stirring with the spoon till there is no pink color left in the meat. Turn off the burner. Remove the skillet from the burner.

 2 Place a **colander** over a **medium mixing bowl**. Spoon the meat mixture into the colander. Let the fat drain into the bowl. Put the meat and onion back into the skillet. Put the fat in a container to throw away.

3 Stir the corn, tomato sauce, enchilada sauce or salsa, green chili peppers, chili powder, and salt into the meat mixture. Put the skillet back on the burner. Turn the burner to medium-high. Cook till bubbly. Turn off the burner. Remove the skillet from the burner.

 4 Spoon ⅓ of the meat mixture into the bottom of a **2-quart rectangular baking dish**. Place 5 tortillas on top of the meat mixture in the baking dish. Spoon ½ of the remaining meat mixture over the tortillas. Sprinkle ½ of cheese over meat. Repeat with remaining tortillas, meat, and cheese.

 5 Turn the oven off. To serve, use a **table knife** to cut casserole into 6 pieces. Makes 6 servings.

Party Ribbon Cake

Ingredients:

1   10¾-ounce frozen loaf pound cake, thawed

⅓   cup raspberry preserves

⅓   cup peach preserves

1   4-ounce carton frozen whipped topping, thawed

2   tablespoons small multicolored decorative candies

Per serving: 204 calories, 2 g protein, 29 g carbohydrate, 10 g total fat (5 g saturated), 52 mg cholesterol, 49 mg sodium, 31 mg potassium.

1 Turn cake on its side. With a **ruler** measure the cake lengthwise into 3 equal slices, marking the cake by inserting several **tooth-picks** at desired levels.

2 Using a **sharp knife,** cut the cake into 3 lengthwise slices. Separate the slices and place the bottom slice, cut side up, on a **serving plate**. Put raspberry preserves in a **small bowl** and stir until soft. In another **small bowl** put peach preserves and stir until soft.

3 With a **table knife** spread the raspberry preserves over the top of the cake layer on the serving plate. Put the second cake layer on top of the raspberry preserves. Spread the peach preserves on top of the second cake layer. Put the last layer of cake, cut side down, on top of the peach preserves.

4 With a **metal spatula**, spread the whipped topping over the top and sides of the cake. Sprinkle decorative candies over top of cake. Chill cake in refrigerator for 1 hour before serving. Makes 12 servings.

Tutti-Frutti Upside Down Cake

Ingredients:

- 3 tablespoons margarine or butter
- ⅓ cup packed brown sugar
- 1 16-ounce can fruit cocktail
- 3 tablespoons flaked coconut
- 1 9-ounce package yellow cake mix
- 1 egg
- ½ cup orange juice

Per serving: 236 calories, 2 g protein, 40 g carbohydrate, 8 g total fat (2 g saturated), 27 mg cholesterol, 276 mg sodium, 117 mg potassium.

1 To drain the fruit cocktail, place a **strainer** over a **small bowl**. Open can of fruit cocktail and pour into strainer. Save syrup for another use, if desired.

2 Turn oven to 350°. Put margarine or butter in a **small microwave-safe bowl**. Micro-cook on 100% power (high) for 1 minute or till melted. With **hot pads** remove bowl from microwave oven. Pour melted butter into **9 x 1½-inch round baking pan**. Sprinkle brown sugar over melted margarine and stir with a **wooden spoon** till smooth. Spread fruit cocktail over brown sugar. Sprinkle coconut over fruit cocktail. Set baking pan aside till Step 3.

3 In a **large mixing bowl** put cake mix, egg, and orange juice. With another **wooden spoon** stir ingredients together. Then beat the mixture very well till smooth.

4 Carefully pour cake batter over fruit in baking pan. With a **rubber scraper**, scrape all the batter from the bowl into the pan and spread evenly.

5 Put the pan into the oven. Bake for 25 to 30 minutes or till a **toothpick** comes out clean when inserted near the center of the cake. Use **hot pads** to remove pan from oven. Turn the oven off. Cool cake on a **wire rack** for 5 minutes.

6 Have an adult place a **plate** upside down on top of the cake pan. Carefully turn the cake pan and plate together right side up. Remove cake pan. Cool about 30 minutes. Serve warm. Makes 8 servings.

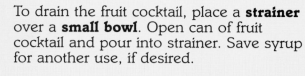

Taco Chicken Sticks

Ingredients:

3   cups corn chips
1   teaspoon chili powder
½   teaspoon ground cumin
¼   teaspoon onion powder
1   pound skinless boneless chicken
        breast halves
¼   cup margarine, melted
½   cup chunky salsa
½   cup shredded cheddar cheese
½   cup dairy sour cream

Per serving: 459 calories, 28 g protein, 18 g carbohydrate, 31 g total fat
(8 g saturated), 80 mg cholesterol, 534 mg sodium, 358 mg potassium.

1 Turn oven to 450°. Put corn chips in a
plastic bag. Use **rolling pin** to finely crush
chips. Add chili powder, cumin, and
onion powder to bag. Set aside till Step 3.

2 Rinse chicken under cold water. Pat dry
with **paper towels**. Use **kitchen scissors**
and a **ruler** to cut each chicken breast
lengthwise into ½-inch strips.

3 Melt margarine in **small saucepan** with
burner set on low. Turn burner off. Pour
margarine into **shallow dish**. Dip chicken
strips into margarine. Put a few strips
into plastic bag with crumb mixture and
shake to coat evenly. Remove from bag.
Repeat till all strips are coated.

4 Place strips on **baking sheet** and put in
oven. Bake 8 to 10 minutes or till no pink
color is left in chicken. Turn oven off. Use
hot pads to remove baking sheet from
oven. Serve with salsa, cheddar cheese,
and sour cream. Makes 4 servings.

Baked Tuna and Rice

Ingredients:

1 12½-ounce can tuna (water pack)

1 10½-ounce can condensed cream of celery soup

1 10-ounce package frozen peas and carrots, thawed

1 cup quick-cooking rice

1 cup milk

½ cup cheese-flavored fish-shaped crackers or ¼ cup shredded cheddar cheese (1 ounce)

Per serving: 441 calories, 53 g protein, 42 g carbohydrate, 9 g total fat (2 g saturated), 47 mg cholesterol, 781 mg sodium, 566 mg potassium.

1 Turn oven to 350°. Put a **colander** in the sink. Open the can of tuna and put tuna in the colander to drain.

2 In a **large mixing bowl** stir together celery soup, peas and carrots, rice, and milk. Stir in tuna. Transfer to a **1½-quart round casserole**.

3 Put the casserole in the oven. Bake for 45 minutes. Use **hot pads** to remove the casserole from the oven. Sprinkle the crackers or cheese over the tuna mixture.

4 Use hot pads to return casserole to the oven. Continue baking for 3 to 5 minutes or till heated through. Remove casserole from oven with the hot pads. Turn oven off. Makes 4 servings.

Cheesy Ham and Broccoli Supper

Ingredients:

1 7-ounce package elbow macaroni

2 10-ounce packages frozen cut broccoli in cheese sauce, thawed

1 cup cubed fully cooked ham

½ cup milk

2 teaspoons prepared mustard

Per serving: 334 calories, 19 g protein, 48 g carbohydrate, 7 g total fat (2 g saturated), 18 mg cholesterol, 916 mg sodium, 526 mg potassium.

1 Turn the oven to 350°. In a **large saucepan** cook the macaroni according to package directions. Turn off the burner. Have an adult help you remove the saucepan from the burner. Place a **colander** in the sink. Carefully pour the macaroni and water out of the pan into the colander.

2 Return the drained macaroni to saucepan. Add the broccoli in cheese sauce, ham, milk, and mustard. Use a **wooden spoon** to stir the ingredients well.

3 Carefully pour the macaroni mixture into a **2-quart casserole**. Cover casserole with a **lid**. Put the casserole in the oven. Bake for 55 to 60 minutes or till hot. Use **hot pads** to remove casserole from the oven. Turn oven off. Makes 4 or 5 servings.

Johnny Appleseed Cabbage Salad

Ingredients:

- 1 small apple
- ½ cup shredded Monterey Jack or cheddar cheese (2 ounces)
- 2½ cups shredded cabbage with carrot
- ½ cup mayonnaise
- 2 tablespoons apple juice
- 3 tablespoons dry roasted sunflower seeds

Per serving: 321 calories, 6 g protein, 9 g carbohydrate, 30 g total fat (6 g saturated), 29 mg cholesterol, 286 mg sodium, 260 mg potassium.

1 Wash and dry the apple. Remove the core by cutting the apple in quarters with a **sharp knife**. Cut the core off of each piece of apple.

2 With a sharp knife, cut the apple into bite-size pieces.

3 To shred cheese, place **cheese shredder** over a piece of **waxed paper** and carefully slide cheese down the side of the shredder.

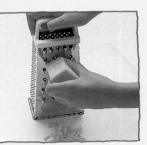

4 In a **small bowl** stir together the mayonnaise and apple juice with a **wooden spoon**. In a **large bowl** stir together the apple, cheese, cabbage, and sunflower seeds. Add the mayonnaise mixture and stir all ingredients together till blended. Cover and chill till served. Makes 4 servings.

Bow Tie Macaroni and Vegetable Salad

Ingredients:

- 1 cup cherry tomatoes
- 1½ cups bow tie macaroni
- 1 10-ounce package frozen mixed vegetables
- ½ cup shredded mozzarella cheese (2 ounces)
- ½ teaspoon dried salad herbs, crushed or ½ teaspoon dried basil, crushed
- ½ cup bottled Italian salad dressing

Per serving: 200 calories, 6 g protein, 19 g carbohydrate, 12 g total fat (2 g saturated), 18 mg cholesterol, 221 mg sodium, 184 mg potassium.

1 Have an adult help you cut the cherry tomatoes in half with a **sharp knife**. Set aside till Step 3.

2 Cook the bow tie macaroni in a **large saucepan** according to the package directions. Turn off the burner. Have an adult help you remove the pan from the burner. Place the frozen vegetables in a **colander**. Place the colander in the sink. Carefully pour the cooked macaroni and water out of the pan over the vegetables in the colander to thaw them. Rinse with cold water and drain again.

3 In a **large mixing bowl,** combine the drained macaroni and vegetable mixture, cherry tomatoes, mozzarella cheese, and salad herbs or basil. Pour the Italian salad dressing over the pasta mixture. Stir well.

4 Cover and chill salad in the refrigerator for 2 to 24 hours before serving. Makes 6 servings.

Cake and Fruit Parfaits

Ingredients:

1 cup fresh strawberries

1 4-serving-size package instant vanilla pudding mix

2 cups milk

4 cream-filled vanilla snack cakes or six ½-inch-thick slices of a frozen loaf pound cake

1 cup fresh blueberries

Frozen whipped dessert topping, thawed

Per serving: 249 calories, 4 g protein, 39 g carbohydrate, 9 g total fat (2 g saturated), 6 mg cholesterol, 213 mg sodium, 213 mg potassium.

1 Cut strawberries into slices and set aside till Step 3. Put pudding mix into a **medium mixing bowl**. Add the milk. With a **rotary beater** or an **electric mixer** on low speed, beat pudding mixture for 1 minute.

2 Cut each snack cake into 6 pieces or each cake slice into 4 pieces. Put 2 pieces of cake in the bottom of each **parfait glass** or **10-ounce custard cup**.

3 Spoon 3 table-spoons sliced strawberries over cake. Spoon 2 to 3 tablespoons pudding over strawberries. Add 2 more pieces of cake.

4 Top with 3 tablespoons blueberries and 2 or 3 more tablespoons of pudding. Top with a spoonful of whipped dessert topping. Fill the other parfait glasses or custard cups the same way. Cover and chill up to 6 hours. Makes 6 servings.

Pork Chops with Fruited Applesauce

Ingredients:

4   pork chops, cut ¾ inch thick
    Salt
    Pepper
1   tablespoon margarine or butter
¼   cup water
¾   cup cinnamon applesauce
¼   cup mixed dried fruit bits
    or raisins
¼   cup orange juice

Per serving: 217 calories, 15 g protein, 17 g carbohydrate, 10 g total fat
(3 g saturated), 47 mg cholesterol, 211 mg sodium, 311 mg potassium.

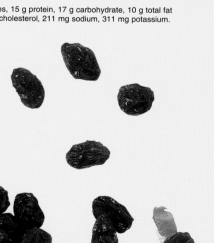

1 Sprinkle pork chops with salt and pepper. Melt margarine or butter in a **large skillet** over medium heat. Put the pork chops in the skillet and brown the chops on both sides. This will take about 5 minutes. Turn burner off. Remove skillet from burner. Have an adult help you drain off the fat.

2 Carefully add water to pork chops in skillet. Return skillet to burner. Cover and simmer over medium heat about 30 minutes or till chops are no longer pink in the center.

3 Turn burner off. Remove skillet from burner. Use a **pancake turner** to place chops on a **serving platter**; cover with **foil** to keep warm. Have an adult help you skim the fat from the pan drippings. Add the applesauce, fruit bits or raisins, and orange juice to the skillet. Stir well with a **spoon**. Return skillet to burner and cook and stir over medium heat till heated through.

4 Spoon the sauce over the pork chops. Makes 4 servings.

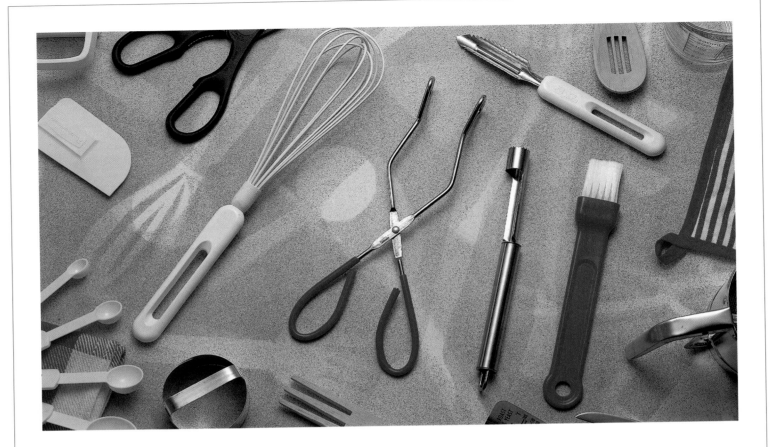

KITCHEN WISDOM TABLE OF CONTENTS

Whether you're just trying your hand at cooking or simply want to have handy tips and pointers for easy reference, *Kitchen Wisdom* is an indispensable guide. Here you'll find the commonly used terms, preparation techniques, and nutrition guidelines that will insure your success every time you make a meal, even if it's the first time. We also review proper kitchen appliances, tools, and gadgets for the task at hand to help you feel like a pro.

KITCHEN WISDOM

Cooking Terms

Al dente: Describes spaghetti or other pasta that is cooked only till it offers a slight resistance to the bite.

Baste: To moisten foods during cooking with pan drippings or a special sauce in order to add flavor and prevent drying.

Beat: To make a mixture smooth by briskly whipping or stirring it with a spoon, wire whisk, rotary beater, or electric mixer.

Blanch: To partially cook fruits, vegetables, or nuts in boiling water or steam. Blanching is also used to loosen skins from tomatoes, peaches, and almonds.

Blend: To process foods in an electric blender, or to combine by hand till smooth and uniform in texture, flavor, and color.

Braise: To cook food slowly in a small amount of liquid in a tightly covered pan on the range top or in the oven.

Butterfly: To split foods such as shrimp or steak through the middle without completely separating the halves, then spreading the halves to resemble a butterfly.

Coat: To evenly cover food with crumbs, flour, or a batter.

Crisp-tender: Describes vegetables cooked until they're just tender but still somewhat crisp.

Cut in: To combine shortening with dry ingredients using a pastry blender or two forks.

Dash: An ingredient measure that equals about half of one quarter of ¼ teaspoon.

Dissolve: To stir a dry substance in a liquid, such as sugar in coffee or gelatin in water, till no solids remain. Heating the liquid is sometimes necessary.

Dollop: To place a scoop or spoonful of a semi-liquid food, such as whipped cream or sour cream, on top of another food.

Fillet: To cut lean poultry or fish into pieces without bones.

Flake: To break food gently into small flat pieces.

Fold: To gently mix ingredients, using a folding motion. With a spatula, cut down through the mixture; cut across the bottom of the bowl, then up and over, close to the surface. Turn the bowl frequently for even distribution.

Garnish: To add visual appeal to finished food by decorating it with small pieces of food or edible flowers.

Glaze: To brush a thin mixture on a food to give it a glossy appearance.

Grind: To use a food grinder or food processor to cut food, such as meat or fruit, into fine pieces.

Knead: To work dough with the heels of the hands in a pressing and folding motion till it becomes smooth and elastic.

Melt: To heat a solid food, such as margarine or sugar, till it is a liquid.

Mix: To stir, usually with a spoon, till ingredients are thoroughly combined.

Mull: To slowly heat beverages, such as red wine or cider, with spices and sugar.

Panbroil: To cook meats in a skillet without added fat, removing any fat as it accumulates.

Panfry: To cook meats, poultry, or fish in a small amount of hot fat in a skillet.

Partially set: Describes a gelatin mixture chilled till its consistency resembles unbeaten egg whites.

Peel: To remove the outer layer or skin from a fruit or vegetable.

Pit: To remove the seed from a piece of fruit.

Preheat: To heat an oven, waffle iron, or electric griddle to the recommended temperature before cooking in it.

Process: To blend a food in a food processor. Also refers to the technique of canning food.

Puree: To chop food into a liquid or heavy paste, usually in a blender, food processor, or food mill.

Reduce: To boil liquids such as pan juices or sauces rapidly so that some of the liquid evaporates, thickening the mixture.

Roast: To cook meats, uncovered, in the oven.

Sauté: To cook or brown food in a small amount of hot fat.

Score: To cut narrow grooves or slits partway through the outer surface of a food.

Shuck: To remove the shells or husks from foods such as oysters, clams, or corn.

Sift: To put one or more dry ingredients through a sifter or sieve to incorporate air and break up any lumps.

Skim: To remove melted fat or other substances from the surface of a liquid.

Stew: To cook food in liquid for a long time till tender, usually in a covered pot.

Stir: To mix ingredients with a spoon in a circular or figure-8 motion till combined or to prevent burning during cooking.

Whip: To beat food lightly and rapidly using a wire whisk, rotary beater, or electric mixer to incorporate air into the mixture and increase its volume.

KITCHEN WISDOM

How To Measure

For consistent cooking and baking results, always measure correctly. Not all ingredients are measured the same way; to ensure accuracy, follow these directions.

Use a glass or clear plastic measuring cup for liquids. Place the cup on level surface and bend down so your eye is level with the marking you wish to read. Fill the cup to the marking. Leave cup on the counter to read.

When using measuring spoons to measure a liquid, pour the liquid just to the top of the spoon without letting it spill over. To avoid unwanted spills, don't measure over the mixing bowl.

Spoon flour or granulated sugar into a dry measuring cup and level it off with the straight edge of a knife or metal spatula. Before measuring flour, stir it in the canister to lighten it. Cake flour should be sifted.

Press brown sugar firmly into a dry measuring cup so that it holds the shape of the cup when turned out.

Use a rubber spatula to press solid shortening firmly into a measuring cup. Level it off with the straight edge of a knife or metal spatula.

To measure stick margarine or butter, follow the guidelines on the wrapper. Cut off the amount needed. For unwrapped margarine or butter, soften it, then measure as directed for solid shortening.
¼ lb. (1 stick) = ½ cup

To measure dried herbs, lightly fill a measuring spoon just to the top (leveling is not necessary). Empty the spoon into your hand and crush the herb with your fingers to release its flavor. (Harder dried herbs, such as rosemary or thyme, are best crushed with a mortar and pestle.)

Measured Equivalents

3 teaspoons = 1 tablespoon
4 tablespoons = ¼ cup
5⅓ tablespoons = ⅓ cup
16 tablespoons = 1 cup
1 tablespoon = ½ fluid ounce
1 cup = 8 fluid ounces
2 cups = 1 pint
4 cups = 1 quart
2 pints = 1 quart
4 quarts = 1 gallon

KITCHEN WISDOM

Ingredient Equivalents

Food	Amount Before Preparation	Approximate Measure After Preparation
Cereals		
Macaroni	1 cup (3½ oz.)	2½ cups cooked
Noodles, medium	3 cups (4 oz.)	3 cups cooked
Spaghetti	8 ounces	4 cups cooked
Long grain rice	1 cup (7 oz.)	3 cups cooked
Quick-cooking rice	1 cup (3 oz.)	2 cups cooked
Popcorn	⅓ to ½ cup	8 cups popped
Crumbs		
Bread	1 slice	¾ cup soft crumbs or ¼ cup fine dry crumbs
Saltine crackers	14 crackers	½ cup finely crushed
Rich round crackers	12 crackers	½ cup finely crushed
Graham crackers	7 squares	½ cup finely crushed
Gingersnaps	7 cookies	½ cup finely crushed
Vanilla wafers	11 cookies	½ cup finely crushed
Fruits		
Apples	1 medium	1 cup sliced
Bananas	1 medium	⅓ cup mashed
Lemons	1 medium	3 tbsp. juice; 2 tsp. shredded peel
Limes	1 medium	2 tbsp. juice; 1½ tsp. shredded peel
Oranges	1 medium	¼ to ⅓ cup juice; 4 tsp. shredded peel

Food	Amount Before Preparation	Approximate Measure After Preparation
Fruits (continued)		
Peaches, pears	1 medium	½ cup sliced
Rhubarb	1 pound	2 cups cooked
Strawberries	4 cups whole	4 cups sliced
Vegetables		
Cabbage	1 pound (1 small)	5 cups shredded
Carrots, without tops	1 pound (6 to 8 medium)	3 cups shredded or 2¼ cups chopped
Cauliflower	1 medium head	4½ cups sliced
Celery	1 stalk	½ cup chopped
Green beans	1 pound (4 cups)	2½ cups cooked
Green peppers	1 large	1 cup chopped
Lettuce	1 medium head	6 cups torn
Mushrooms	½ pound (3 cups)	1 cup cooked
Onions	1 medium	½ cup chopped
Potatoes	3 medium	2 cups cubed or 1¾ cups mashed
Spinach	1 pound	12 cups torn
Tomatoes	1 medium	½ cup chopped
Miscellaneous		
Cheese	4 ounces	1 cup shredded
Whipping cream	1 cup	2 cups whipped
Ground beef	1 pound raw	2¾ cups cooked
Cooked meat	1 pound	3 cups chopped
Chicken breasts	1½ pounds (2 whole medium)	2 cups chopped cooked chicken

Handy Substitutions

For best results, use the ingredients specified in the recipe.

If you don't have:	Substitute:
1 cup cake flour	1 cup *minus* 2 tablespoons all-purpose flour
1 tablespoon cornstarch (for thickening)	2 tablespoons all-purpose flour
1 teaspoon baking powder	½ teaspoon cream of tartar *plus* ¼ teaspoon baking soda
1 package active dry yeast	1 cake compressed yeast
1 cup sugar	1 cup packed brown sugar *or* 2 cups sifted powdered sugar
¼ cup fine dry bread crumbs	¾ cup soft bread crumbs, *or* ¼ cup cracker crumbs, *or* ¼ cup cornflake crumbs
1 cup honey	1¼ cups sugar *plus* ¼ cup liquid
1 cup corn syrup	1 cup sugar *plus* ¼ cup liquid
1 square (1 ounce) unsweetened chocolate	3 tablespoons unsweetened cocoa powder *plus* 1 tablespoon shortening *or* cooking oil
1 cup whipping cream, whipped	2 cups whipped dessert topping
1 cup buttermilk	1 tablespoon lemon juice *or* vinegar *plus* enough whole milk to make 1 cup (let stand 5 minutes before using), *or* 1 cup whole milk *plus* 1¾ teaspoons cream of tartar, *or* 1 cup plain yogurt
1 cup whole milk	½ cup evaporated milk *plus* ½ cup water *or* 1 cup water *plus* ⅓ cup nonfat dry milk powder
1 cup light cream	1 tablespoon melted butter *plus* enough milk to make 1 cup
2 cups tomato sauce	¾ cup tomato paste *plus* 1 cup water
1 cup tomato juice	½ cup tomato sauce *plus* ½ cup water
1 small onion, chopped (⅓ cup)	1 teaspoon onion powder *or* 1 tablespoon dried minced onion
1 teaspoon dry mustard (in cooked mixtures)	1 tablespoon prepared mustard

Cooking Tools

Whisk, Rotary Beater, Mixers:
Use a wire whisk for light mixtures (puddings, sauces, and egg whites) or rotary beater operated by a hand crank. For light to medium mixtures use an electric hand mixer. For heavy batters and doughs and long mixing periods, the stand mixer is recommended.

Spoons: Wooden spoons are recommended for beating because they make little noise against the sides of a glass or metal bowl. When stirring hot mixtures, wooden spoons help prevent burned fingers. Metal spoons are essential for testing custard and jelly and for skimming off fat. Use a slotted spoon to lift large pieces of food out of liquid.

Spatulas, Turners: Spatulas differ in design and purpose. Use a rubber spatula to scrape a bowl clean. Use a flexible metal spatula to frost a cake or loosen bread or cake from pan. The large metal spatula is used primarily as a pancake or egg turner. Some spatulas or turners are made from materials that will prevent scratching nonstick surfaces of pans and skillets.

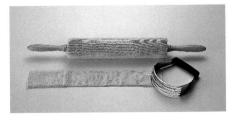

Pastry Blender, Rolling Pin: Use a pastry blender to cut in shortening for flaky baked products, such as pie crusts and biscuits. You'll also need a rolling pin to roll out pastry, breads, and cookies. To keep dough from sticking, slip the rolling pin into a cotton knit rolling pin cover.

Knives: Use a paring knife or utility knife for peeling fruits and other small cutting jobs. A chef's knife is best for chopping and for large cutting tasks. A serrated knife works well when slicing tomatoes and bread. Other useful types of knives include boning, grapefruit, butcher, and carving knives.

Vegetable Peeler, Kitchen Shears, Meat Mallet: A vegetable peeler helps reduce waste. Use kitchen shears to snip fresh herbs and dried fruits; heavy-duty shears will even cut up chicken. Use the flat side of a meat mallet for flattening boneless pieces of chicken or veal. The grooved side can be used for tenderizing meats.

Sieves, Colanders: Sieves (or strainers) and colanders vary in size and design. A sieve is made of fine wire mesh, while a colander has larger holes and is freestanding. Both are used to separate small particles from large ones or liquids from solids. They are also useful for rinsing fruits and vegetables.

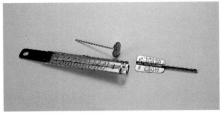

Thermometers: A candy/deep-fat frying thermometer is marked with different stages of candy making, (thread, soft-ball, etc.) and usually gives deep-fat frying temperatures as well. A meat thermometer is used for checking the internal temperature of meat and poultry.

Saucepans, Skillets, Dutch Ovens: Saucepans are basic for range-top cooking. Skillets are wider and shallower than saucepans. A kettle or Dutch oven is required for cooking large quantities of food, such as soups or stews.

Cooking Equipment

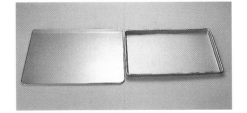

Baking Pans and Dishes: Metal baking pans and non-metal baking dishes are commonly used in the oven. They come in a variety of sizes and shapes but round, square, and rectangular are most often used. Glass dishes usually require a lower oven temperature.

Baking (Cookie) Sheets, Jelly-Roll Pans: A baking sheet or cookie sheet is a flat metal pan that may have a raised edge on one or two sides. It differs from a jelly-roll pan (also called a shallow baking pan) in that the jelly-roll pan has 1-inch sides and can be used to make jelly-rolls or bar cookies.

Muffin Pans, Popover Pans: The standard muffin cup measures 2½ inches across the top; smaller sizes are available. Six or twelve cups are usually included in a single pan. Popover pans are deep individual cups mounted on a wire frame. They are designed so that popovers will rise high and have a crisp brown crust.

Custard Cups, Ramekins: Custard cups are 6- or 10-ounce glass or ceramic dishes for oven use. They may be used in place of muffin pans or for making custards. Ramekins, made of porcelain or earthenware, resemble miniature soufflé dishes and are used for individual servings.

Loaf Pans and Dishes, Casseroles: Metal loaf pans and non-metal loaf dishes are deeper than baking pans and dishes. They are used for making breads, cakes, and meat loaves. A casserole dish is deeper than a baking dish and is usually round or oval and made of glass or ceramic materials.

Pie Plates, Pie Pans, Tart Pans: A pie plate or pan is used for making pies. Choose one of glass or dull metal; shiny metal keeps the crust from browning properly. Tart pans have fluted sides and removable bottoms. They are used for pies with shallow pastry sides and no top crust.

Roasting Pans, Broiler Pans: A roasting pan is a shallow pan with a rack designed to keep the meat out of the drippings while roasting. A broiler pan is a shallow pan with a fitted rack designed to keep meat out of the drippings while broiling. Broiler pans can also be used for roasting.

Tube Pans, Bundt Pans: A tube pan has a cylinder in the middle and is used to make angel and chiffon cakes. It may or may not have a removable bottom. Bundt pans (fluted tube pans) are used for making pound cakes and other creamed cakes when a fancy shape is desired.

Springform Pans: Springform pans have removable sides. They are used for making desserts with delicate crusts (such as cheesecakes) that could be disturbed when removed from the pan.

Preparation Techniques

To snip fresh herbs, put the herb in a deep container, such as a 1-cup glass measure, and snip it with kitchen shears. Or, chop fresh herbs with a sharp knife. To substitute fresh herbs for dried, use three times more of the fresh.

To peel tomatoes easily, spear a tomato in the stem end with a fork, then plunge the tomato into boiling water for 30 seconds or just till the skin splits (or you can hold the tomato with a slotted spoon). Immediately dip the tomato into cold water. With a sharp paring knife, pull the skin off the tomato.

To dissolve unflavored gelatin, place one envelope of unflavored gelatin in a small saucepan. Stir in at least ¼ cup water or other liquid. Let stand 5 minutes to soften. Heat and stir over low heat till the gelatin is dissolved. (When unflavored gelatin is combined with at least ¼ cup sugar, softening is not necessary. Combine the gelatin-sugar mixture with liquid and heat immediately to dissolve the gelatin and sugar.) Once it's dissolved, the gelatin can be combined with other ingredients.

To chop canned tomatoes easily, use kitchen shears to snip tomatoes into pieces while still in can or pour them into a bowl.

To separate eggs, carefully crack open an egg into a small bowl or custard cup. Over another small bowl, pour egg into an egg separator. When white has drained from yolk, place the egg white and egg yolk in separate bowls. Repeat procedure with additional eggs. Do not allow any yolk to spill into the white or the whites will not beat properly.

To beat eggs slightly, use a fork to beat the egg till the white and yolk are combined and no streaks remain.

Preparation Techniques

To beat egg yolks, place the egg yolks in a mixer bowl. Beat with an electric mixer on high speed about 5 minutes or till thick and lemon-colored.

To sift powdered sugar, spoon the powdered sugar into a sifter or sieve. Sift into a bowl or directly onto cakes, bars, or cookies. (Sifting prevents powdered sugar from clumping.) If desired, place a paper doily on top of the food. Lightly sift the powdered sugar over the doily then remove the doily carefully.

To section grapefruit and oranges, cut a thin slice from each end of the fruit. Using a very sharp knife or serrated knife for peeling citrus fruits, cut from the top of the fruit down. Cut off the peel and the white membrane. Working over a bowl to catch the juices, cut between one fruit section and the membrane to the center of the fruit. Turn the knife and slide it up the other side of the section next to the membrane; repeat. Remove seeds.

To juice citrus fruits, cut each piece of fruit in half crosswise. Hold a citrus juicer atop a measuring cup or bowl. (Or, use a freestanding juicer.) Press each half of fruit into the citrus juicer, turning the fruit back and forth till all the juice has been removed. Discard the pulp and seeds that collect in the juicer.

To cut fresh pineapple, remove leafy crown by holding pineapple in one hand and the crown in the other; twist in opposite directions. Trim top of pineapple and cut off the base. Set pineapple upright on a cutting board. Starting at the top of the fruit and working down, cut off wide strips of peel with a sharp knife. Remove the eyes from the pineapple by cutting narrow wedge-shaped grooves diagonally around the fruit. Cut into spears, slices, or chunks, removing the hard core from the center.

To sieve berries, in a blender container or food processor bowl blend or process berries till smooth. Place a sieve over a bowl. Pour the pureed berries into the sieve. Using the back of a wooden spoon, stir and press the fruit through the sieve. Discard seeds that remain in sieve.

Seasoning with Herbs

Basil has broad shiny leaves; several varieties are available. Its aroma and flavor range from peppery and robust to sweet and spicy. Basil is an important herb in Mediterranean cooking. Use it to flavor meats, egg dishes, pesto, salads, and vegetables, especially eggplant and tomatoes.

Chives are related to onions and leeks. Their hollow stems are bright green and slender. Chives have a delicate onion flavor; use to flavor poultry, tuna, cream soups, green salads, sauces, and salad dressings.

Dillweed has delicate, feathery leaves and a distinctive flavor. Dillweed enhances the flavor of chicken, egg, and fish dishes; mustard-based sauces; salad dressings; and vegetables, such as carrots, peas, and cucumbers.

Oregano has small, slightly oval leaves. It has a strong, spicy flavor with pleasantly bitter undertones. Use it in moderation to flavor marinades, meats, vegetables, tomato-based dishes, and pizza.

Rosemary has silvery-green, spiky leaves. Highly aromatic, its strong flavor is a combination of both lemon and pine. Rosemary is a welcome addition to marinades for grilled meats, chicken, and fish; beef stews; soups; and vegetables.

Sage can be recognized by its long, velvety, gray-green leaves. It has a pungent, slightly bitter flavor and aroma. Sage is used in meat recipes (especially pork and sausage), poultry and egg dishes, stews, stuffings, and tomato-based sauces.

Spearmint is the most commonly-used variety of more than 30 species of mint. Its leaves are large, pointed, and a bright green. It has a sweet, pungent aroma and refreshing flavor. Use to season lamb, stuffings, tea and fruit-based beverages, fruit salads, and vegetables such as carrots and peas.

Tarragon has pointed long and slender dark green leaves. Its assertive flavor is spicy-sweet and akin to licorice. Tarragon combines well with poultry, veal, fish, and shellfish; egg salad; salad dressings and marinades; asparagus; and mushrooms.

Thyme can be identified by its small, pointed, gray-green leaves. Its flavor and aroma are both minty and faintly lemon-like. Use thyme in meat, fish, chicken, and egg dishes; soups and stews; barbecue sauces; marinades; and with vegetables such as tomatoes and zucchini.

Easy Garnishes

Radish Accordions: Place radishes between two parallel wooden sticks to keep from cutting through the radishes. Make 8 to 10 narrow cross-wise cuts ⅛ inch apart in radishes. Place in ice water so the slices fan out. Use with meats or salads.

Citrus Twists: Thinly slice lemons, limes or oranges. Cut into center of each slice; twist ends in opposite directions. Use with main dishes, salads, or desserts.

Fluted Mushrooms: Hold a paring knife at an angle and begin at the top of each mushroom cap, making V-shaped cuts. Turn mushroom slightly, making V-shaped cuts around mushroom cap. Or, make a series of slight indentations in the mushroom cap with a punch-type can opener. Use with salads and meats.

Tomato Roses: Cut a base from the stem end of a tomato (do not sever). Cut a continous narrow strip in spiral fashion, tapering end to remove. Curl strip onto its base in a rose shape. Use with salads and dips.

Scored Cucumbers: Make a V-shape cut lengthwise down each cucumber (or run the tines of a fork lengthwise down each cucumber, pressing to break the skin). Repeat at regular intervals around cucumber. Slice or bias-slice. Use with salads and dips.

Onion Brushes: Slice roots from ends of green onion; remove most of green portion. Slash both ends of the onion pieces to make fringes. Place in ice water to curl. Use with meat, poultry, fish, or on appetizer trays.

Carrot Curls/Zigzags: Using a vegetable peeler, cut thin lengthwise strips from carrots. For curls, roll up; secure with toothpicks. For zigzags, thread on toothpicks accordion-style. Put curls and zigzags in ice water; remove toothpicks before using. Use with salads, sauces, and thick soups.

Chocolate Curls: For curls, use a bar of chocolate at room temperature. Carefully draw a vegetable peeler across the chocolate, making thin strips that curl. Use to garnish cakes, tortes, custards, or ice-cream drinks.

Strawberry Fans: Place strawberry, hull side down, on cutting board. Make narrow lengthwise cuts; do not slice all the way through. Hold gently with one hand and twist in the opposite direction with the other so slices fan out. Use for salads and desserts.

277

Nutrition Basics

The secret to healthy and delicious meals lies in "pyramid power." The Food Guide Pyramid has replaced the once-familiar Four Food Groups as the standard for balancing your diet everyday.

Why A Pyramid?

Nutritionists believe that a picture is a useful way to illustrate the ideal daily diet—one planned with an eye toward variety, moderation, and proportion. Graphically, the pyramid is an easily understood symbol.

What The Pyramid Tells You

At the pyramid's broad base lies the breads, pasta, and grains food group, followed next by vegetables and fruit. These foods are emphasized because they are low in fat and supply vitamins, minerals, complex carbohydrates, and dietary fiber—important nutrients that contribute to overall good health. They may also help to postpone or prevent certain diseases, such as cancer and heart disease.

On the third tier of the pyramid, you'll see the food groups that include dairy products, meat, poultry, fish, dry beans, and nuts. These two food groups, although high in many nutrients, also contain higher levels of fat than those foods at the base of the pyramid. Consequently, they should be eaten in moderation.

Fats, oils, and sweets appear in the small triangle at the top of the pyramid. These foods are necessary but should play a very small role in your diet.

Foods high in fat contribute to obesity and are linked to an increased risk for heart disease and some forms of cancer. In fact, food experts recommend that the number of calories from fat not exceed 30% of our daily caloric intake.

Since fats and sugars are present in foods within the other groups, tiny circles (fat) and triangles (sugar) indicate where fats and sugars may be found.

In addition to showing the recommended proportion of each food group, the pyramid also illustrates how many servings in the major groups you should be eating each day.

Menu Planning and The Pyramid

It's easy to meet the daily recommendations on the Food Guide Pyramid with a little planning. These tips will help you achieve deliciously satisfying meals and snacks and establish a pattern for healthy eating habits.

Breakfast is the place to start:
- Drink a glass of juice.
- Enjoy fresh or dried fruit on cereal or as a topper for pancakes and French toast.

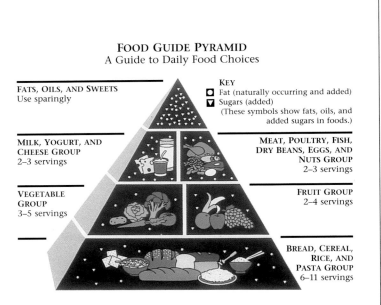

FOOD GUIDE PYRAMID
A Guide to Daily Food Choices

FATS, OILS, AND SWEETS
Use sparingly

KEY
□ Fat (naturally occurring and added)
▽ Sugars (added)
(These symbols show fats, oils, and added sugars in foods.)

MILK, YOGURT, AND CHEESE GROUP
2–3 servings

MEAT, POULTRY, FISH, DRY BEANS, EGGS, AND NUTS GROUP
2–3 servings

VEGETABLE GROUP
3–5 servings

FRUIT GROUP
2–4 servings

BREAD, CEREAL, RICE, AND PASTA GROUP
6–11 servings

- Stir chopped vegetables into scrambled eggs or use as fillings for omelets.
- Sample the plentiful variety of bagels and whole grain breads available at delis, bakeries, or your supermarket.
- Enjoy the stick-to-the-ribs goodness of hot oatmeal prepared super fast in the microwave oven.

Lunches can be fast and healthy too:
- Stir chopped fresh or frozen vegetables into canned reduced sodium-soups, macaroni and cheese, or mashed potatoes.
- Perk up sandwiches with chopped or shredded veggies.
- Go creative at the salad bar, but take it easy on the dressing, high-fat toppings, and cream salads.
- Have thick-crust, whole-grain pizza with assorted vegetable toppings. And hold the cheese, please.

Make a dinner date with good nutrition:
- Serve pasta, rice, or bean dishes as the entree instead of meat several times a week.
- Toss leftover cooked vegetables and grains into green salads.
- Serve brown rice, barley, or couscous as tasty side dishes.
- When grilling meat, plan to grill some vegetables or vegetable kabobs as well.
- Include warm whole-grain rolls or crusty sliced bread as part of the meal.
- Serve poached fruit for dessert. Try topping it with vanilla yogurt or a sauce made from pureed fresh fruit.

KITCHEN WISDOM

Menu Planning and The Pyramid *(continued)*

Snacks needn't be sinful:
- When you crave something sweet, reach for an orange, apple, banana, or grapes.
- Munch on crunchy pretzels, rice cakes, or unbuttered or air-popped popcorn.
- Make tasty dips by blending low-fat yogurt or sour cream, yogurt cheese, or fat-free cream cheese with chopped vegetables and herbs. Or, drain and mash canned beans; combine with chopped onion, garlic, herbs, and spices.
- Keep carrot and celery sticks, sliced zucchini, broccoli and cauliflower flowerets in the refrigerator for handy snacking.

Remember, the pyramid is a guide. You may not meet all of its recommendations every day, but strive to balance your diet over time, compensating for day-to-day deviations as necessary.

Pay Attention to Food Labels

Nearly all food packages display nutrition labels that adhere to regulations established by the Food and Drug Administration (FDA).

These food labels have been revised to give more complete, accurate, and easy-to-understand information. The labels will help you make informed choices about the food you buy—choices that follow the dietary recommendations on the pyramid.

Learning from the Labels

Serving sizes: Serving sizes of all similar foods, regardless of brand, must be consistent. Compare the amount you normally eat to the amount listed. If you eat more, you are consuming more calories.

Calories and calories from fat: The total calories per serving and the number of calories coming from fat are shown.

Daily Values for nutrients: This section of the food label shows the proportion (total amount of fat, for example) provided by one serving of food for a person eating 2000 calories a day. This guide makes it easier to compare food choices. Daily Values appear for total fat, saturated fat, cholesterol, sodium, total carbohydrate, dietary fiber, vitamins A and C, calcium, and iron.

Calories per gram: The label will tell you how many calories are in each gram of fat, carbohydrates, and protein.

Coming to Terms With Definitions

Terms such as light, less, fewer, free, low, more, lean, extra lean, and fresh have meaningful definitions based on specific guidelines and standards. For most people, memorizing definitions for these terms would not be practical. Just be aware that you can trust the terminology to help you shop wisely.

Health Claims

Research has shown that some foods or nutrients may help decrease the risk of certain diseases or health-related conditions. Food packages displaying these claims must meet established criteria thought to lower the risk of specific diseases. Package labels will allow claims regarding the following food-health relationships.

1. Calcium and osteoporosis
2. Fat and cancer
3. Saturated fat and cholesterol and coronary heart disease
4. Fiber-rich grain products, fruits, and vegetables and cancer
5. Fiber-rich fruits, vegetables, and grain products and risk of heart disease
6. Sodium and high blood pressure
7. Fruits and vegetables and cancer

Want to Know More?

Additional information on the Food Guide Pyramid and food labels is available. To find out more, contact your county extension agent or call the Consumer Nutrition Hot Line (800-366-1655) at the National Center for Nutrition and Dietetics, 10 a.m. to 5 p.m. CST Monday through Friday.

RECIPE INDEX

RECIPE INDEX

RECIPE INDEX

RECIPE INDEX

RECIPE INDEX

TECHNIQUE INDEX

Keep track of your daily nutrition needs by using the information we provide at the end of each recipe. We've analyzed the nutritional content of each recipe serving for you. When a recipe gives an ingredient substitution, we used the first choice in the analysis. If it makes a range of servings (such as 4 to 6), we used the smallest number. Ingredients listed as optional weren't included in the calculations.

Metric Cooking Hints

By making a few conversions, cooks in Australia, Canada, and the United Kingdom can use the recipes in Better Homes and Gardens® *Picture-Perfect Home Cooking* with confidence. The charts on this page provide a guide for converting measurements from the U.S. customary system, which is used throughout this book, to the imperial and metric systems. There also is a conversion table for oven temperatures to accommodate the differences in oven calibrations.

Volume and Weight: Americans traditionally use cup measures for liquid and solid ingredients. The chart (top right) shows the approximate imperial and metric equivalents. If you are accustomed to weighing solid ingredients, here are some helpful approximate equivalents.
- 1 cup butter, caster sugar, or rice = 8 ounces = about 250 grams
- 1 cup flour = 4 ounces = about 125 grams
- 1 cup icing sugar = 5 ounces = about 150 grams

Spoon measures are used for smaller amounts of ingredients although the size of the tablespoon varies slightly among countries. However, for practical purposes and for recipes in this book, a straight substitution is all that's necessary.

Measurements made using cups or spoons should always be level, unless stated otherwise.

Product Differences: Most of the ingredients called for in the recipes in this book are available in English-speaking countries. However, some are known by different names. Here are some common American ingredients and their possible counterparts:
- Sugar is granulated or caster sugar.
- Powdered sugar is icing sugar.
- All-purpose flour is plain household flour or white flour. When self-rising flour is used in place of all-purpose flour in a recipe that calls for leavening, omit the leavening agent (baking soda or baking powder) and salt.
- Light corn syrup is golden syrup.
- Cornstarch is cornflour.
- Baking soda is bicarbonate of soda.
- Vanilla is vanilla essence.

Useful Equivalents

⅛ teaspoon = 0.5 ml
¼ teaspoon = 1 ml
½ teaspoon = 2 ml
1 teaspoon = 5 ml
¼ cup = 2 fluid ounces = 50 ml
⅓ cup = 3 fluid ounces = 75 ml
½ cup = 4 fluid ounces = 125 ml
⅔ cup = 5 fluid ounces = 150 ml
¾ cup = 6 fluid ounces = 175 ml
1 cup = 8 fluid ounces = 250 ml
2 cups = 1 pint
2 pints = 1 litre
½ inch = 1 centimetre
1 inch = 2 centimetres

Baking Pan Sizes

American	Metric
8x1½-inch round baking pan	20x4-centimetre sandwich or cake tin
9x1½-inch round baking pan	23x3.5-centimetre sandwich or cake tin
11x7x1½-inch baking pan	28x18x4-centimetre baking pan
13x9x2-inch baking pan	32.5x23x5-centimetre baking pan
2-quart rectangular baking dish	30x19x5-centimetre baking pan
15x10x2-inch baking pan	38x25.5x2.5-centimetre baking pan (Swiss roll tin)
9-inch pie plate	22x4- or 23x4-centimetre pie plate
7- or 8-inch springform pan	18- or 20-centimetre springform or loose-bottom cake tin
9x5x3-inch loaf pan	23x13x6-centimetre or 2-pound narrow loaf pan or paté tin
1½-quart casserole	1.5-litre casserole
2-quart casserole	2-litre casserole

Oven Temperature Equivalents

Fahrenheit Setting	Celsius Setting*	Gas Setting
300°F	150°C	Gas Mark 2
325°F	160°C	Gas Mark 3
350°F	180°C	Gas Mark 4
375°F	190°C	Gas Mark 5
400°F	200°C	Gas Mark 6
425°F	220°C	Gas Mark 7
450°F	230°C	Gas Mark 8
Broil		Grill

Electric and gas ovens may be calibrated using Celsius. However, increase the Celsius setting 10 to 20 degrees when cooking above 160°C with an electric oven. For convection or forced-air ovens (gas or electric), lower the temperature setting 10°C when cooking at all heat levels.